THE COMPLETE IDIOT'S GUIDE® TO

Buying and Selling a Business

by Ed Paulsor

D1275523

alpha
books

ALPHA DEVELOPMENT TEAM

Publisher
Marie Butler-Knight

Editorial Director
Gary M. Krebs

Associate Managing Editor
Cari Shaw Fischer

Acquisitions Editors
Randy Ladenheim-Gil
Amy Gordon

Development Editors
Phil Kitchel
Amy Zavatto

Assistant Editor
Georgette Blau

PRODUCTION TEAM

Development Editor
Al McDermid

Production Editor
Michael Thomas

Copy Editor
Christy Parrish

Cover Designer
Mike Freeland

Photo Editor
Richard H. Fox

Illustrator
Jody Schaeffer

Book Designers
Scott Cook and Amy Adams of DesignLab

Indexer
Chris Wilcox

Layout/Proofreading
Juli Cook
Diana Moore

Contents at a Glance

Contents

Foreword

Whether you are buying or selling a business, hang on for your life because this is one of the biggest adventures you'll ever experience. Even a simple concept like selling cookies that people love to eat can become a wild mixture of excitement, negotiation, and uncertainty when it comes time to sell. And take it from me, you don't want to wait until the last minute to prepare to either buy or sell a business.

In this book, Ed Paulson's street-smart advice takes a prospective seller or buyer through each step of the process. You learn the important ingredients that go into creating the right recipe for buying or selling a business. Subjects such as taxes and legal issues, which are often intimidating, are covered in a simple-to-understand format. In short, you learn all of the important aspects associated with managing this complicated process.

Regardless of which side of the negotiating table you occupy, keep a positive attitude. The whole process is easier and more enjoyable when you remember that people—not companies—negotiate these transactions. A good attitude along with proper preparation will make this part of your business journey more profitable and more fun.

Your search for a book on buying and selling a business can stop here. *The Complete Idiot's Guide to Buying and Selling a Business* is the advice you need to be one smart cookie!

—Wally "Famous" Amos, founder of Famous Amos cookies

Wally Amos is credited with being the father of the gourmet cookie industry. He opened his first Famous Amos store on Sunset Boulevard in 1975. By 1985, sales had grown to more than $10 million. However, adverse financial results forced Amos to relinquish ownership. Turning adversity into opportunity, he launched a new venture, The Uncle Noname Company, now known as Uncle Wally's, which features high quality, fat-free, sugar-free gourmet muffins. In 1999, Wally came full circle as he rejoined Famous Amos, the company he founded over two decades ago.

An inspiring public speaker, Amos shares his insights on managing change and overcoming adversity. He also addresses audiences on the topics of adult illiteracy and school dropout prevention. Since 1979, Wally has been National Spokesman for Literacy Volunteers of America. He is also a Board Member of the National Center for Family Literacy and Communities in Schools.

Wally has been the recipient of many honors and awards. He gave the shirt off this back and his battered Panama hat to the Smithsonian Institution's Business Americana Collection. Dr. Amos received an honorary Doctorate in Education from Johnson & Wales University. He has been inducted into the Babson College Academy of Distinguished Entrepreneurs, and he received the Horatio Alger Award, The President's Award for Entrepreneurial Excellence, and The National Literacy Honors Award.

He wrote his autobiography, *The Famous Amos Story, The Face That Launched a Thousand Chips,* in 1983. He collaborated with his son, Gregory, on *The Power In You, Ten Secret Ingredients To Inner Strength*, a hopeful, inspirational book sharing Wally's philosophy and life experiences. His book *Man with No Name, Turn Lemons Into Lemonade* tells how Wally lost everything, including his name, and turned adversity into opportunity. Wally's most recent book, *Watermelon Magic: Seeds of Wisdom, Slices of Life*, was published in 1996 by Beyond Words Publishing. In it, he uses watermelon as a metaphor of life, sharing his personal path to wisdom, humor, joy, and a positive outlook on life.

Introduction

Your business is thriving, but you are growing restless. Or, perhaps your business is thriving, and you are hungry for more business. Perhaps your business is in trouble, and you are looking for a way to capture some of its value before all of its value disappears. Perhaps there has been a death in the family, and it is your job to sell the family business. If any of these situations is even close to yours, this book is for you.

There is nothing idiotic about wanting to buy or sell a business. In fact, a solid case can be made for it being idiotic if you don't buy or sell when the right opportunity presents itself.

It is a natural progression for any business owner either to sell a successful business or to purchase another business so that existing success can grow to new heights. These large-risk/large-reward situations make for exciting and, potentially, for very lucrative business times.

The process associated with selling or buying a business is complicated, but it can be divided into several stages.

First, you must make the decision to either buy or sell. The process then moves on to preparing to buy or sell, finding the prospective buyer or seller, closing the deal, and making the post-transaction stage a success. The general aspects of buying and selling are similar, but the details are highly dependent upon whether you are the buyer or the seller. To be an effective buyer, you should better understand the seller's perspective, and vice versa. Therefore, this book presents both sides of the transaction. After all, you might be a buyer today, but you could easily become a seller tomorrow.

My intent with this book was to take advantage of your already successful business background. I do not intend to make you an M&A attorney or a CPA, but I do intend to make you the best possible manager of these professionals as they pertain specifically to buying a selling a business.

You will find an introduction to more advanced financial principles, such as discounted cash flows and present value analysis. Why? Because these are the tools with which professionals determine the value of a business. To optimally manage the value determination process, you should understand the fundamental underpinnings of this important, abstract, yet powerful analysis technique. By the way, other, simpler valuation techniques are also presented. You are no longer in simple accounting. Wow!

By the time you finish this book, you should have performed an in-depth survey of your own motivations for buying or selling, you should be comfortable with the general valuation placed on the business, and you should have a solid idea of what you intend to get out of the transaction. The rest is up to you.

Isn't that the way it is with every major business decision? You can read, analyze, and consult about a decision for months or even years. At some point, however, you, as the key decision maker, must make a decision and recommendation. My intention is to make you as prepared and as comfortable as possible with making that decision. I want you to understand the information presented by your professional advisors and to be able to instruct them on how best to serve your needs.

After all, the accountants and lawyers work for you. Although they sometimes forget this, they can only work within the guidelines you give them, and if you provide no guidelines, they will do the best that they can to define them on their own.

Making big decisions is part of doing business. The bigger the decision the better prepared you had better be. Without proper preparation, a large decision can quickly undermine or completely erase years of hard work. Take the time to read this book. Understand its management recommendations. Grapple with its financial analysis techniques. Finally, apply this information to your particular situation.

You can and will make the right decisions for you and your company. You are no idiot. You and I both know that. Time to get to work.

How to Use This Book

This book is divided into seven parts. Some parts apply equally to both buyers and sellers, whereas others are oriented specifically toward the buyer or the seller. Remember, though, that the more you understand about the other person's objectives the more likely you are to negotiate a successful buy or sell transaction. My point being that you should read both the buying and selling sections no matter which side of the table you occupy.

Part 1, "Common Stuff for Buyers and Sellers," presents information that is common to both buyers and sellers. It presents the overall issues that apply to both the buying and selling process, including the general ways to manage the process and/or structure the final acquisition.

Part 2, "We Have Ways to Make Money Talk," is your financial primer for this book. It presents some general information about financial statements, and it provides a look at the effective use of financial ratios for a healthy financial checkup. Finally, the tax implications of specific transaction types are presented.

Part 3, "Checking Out a Target Business," is aimed at the buyers. Here is where you start the due diligence investigation process, start collecting detailed information about the company and its personnel, and look at the possibility of buying a competitor. If your target company is involved with franchising, Chapter 12 is a must read.

Part 4, "Actually Buying the Business," gets into the details of the decision of whether to buy or not. Placing a value on the company along with methods of financing are presented in enough detail for you to understand their possibilities and complexities. This is a must read section for both buyers and sellers.

Part 5, "Preparing to Sell Your Business," is aimed at the seller's side of the table. Here you learn the various preparation techniques, motivations for selling, financial report readiness/preparation, and the tax implications of selling. This is also a must-read section for both buyers and sellers.

Part 6, "Putting Your Baby on the Market," deals with the actual sale process from preparing the company marketing brochure (the prospectus), setting the asking price, to dealing with the unfortunate possibility of your company not selling. Chapters 21, 22, 15, and 16 are critically important chapters, and they should be well digested by both buyers and sellers.

Part 7, "After You Say 'I Do,'" presents the various aspects of making the acquisition perform to its maximum potential. This section is aimed at both buyers and sellers, although Chapter 26 is oriented more toward the buyers.

The appendixes are provided as supporting sections for the chapters. The glossary presents many common business and acquisition buzzwords. The other appendixes present reference and resource information that you might find useful.

Extras

A visual reference is provided throughout the book in the form of various tips, cautions, and advice that pertains to the topic under discussion.

Straight Talk

This is information learned from the street and experience. The managers in the group might find the personal stories, lessons, and comments contained in these of particular value. This is the stuff you don't learn in school.

Terms of Acquisition

Terminology and buzzwords are presented here. Many of these buzzwords are included in the glossary, so, if you forget where in the book a term was defined, make sure to check out Appendix A in the back of the book.

Buyer/Seller Beware

These items are designed to warn the buyer, the seller, or both about a particular aspect of the topic under discussion. You should make a point of reading and thinking about these points, since they usually can have a dramatic effect.

Hot Tip

Just as the name suggests, Hot Tips are items that make your life easier and provide that little extra to make a little effort go a long way. These guys can save you tons of time and frustration if you read them and follow them.

Acknowledgments

There are so many people to acknowledge that it is hard to know where to start. I don't want this to sound like an Academy Award acceptance speech. Therefore, I will keep the list to people who were directly involved with the production of this book, because the people who shared their stories preferred to remain anonymous.

Thank you, Alpha Books, for your continued success with the *Complete Idiot's Guide* series, and to Gary Krebs and Kathy Nebenhaus for seeing the value in this book. An initial thank you goes to my mother, Jean, who continues to put her professional secretary skills to work by reviewing and editing the original drafts. Thank you, Al McDermid, for your development work that has made this book a better learning tool for its readers. To Christy Parrish and Mike Thomas for getting the manuscript into its final form. A thank you goes to the various production, sales, and marketing personnel who made this work more readable and got it onto the bookstore shelf. Thanks to Arbor Hill Restaurant for more of that bottomless cup of coffee and a morning work space.

Finally, I want to acknowledge you, the reader, for your willingness to grow on both a personal and a professional level. Without you, this book would not exist.

Dedication

To my mother, for her personal commitment to me combined with her prompt, accurate copy editing skills, and to my wife, Loree, for her faith in me and her willingness to chain me to the keyboard.

A Special Thank You to the Technical Reviewer

In particular, I want to gratefully thank Ken Daemicke, a C.P.A with Mulcahy, Pauritsch, Salvador, and Co., Ltd., in Hinsdale, IL for providing a financial reality check along with his insights.

Trademarks

All terms mentioned in this book that are known to be or are suspected of being trademarks or service marks have been appropriately capitalized. Alpha Books and Penguin Group (USA) Inc. cannot attest to the accuracy of this information. Use of a term in this book should not be regarded as affecting the validity of any trademark or service mark.

Part 1

Common Stuff for Buyers and Sellers

There is common information that pertains to any company purchase, whether you are a buyer or a seller. Part One presents this information to help the buyer better appreciate the seller's point of view, and vice versa.

Chapter 1

Timing Is the Secret to Success

In This Chapter

➤ The importance of timing when selling and buying

➤ The three ingredients of timing

➤ The use of brokers when buying and selling

➤ The importance of relating small and large businesses

➤ Strategic reasons for buying and selling

"So how long do you think that this current market frenzy will continue?" asked Bill of his stock trader friend, Judy.

"That's a good question, and everyone has his or her own right answer. Just ask them," said Judy shaking her head. "I do know that if you are interested in selling your business, this is a good time to do it. Interest rates are low and overall market confidence appears to still be strong."

Bill put down his coffee cup and started to pace the room. Clearly he was agitated, but Judy wasn't sure about what. "Okay, what's wrong?" she finally asked.

"Just this. The markets might be ready, but I'm not ... or rather we're not. I could sell the company now, but would probably only get a fraction of what I could get if we were ready."

Bill went on to explain how the company's processes were not properly documented, that the financial statements received some flags on the last audit, and that he hadn't emotionally prepared himself or his staff for the prospect of selling.

Judy poured Bill another cup of coffee and set it in front of him. Putting her hand on his shoulder she said, "Well, there's no time like the present to get started. If you're lucky, the market surge will continue for another few years, when you are ready to sell. What the heck? You've got nothing to lose by getting ready."

"I know you're right," sighed Bill. "I'm just mad at myself for not being ready now."

Most of us have had opportunities pass us by simply because we did not recognize them as such at the time or because we just weren't ready to take advantage of them when they presented themselves. You can count on luck alone, or you can prepare and hope that you are also lucky. Some people call the second approach "making your own luck," and I think there's some truth to that. The more prepared you are, the more likely you are to see an opportunity when it presents itself.

Timing Creates Better Deals

So much of life's success is built on timing. Whether it is timing of your own choosing or simply luck, we all know that being in the right place at the right time can spell the difference between success and disappointment.

The same applies when buying or selling a business. Business timing is dependent upon a number of factors that can all influence whether the deal works out in your favor. Optimal timing is also dependent upon whether you are the buyer or the seller. We will cover both in their own sections.

Here are a few timing-related points that are common whether you are buying or selling a business:

➤ The general state of the economy

➤ The state of the company's specific industry

➤ The financial condition of the company itself

The general state of the economy plays a large role in determining the availability of financing for the buyer, while also setting a general level of financial optimism about the future. As you will hear repeatedly throughout this book, the value of any asset is heavily dependent upon the buyer's perceived economic view of the future. The better the economic view of the future, the more people are willing to pay for something today since the perceived risk of losing it in the future is perceived as minimal. On the other hand, if the future looks less rosy, people will want to risk less (which means pay less) today just in case things do take a future turn for the worst.

Take the comments made about the general state of the economy, and apply them to a company's specific industry. If the industry is booming, the level of perceived risk is lower, usually allowing the seller to obtain a higher sale price from the buyer. If the industry is in decline, the buyer is usually willing to pay less since the future is less certain. More discussion of this important topic is presented later in this chapter and throughout the book.

Overall market conditions are important, but eventually the price of a business is mostly dependent upon the business itself. If the business is doing well both operationally and financially, a buyer is usually willing to pay a higher price since the level of perceived risk is lower. If, on the other hand, the business is in shambles and losing money, the buyer will be less willing to purchase, meaning that the seller must reduce the price substantially to close the deal.

What I just said shouldn't come as too much of a surprise. Which would you rather pay top dollar for: a solidly built house in a booming market or an older house in a region experiencing an economic slump? Get the picture?

Here's the reality check. You do not control the general state of the economy or your particular industry unless you are a major player with a large percentage market share. Almost always, you are going to have to make your best guess as to when both the general economy and your particular industry will be in their best shape. Based on that guess, you can then assess the best time to buy or sell.

Timing Your Business Buy

Buyers might want to watch for high and low trends in the economy and specific industries. Either situation presents its own set of unique opportunities.

If you are a buyer with a lot of purchasing power and are looking for a bargain, buying when the markets are low can provide excellent opportunities. For example, assume that the overall economy is in a slump but a particular industry is maintaining a consistent level of economic growth. A slow market usually means that finance money is less available, which limits the number of buyers. When the number of buyers is limited and the supply of companies for sale is on the rise, you have a buyer's market.

By the way, a limited availability of financing might also force companies to sell simply to meet their financial obligations, which also plays well for the buyer. Limited financing means that interest rates are probably higher, making it more expensive to operate a business using credit.

Do you see a pattern forming here?

But there are also risks associated with a declining economy or industry. When you buy during a decline, you are probably doing so with the expectation that the economy will turn around and that your particular industry and/or company will maintain a viable financial level of performance during the economic turn around process. Should your expectation be incorrect, you might have purchased a company that requires a higher level of financial investment than you initially expected, thus turning a great purchase into a marginal one, or worse.

Hot Tip

Cash is king in a declining economy, and buyers with ready supplies of cash and financing might find some excellent bargains during hard economic times.

You can see that buying in a down economy presents both opportunities and risks, as with any financial situation. Remember, any investment that provides a return higher than that of a standard savings plan also comes with a higher level of risk attached. It is just the name of the game; watch out for anyone who tries to convince you otherwise.

Buying a company in a hot industry in an "up" economy also has its fair share of risk attached and, perhaps, a lower potential financial return.

An *up economy* means people are more optimistic about the future, which generally increases the perceived value of a company. After all, if a company's future profits are assumed to be as good as, if not better than, its current profits, you can afford to pay more for the purchase.

A higher purchase price means a higher initial investment, which usually involves more cash and debt. Should the future turn out as good as, or better than, you expected, life is good. Congratulations.

If the future should instead take an unexpected turn for the worst, you might be the owner of a company that is heavily in debt, overvalued for the future economic climate, and perhaps experiencing a downturn in its business due to economic forces beyond the company's control.

Terms of Acquisition

Up economy   A period of positive overall economic growth.

Risk   The possibility that things will not turn out as you expect and will cost you a portion or all of your investment.

You might be in a the position of having to sell a company that is struggling economically in a down economic climate. Rarely an enviable situation.

In summary, buying in a down economy presents bargains but also involves risks related to future economic trends. Down markets eventually do go back up, but holding on until things turn around can be a tricky and an expensive process.

Buying in an up economy means that the company purchased will likely cost more, involving more cash and debt, but also will not involve the risks of a down economy at the time of purchase. It does, on the other hand, involve the risk of a future economic downturn that is completely beyond your control. As always, risk and reward must be assessed for every particular situation, and only you can ultimately make the determination as to the right time to buy.

Timing the Sale

As mentioned at the beginning of this section, you do not control the overall economy at all, and in general, you do not control the performance of your particular industry segment.

On the other hand, if you are selling, you should be clear that you do control both the operation and the financial health of your business. So, my suggestion is that you sellers focus on the things that you do control and get your business in order. In this way, when the economy and your industry look attractive, your business will shine like a diamond.

As a seller, you want to obtain the highest possible value for your company. This generally means selling your company when both the overall economy and your particular industry segment are up. Obviously, you will obtain the highest possible value when selling a well performing company in a positive economic climate. This sounds good on paper, but is often difficult to come by in reality. The trick is to have your company operations prepared so that you can act promptly when the economy turns positive.

Buyer/Seller Beware

Independent of the economic state, you should make sure that you have more money on hand than you expect to need. Good economies turn sour and bad economies can linger longer than expected. Having more cash is always better than having less.

Oddly enough, a down economy presents its own set of opportunities for well-run companies. Your company might be profitable and be part of an industry segment that has maintained a positive growth even though the overall economy has taken a downturn. This is often the case with the entertainment industry since people use entertainment as a way of escaping from their daily troubles. Entertainment revenues often remain the same or increase whereas other industries suffer.

Notice that selling an entertainment company, under the previously mentioned circumstances, might allow you to command a higher sale price. Why? Think of it this way.

There are a limited number of investment options available to investors. If the overall economy is sluggish or full of uncertainty, then higher investment returns are probably available but with much higher associated risks. If, on the other hand, you can show an investor that your company presents only a moderate risk level, you should be able to command a higher price for your company since it presents the best risk/ reward trade off for investors.

Once again, the right time for selling a business is based on your personal assessment. If conditions are optimal, the decision is easy. If conditions are mixed, which are typically the case, you must make the decision based on your own assessment of the information at hand. Only history will tell if you made the right decision or not.

Timing Based on Strategy

There are times when overriding strategic concerns or completely unexpected occurrences will drive a decision to buy or sell. Here is a partial listing of events that might fall into this category:

> ➤ A partner in your company passes away, leaving you with the entire company and the responsibility of dealing with the heirs. This set of conditions often prompts the sale of smaller companies.

Straight Talk

I once asked a professor friend of mine for advice on a particular business topic. His response stayed with me.

He mentioned that I already had all of the information and knowledge I needed to make this decision and nobody could make this decision any better than me given the specific set of circumstances.

"Your job is to make the decision," he said. "My job is to evaluate it three years from now and critique whether you made the right or wrong one."

➤ One of your biggest competitors decides to sell and you are afraid that another competitor will purchase the company, putting you at a market disadvantage.

➤ Your particular financial situation changes due to any of a number of unexpected possibilities such as a medical problem or a divorce, which creates the need for additional cash and prompts the sale of the company.

➤ A larger company decides to enter your particular market and is looking to buy an existing company for its toehold. This chance will go to either you or one of your competitors, and it might prompt your decision to sell earlier than expected.

Hot Tip

As my father used to say, "Some help by staying and some help by going."

➤ You might find that the family business that you planned to hand to your children isn't wanted by any of your children. Whereas you might have otherwise worked the company until your children were ready to take over the reins, you might instead decide to sell the company, freeing you up to do other things with your hard-earned equity.

➤ Legislation or zoning might change, making your business either more or less desirable, prompting you to sell when not previously planned.

Notice that most of these items are completely outside of your control, but they can put you in a position where you are better off selling or buying at an unexpected time.

Like John Lennon says, "Life is what happens when you are busy making other plans." This rule also applies in business.

Using a Business Broker

There are companies out there that act as intermediaries between business buyers and sellers. They are the equivalent of a real estate broker except that the property being handled is a business. These brokers can work for either buyers who are looking for particular types of properties or sellers who are putting their firms on the market.

There are pros and cons associated with using a business broker. A major benefit is that you are not alone in trying to sell or buy a business. If you have selected an experienced broker, this person can act as a resource in determining the right price and prospect.

In addition, this broker should have contacts in the industry, meaning that finding the right buyer or target company should be a more focused activity. As a seller, this means dealing with fewer *"tire kickers,"* and as a buyer, this means having fewer false starts evaluating companies that will not meet your criteria.

However, business brokers do not provide their services for free; they take either a flat fee or a percentage of the sale price as compensation for their services. This fee is negotiable and depends in large part on the size of the company being sold. For companies that sell for under $500,000, the fee is usually in the range of 10 percent or more. Notice that this equates to as much as $50,000 in selling fees, which can be a large portion of the sale's profits, making the use of a broker a last resort option for many small companies. For companies larger than $500,000, the fees range from 2 to 7 percent of the sale price depending on the size of the company sold. A common formula applies 5 percent to the first $1 million, 4 percent to the next $1 million, 3 percent to the next $1 million, 2 percent to the next $1 million and 1 percent to the rest of the sale price. Fees are always negotiable; however, these figures should give you a budgetary starting point.

Terms of Acquisition

Tire Kickers People who appear to be interested in buying a car (or your business), who ask a lot of questions (kick the tires), who take up a lot of your time, and who ultimately decide that they really aren't interested.

Should you decide to use a broker, it is important that you carefully qualify the broker's credibility. The qualification criteria should include experience with businesses of your type, preferably experience with your particular industry; access to M&A (Mergers and Acquisitions) attorneys, accountants, and tax attorneys; a proven track record; high integrity; and no potential conflicts of interest. A typical conflict of interest could be something like representing one of your competitors while also trying to sell your company, or having a business interest in your transaction that extends beyond the standard broker/client relationship.

Business sale/purchase arrangements are complicated enough without adding any unnecessary personal or business entanglements to the arrangement. Keeping it simple yet competently professional is the right, and only, way to go when using a broker. Your broker will represent you and your company to potential buyers, and a poor choice can actually do you more harm than good. So don't rush this selection.

Being Small Is Special

When compared to the bigger companies, smaller companies sometimes feel that they are at a disadvantage when either buying or selling. In fact, smaller companies can bring to these transactions many advantages that are usually not found with larger companies.

Hot Tip

Make sure that you have prospective brokers sign a non-disclosure document before revealing any information that you would not want the general public to know. This document protects both you and the broker, and it ensures that both sides understand that secrecy is paramount.

Terms of Acquisition

Reverse Acquisition   When a smaller company purchases a larger one.

For starters, a large percentage of the innovations made in technology and other business arenas is often done within smaller companies. Why? It is really a matter of survival. There is no way for a smaller company to compete with larger firms by offering the same breadth and depth of products and services. Smaller firms survive through innovation and creativity. They thrive by providing these attributes to niche markets typically ignored by the larger firms. As these niches grow, they attract the attention of larger firms that eventually see the niche as a viable major business opportunity.

At this point, a larger firm might choose to develop its own products and/or services to address this evolving market, or they might simply purchase the expertise in the form of a smaller company already established in this market. Developing the expertise has risk associated with it and takes time. Purchasing an established firm takes less time and immediately provides the larger firm with a foothold into the market. In terms of time saved and market access gained, it often makes more sense for the larger firm to purchase the smaller one.

A smaller firm can also purchase a larger firm, depending on the companies and finances involved. As a strange twist, larger firms occasionally want to be purchased by a smaller company to gain access to the smaller firm's management and technology. The strong entrepreneurial temperament of a smaller business can then be infused into the larger firm since the parent company is now the smaller, more entrepreneurial firm. Both finances and shareholder temperament have to be just right for this to work out, but it does happen.

Large Businesses Are Special, Too

The purchase of a smaller company by a larger one does not always sound the "death-knoll" for entrepreneurialism and innovation. In fact, it can actually foster this creativity if it is handled properly. But, if you are the seller, you will probably want a clear commitment and understanding with the larger company regarding the preservation of the successful essence of your company before the deal is signed or too much proprietary information is revealed. Sellers often retain an emotional attachment to their sold company and want to ensure that the important essence is retained by the purchasing company's management.

A larger company can provide resources that would just not be readily available otherwise to smaller ones. These resources may include extended distribution of products and services, increased operating budgets, synergy with other existing technologies, along with more professional management personnel and procedures. Unfortunately, along with these resources often come policies, procedures, and oversight that have squashed innovation within more than one company.

Straight Talk

Back in the early 1980s, I worked with the IBM PC team in Boca Raton, Florida. At that time, the engineering and manufacturing was done in a series of semi-permanent buildings that often suffered from insufficient air conditioning.

This was set up as a rogue group within IBM to keep it from being stifled by the IBM bureaucracy. Well, success caught up with them around the time of the PC AT introduction, and IBM decided to get this rogue group under control. I think we all know what happened to IBM's dominance of the PC marketplace from that point forward.

Hey—Give Me That: Hostile Takeovers

Unfortunately, under certain conditions, it is possible for somebody to purchase your company even if you don't want them to. This is called a "hostile takeover," which is pretty self-explanatory.

A hostile takeover is usually only attempted with publicly owned companies, but it can be accomplished in less obvious ways with privately owned companies.

A publicly held company can be taken over if a buyer purchases enough shares to have a majority voting say in the financial operation of the company. The corporation that

11

issued the shares has no direct say over who can and cannot purchase these shares. If the existing shareholders choose to sell their shares to the buyer, so be it.

There are various defensive strategies that the corporation can implement to fight off a hostile takeover. Unfortunately, these almost always leave the company in worse financial shape than it was in before the takeover attempt started.

Privately held companies can get themselves into a compromised position in a number of ways that do not involve the selling of shares, although the selling of shares is the easiest takeover method.

Suppose that your corporation has outstanding loans and that these loans can be sold to another lender. If that lender is a party interested in owning your company, the new lender can apply exceptional pressure on the corporation by employing tactics such as strictly enforcing the rules of its contract in an unreasonable way that might possibly cause the note to be called. The corporation must then restructure its debt under a compressed timeframe. This is often difficult to accomplish, and it could force the company into a sale simply to pay its debts.

Is this a "nice guy" approach to business? Absolutely not, but that doesn't mean that there isn't someone out there willing to try it on you and your company if you have something that they want.

Hot Tip

Always make sure that the people you borrow money from are worthy of the trust you are giving to them. As with lending money, it is always good to check out the other party before finalizing your relationship.

The Least You Need to Know

➤ Keeping your company in ready-to-sell condition ensures that you will be able to sell when overall market conditions are right.

➤ You cannot control the overall economy, but you can track it and guess for yourself what will happen next.

➤ Buying a company during poor economic times often allows you to buy at a lower price.

➤ Smaller companies add entrepreneurial spirit to larger companies, which can be valuable to that larger company.

➤ Selecting the right business broker is an important decision that should be made carefully and only with signed non-disclosure agreements.

Chapter 2

Start at the Very Beginning ...

In This Chapter

➤ The difference between buying and selling

➤ The stages of the buy/sell process

➤ Bring in the right professionals when needed

➤ Find the right buyer or acquisition target

Frank thought that he had everything under control. He had found a solid prospective buyer, had prepared the sales documents, and had presented the company effectively enough to get an offer. But his fears had found him as well; he had an offer and he couldn't determine if it was a good one or not.

The advice he had received from his attorney was that everything looked to be "in order." His accountant told him that the numbers all seemed to "add up." But nobody could tell him if it was a "good deal." And the buyer wanted an answer by early next week, leaving him with only a few days to evaluate the offer.

Frank believed that he understood the finances involved, but he had questions about a couple of clauses in the agreement. When he ran them by his corporate attorney, the response was less confident than he would have liked. And these clauses could seriously restrict his business options for a few years after the sale.

There had to be someone out there who could confidently advise him on the "reasonableness" of these clauses, and he only had a few days to find that person.

Buying and Selling Are Similar ... but Different

This might seem obvious, but it takes both a buyer and a seller to complete a business transaction. What is not so obvious is that the interests of the buyer and seller are related but very different. And these differing interests often cause miscommunications that, if not resolved early in the process, can cause an otherwise excellent transaction to fall apart.

For example, both the buyer and the seller want the company sold but for different reasons. The buyer is looking to the future when determining the value of the company, and filters all discussions through a "future" filter. The seller, on the other hand, is usually looking at the company from a historical perspective, and filters all buyer comments through that "historical" filter.

Although each party shows up for each of the meetings, it is very possible that each party also attended a different meeting in his or her own mind. Getting the buyer and seller to agree on important points is often more of an art form than a science, but whether art or science, both parties must be agree to ensure a solid transaction that works for both parties.

Hot Tip

Buyers and sellers approach negotiations with their own best interests in mind. Mentally putting yourself in the other party's shoes may both speed up and smooth out the transaction.

Both parties are trying to sell the other on being the right candidate. The seller is trying to convince the buyer that his or her particular company is the best value available. The buyer is trying to convince the seller that he or she can perform financially as agreed to in the contracts and that the various personal covenants stipulated will be adhered to. For some sellers, personal covenants such as retaining certain employees or managing company resources in specific ways might be more important than the actual purchase price. If the buyer is talking price and the seller is thinking employee and customer protection, there is fertile ground for misunderstanding.

Preparing to Buy

You folks who plan to sell your business will find detailed information about reasons for selling in Chapter 17, "Why Sell, Anyway?"

I want to spend a few moments here talking to you buyers about your purchasing motivations. Purchasing a company is a lot like taking on a roommate, and it should not be pursued lightly. The right roommate can enhance the quality of your life, making your life better than it was previously. The wrong roommate can turn a good situation sour quickly and even put your emotional, physical, and financial health in jeopardy. The same can happen with a poor company acquisition.

You and your company have worked hard for the money and reputation you currently enjoy. When you buy a company you attach your finances, personnel, and reputation to that company. Even if you plan to leave the company as its own stand-alone entity, you still make a financial commitment to the company that must be maintained, perhaps at the expense of your core company's operation.

So, where do you start the purchasing process? You first start by knowing where you plan to go with the purchase, which means some type of strategic planning function. From your strategic plan, you can determine the areas of company operation that would be improved with the purchase of another company. Once you determine this, you can then effectively start looking for potential acquisition targets.

Terms of Acquisition

Acquisition Target A company that you decide to investigate in earnest for potential purchase.

M & A Merger and acquisition.

Strategic Plan A business plan that sets the overall direction of a company over the next three to five year period.

At a minimum, you should start by first asking yourself a few questions:

➤ What is right with our current company operation?

➤ What can be improved with our current company operation?

➤ What would be our incremental revenues and profits if we were to address these deficiencies?

➤ How much can we spend to remedy these deficiencies?

➤ What must we do today to remain competitive within our market segment, and what must we do within the next three to five years?

➤ Do we need additional business resources in specific marketing, sales, manufacturing, personnel, or financial areas?

➤ Can our current financial, marketing, sales, personnel, engineering, and other operational resources be used effectively to achieve our overall strategic business goals?

➤ Would any particular technology or business strategy fit well with our current strengths making the combination more successful than the sum of its parts?

➤ Can we afford the time and/or money needed to develop the required capabilities using in-house resources?

➤ Are we willing to purchase this expertise or capability instead of developing it internally?

➤ Have we performed our self-evaluation to make sure that we are purchasing the business that matches our personal and business goals?

➤ If we are using our own money to fund the purchase, could we prove to someone else that this purchase justified *their* putting up the money? If we cannot convince someone else, we aren't ready.

Treat this list as a starting point for generating more questions. The more questions you ask before starting your purchasing search, the more efficiently the process will proceed, and the more likely you are to wind up with a satisfactory purchase. You are always better off determining your problems earlier in the process than later so that you save your time, money, and reputation.

Buyer Beware

Purchasing a business is like any other business decision. It must make good business sense, or it will make little sense at all.

There are all kinds of reasons for buying a company, but unless these reasons eventually lead to improved shareholder value in the form of dividends and/or increased price-per-share, the purchase should be re-evaluated. This is especially true for publicly held companies; although, it applies to privately held companies as well. No business stays in business for very long if it fails to minimally maintain and, optimally, improve its financial health.

Finding the Candidate

Whether you are buying or selling, you must find your candidate. For the seller, the candidate is the person or other company interested in potentially buying your company. For the buyer, the candidate (target company) is the company that is a solid potential fit with your purchase goals.

Finding that candidate can be a tricky business, which is why many companies turn to a business broker. Just as a real estate broker is familiar with both the properties and buyers currently on the market, a good business broker will also be familiar with the current set of buyers and sellers.

If you choose to go without a business broker, then you must do this legwork on your own.

Finding a Company to Buy

As the buyer, you must first determine the general criteria for your target company. Here are some things to consider when narrowing down the list of potential candidates:

➤ Is the company in a geographic location that meets your needs?

➤ Is the market segment growing or shrinking?

➤ Is this company's reputation one that you want associated with your organization?

➤ Is the company culture compatible with your own organization, or will there be a clash?

➤ Is the target company a leader or follower in its market segment?

➤ How long has the company been in business and under how many different ownership structures?

➤ Is the company publicly or privately owned?

➤ What special attributes make this particular company an attractive purchase candidate?

➤ Are there members of the executive management team that would make welcome additions to your own organization?

➤ Does the target company's general direction appear compatible with the direction you want for the company you choose to purchase?

Hundreds of other items can be, and will be, added to this list as you get farther into the purchase evaluation process. At this stage, you are simply trying to make a first-cut determination about which companies are worth further evaluation. Notice that most of this information is publicly available and requires the disclosure of no confidential information. Should a company fail this first set of evaluation criteria, you are best served dropping it from the list unless other attributes are such a strong fit that they warrant further investigation.

Once you narrow the list down to 10 companies or less, then you should perform an in-depth newspaper or other media analyses. A tremendous amount of information is provided by industry publications, and most of them are in your public library. A few days in the library can round out your initial assessment. It might even let you know whether the company is currently for sale, whether deals have recently fallen through, and/or whether the company has extenuating circumstances that make it an even better acquisition target.

Hot Tip

If you are purchasing a smaller company, you should pay special attention to the top management team in general and the owners in particular. As a way of ensuring a smooth transition these people will quite often become your employees for a period of time after the sale. If the top management team has a reputation for being difficult to work with, you might want to just look elsewhere from the start.

By the way, note that at this stage you do not even know if the company is for sale or not. You are simply determining whom you should talk to.

It is very possible, and probable, that your list of 10 companies will now be down to five or less. But notice that your information on these companies should now be as current as is possible with publicly available information. You can talk intelligently to the company's management and represent yourself as a credible buyer. This may not close the deal for you, but it will certainly give you a better chance of initially getting their attention.

If your target company is a publicly traded company, getting your hands on the latest annual report, along with other required filings and reports, is a must. You should also check out the stock's history over the last 12 to 36 months, just to round out the media information with hard financial data. Part Three of this book will cover targeted company evaluation procedures in greater detail. Remember that at this stage you are simply trying to determine which companies to further investigate.

Finding a Buyer

If you are on the selling side, your marketing challenge is finding the right buyer. As with most things in business, determining the right buyer is usually not a simple process. Simply having the money to purchase your company might be enough for some sellers, but most sellers will want the buyer to provide something more than money. This is particularly true for sellers who accept a portion of the sale price in the form of stock in the acquiring company.

The seller who accepts stock in the acquiring company now becomes actively concerned with the future financial performance of the acquiring company. In fact, the seller is often given (or requires) a seat on the acquiring company's board of directors, giving the seller some management say regarding future operations.

Many of the initial research activities recommended for buyers in the earlier section of this chapter apply to sellers as well. If you choose not to employ the services of a broker, then you are on your own in finding the right buyer.

Seller Beware

Don't expect to sell your business and leave like you would when selling a house. This is particularly true with a small business that is often heavily dependent on its owners. Evaluate the acquiring company like you would a future employer, because that is probably what it will become.

Ideally, your perfect buyer is not only willing to pay you a solid price for your company (and is able to come up with the money) but is also willing to provide some other business benefits to your company's operation. These benefits may be in the form of a wider distribution channel for your company's products, more advanced technical support, or an international manufacturing capability. These capabilities are beyond the capacity of many smaller companies, and simply joining forces with a larger company can provide the small company with an instant national, or international, presence. And if your products or services fill a void in the acquiring company's offerings, both companies and their customers will win.

It is also important that you be willing to work for the acquiring company after the sale is completed, which is often a stipulation attached to the purchase of a smaller company. There is little reason to sell your company only to find yourself shackled to a company and job that you would never have taken under other circumstances, unless the money or other benefits outweigh the disadvantages. We are all negotiable, and you don't want to sell out too quickly to a demanding buyer unless it is personally and/or financially worth your while.

So, researching the right companies, in the right markets, with the right products, with enough money, and with a potential interest in buying your company takes some effort and creativity. You might already have several prospects in mind simply from your familiarity with the industry and its players.

Excellent candidates are those with whom you do not directly compete but who share a common customer base. Companies are always looking for ways to sell more products or services to their existing customers, and purchasing an established company with a proven track record allows them to provide new items in a much shorter time frame than developing these new capability on their own. Plus, your company has its own name recognition that adds to their existing offering, which should make the total package that much stronger. And, compared to a direct competitor who would like nothing more than to see you and your company disappear, these companies are less likely to use your private information against you.

Alternative candidates for consideration are companies in other industries who could benefit from either the business or technological strengths of your company. If the selling company is a manufacturing concern, you might find that your company's manufacturing equipment and personnel could be easily cross-trained to create products for another industry. Your newer equipment and efficiencies might be of value to company that hasn't upgraded in a while.

Straight Talk

For you small businesses, the right buyer might be someone you would never expect at first glance. I know an attorney in New York who bought a law practice in Hawaii so that he had a reason to write off his frequent trips. He intends to retire there eventually and is feathering his nest now for when that time comes. If you are the owner of a small Hawaiian law firm, you might look for law firm executives who make frequent trips to Hawaii as your initial buyer prospect list.

As with much of sales, success depends in large part on understanding what you have to offer, understanding who benefits most from what you have to offer, and understanding how to present your company in such a way that the benefits are clear.

Presenting a viable product or service to a credible buyer in an easy-to-understand way is a great recipe for sales success. Making it easy for the buyer takes a lot of work on the front end, but the rewards are well worth your time.

It All Happens in Stages

Selling a business takes time. Period. It also takes planning if you expect to make as much off of the sale as possible.

It might help you to divide the pre-selling process into a few steps.

1. **Solidify Operations Stage:** At this stage you perform the functions needed to ensure that a buyer believes that the value of your company will transfer with minimal loss to the new owners. By the way, the steps accomplished at this stage are good business practice whether you choose to sell or not. This stage usually lasts at least one year and may start as many as five years ahead of when the company is actually placed on the market. This stage is covered in more detail in Chapter 18, "Getting Ready to Sell."

2. **Pre-Sale Stage:** You have reached this stage when you have a solid start on the completion of stage one and have decided in earnest to sell your company. In this stage, you decide on the members of the sales team, including key employees, an M&A attorney, an accountant and/or tax attorney, and any other owners. You must also get the other owners to subscribe to your belief that selling the company is the right thing to do. Investigation is started to determine prospective buyers along with a reasonable asking price. Any sales-related documents, such as a prospectus, are created during this stage, which can last up to year, during which time secrecy is critical. See Chapters 19 to 22 for more details on this stage.

Hot Tip

Sales success is achieved by moving the customer, in a controlled fashion, from one stage to the next. Buyers are never comfortable if they feel like a stage was skipped, whether they think of them as stages or not. Cover your bases with each of the stages, and you will be more successful and have a happier buyer.

3. **Initial Marketing Stage:** During this stage you start to put out feelers with various prospective buyers to see who might be interested in purchasing your company. The challenge here is to approach enough companies to find an interested buyer or two, while not telling so many people that your pending sale becomes common industry knowledge. During this stage you might contact people by mail or telephone and will have probably have a meeting or two before moving to Stage 4.

4. **Due Diligence Stage:** This is the most frightening stage for most sellers since this stage requires revealing detailed information about the overall

operation of your company. You want to make sure that whoever gets to this stage as a prospective buyer is truly interested, because confidential information will almost definitely be revealed during this stage. It is always best to be selective about who actually gets to this stage. This stage might last anywhere from a few weeks to a few months, depending on the size of the companies involved and the overall business complexity.

5. **Proposal, Negotiations, and Closing Stage:** This is where purchase price numbers are discussed along with terms and conditions. The lawyers are usually pretty actively involved at this point, and many contractual terms and conditions might actually be worked out between the attorneys who then come to you for final approval. This stage ends when the purchase agreements are signed, money has changed hands, and you have given the new owners the key to the front door.

6. **Post Sale Stage:** Many people forget about this stage, which in some ways can be the most important. Everything done in the first five stages lead to this stage. The new owners meet with the employees, customers, and vendors while taking over the reins of your company. It is in your best personal and business interest to ensure that this stage goes smoothly since your reputation and income will depend on it. This stage is particularly important if the purchase agreement involves stock, loans, or other financial vehicles that are tied to the company's future financial performance.

As you can see, this is not a one-step process and you should be willing to sign up for the whole trip once you reach stage three. This doesn't mean that you cannot take your company off the market at any time before it actually sells, but don't expect to do that without suffering some type of professional, financial, personal, or legal repercussions.

The Sales Meetings

If you are the seller, you cannot expect the buyer to intuitively understand the value that you know to be in your company. It is your job to present your company in such a way that the buyer understands and believes in the benefits associated with owning your company.

Every contact that you have with a prospective buyer should lead the buyer through the various stages of the sales process.

Here are a few major points regarding effective selling techniques adapted from my *StreetWise Guide to Professional Selling* training course:

Terms of Acquisition

Close A request for action by the other party. It might be as simple as requesting additional information or as important as asking them to purchase your company for your asking price. Every sale process will have many smaller closing points that lead to the ultimate purchase.

➤ Buyers purchase based on the benefits that they perceive will come their way from the purchase.

➤ Buyers must believe that the various features of what you sell will actually provide them with those benefits, or they will not make the purchase.

➤ Buyers purchase only when they need something, whether something intangible like the need to spend money (like my wife) or a tangible need like a new car to go to work. The level of need will define the buyer's level of interest.

In summary, a customer has a need that prompts him or her to look for a product or service (or business) that has the features that will address that need. However, the purchase decision is ultimately made based on the benefits that the buyer perceives will come his or her way once the purchase is accomplished.

Talking to buyers who do not need what your company has to offer is basically a waste of time. If they don't need it, they won't buy it.

Presenting the various aspects (features) of your company without translating them into ways that those features benefit the buyer is doing yourself, and your company, a disservice. Don't leave it up to the buyer to determine how your company makes his or her life better. Determine this for them and then present your case in the most beneficial light possible.

Keep a focused eye on qualifying the buyer's needs and then present the features of your company that address those needs in such as way that the benefits to the buyer are obvious. Doing this well is the best way to get top dollar for your company in a reasonable time frame.

Getting the Right Professional Help

As you get deeper into buying and selling a business, you will find that each question generates a few more. And, the more complicated the transaction, such as one involving a publicly held company, the more you will appreciate having on your team professionals whom you trust and who have walked these paths before.

Let's start with your accountant. This person is important in that he or she presents your financial information as a sort of objective observer. Depending upon the level of involvement with your company's accounting, he or she may be able verify the bookkeeping and

---

Buyer/Seller Beware

Just because a person, such as a CPA, understands accounting doesn't make him or her a good financial and business manager. Just because an attorney understands business law doesn't mean that he or she understands mergers and acquisitions law. Get the right professionals with the right expertise for your team and don't rush into a selection. Time spent here will save time, money, and aggravation later in the process.

accounting accuracy of the information presented in the financial statements. If your accountant is an employee or Chief Financial Officer for your company, then his or her level of detailed knowledge about the information presented in the financial statements will be substantial. If you use a hired accountant who simply arranges the number that you provide, then he or she can only verify that portion of the process.

The difference between someone with an accounting background and a CPA (Certified Public Accountant) is that the CPA is licensed by the state in which he or she operates. This licensing procedure is rigorous and defines specific ethical and legal codes of conduct. CPAs typically know accounting and taxes, but they might not understand business. It is important for you to understand the limitations of your accountant's abilities. In particular, accountants are detail-oriented people who deal primarily with historical information. This information is well defined since it has already happened. Accountants often have a hard time risking the future based on a hunch, which is what most entrepreneurial business types thrive on.

So, get a clear understanding about your particular accountant's personal orientation toward speculative ventures and risk. You are the business manager. He or she is the accountant whose primary job is to make sure that the financial numbers shown on the statements accurately reflect the current and historical status of a company. Your job is to use that information to make business decisions. If you are lucky, you will get both a financial manager and an accountant in the same person, but don't expect it.

The same general advice applies to attorneys. Attorneys are excellent at making sure that contracts and other documents are "legal," but they are not really trained to determine whether something makes good business sense or not.

For example, a "legal" agreement could be one that allows your vendors to instantly change, without prior notification or your consent, the terms on your accounts payable debt so that it is due within 48 hours instead of the initially agreed to 30 days. If you signed an agreement containing these conditions, you would be legally bound by the agreement even if it made no business sense. Counting on your attorney to make business decisions for you is usually an unrealistic expectation, unless you are lucky enough to have an attorney who is also a solid businessperson.

You will also find that attorneys have little accounting background, which puts you and your accountant in the role of interpreting any financial numbers involved with your agreements.

Merger and acquisition (M&A) law is a specialized animal that involves specialized areas of the law. It is likely that your standard corporate attorney will not have the specialized expertise needed to assist with the creation and/or review of M&A documents. For this reason, it is best to have an

Hot Tip

If you can find an attorney–CPA with M&A experience, you will pay more for this person's time, but it might turn out cheaper than having to work with multiple professionals. It will certainly be easier to work with a single person than with several.

experienced M&A attorney onboard from the beginning of your buying or selling process. If the transaction involves a publicly traded company, your attorney's expertise in the area or public disclosure should also be carefully reviewed. If the transaction involves a franchise, you might even need an additional lawyer since franchise law is another one of those specialized legal areas.

There are significant benefits to having a tax attorney on your team in addition to an M&A attorney. The tax attorney will understand both the accounting and legal aspects of your particular company. The M&A attorney will understand the legal aspects of the agreements you will sign as part of the transaction. The skill sets involved are unique and usually require the involvement of different people. Having a tax attorney who is also a CPA is an ideal combination. If this person also has M&A experience, you should lock him or her in a room and not let them out.

The Least You Need to Know

➤ Both buyers and sellers participate at each stage of the sales process but sellers typically have a historical perspective, whereas buyers are evaluating the future.

➤ General business attorneys will probably not have the specialized M&A skills needed to evaluate the purchase agreements you will encounter or need to generate. Finding a competent and experienced M&A attorney whom you trust is an important part of the process that should not be rushed.

➤ Both buyers and sellers must sell each other as part of their negotiations. Honing your sales skills will pay off as you move into the sales and marketing stages of the process.

➤ Selling or buying without a business broker means that you must find potential buyers or acquisition targets on your own. Extensive research in trade publications and reports and at the library are invaluable in determining likely prospects.

➤ Expect the sale/acquisition process to take between one and five years, depending on market conditions, your team's readiness, and the overall complexity of the transaction.

Chapter 3

Making Sure You're Legal

In This Chapter

➤ Understanding seller's legal disclosure requirements

➤ Legally protecting yourself as a buyer

➤ Selecting the right attorney

➤ SEC and antitrust considerations

➤ Protecting employees

"How much of this should we take at face value?" Mike asked Bill, his attorney. "I think that they are being forthright with answering all of our questions, but I still have an uneasy feeling about accepting their assertions as fact."

Bill nodded, in agreement. "Face it. Once the deal is closed, you have to live with the future fallout, not with them. Especially the way the deal is structured. They are getting a lot of cash up front and taking the rest in stock. If the future turns out to be less than expected, they won't suffer much."

"It means more money, and a lot more overtime over the next few weeks, but I will feel more comfortable if we get to know the area a little better than we do now," replied Mike. "I know that their location is a prime one today, and we also know, from experience, that things change. Let's get a few of our people on the streets in the area to do a little digging of their own."

It is not that you don't trust someone. It is that everyone sees things in their own light and with their own interests at heart. People tend to favor their side more than someone else's; I really don't think this makes them dishonest. Where judgement errors stop and fraud begins is a case for the attorneys and courts. And I hope that you are never in a situation where you must address this issue in a legal fashion.

Sellers, buyers, and their negotiators have specific ethical and legal standards to which they must adhere. This chapter presents a number of legal actions that you can take, as either a buyer or a seller, to better ensure a smooth and ethical negotiation and final transaction.

Your Legal Requirements When Selling

Ever sold a house? Remember all of the legal documents you had to sign attesting to the solid nature of the house, neighborhood, city, state, country, and universe? Or so it seemed. All of these documents are there to protect the buyer from any material, undisclosed negative seller information, and the same cautions pertain to the buyer of a business. Except that these folks have more, and usually better, lawyers.

Selling a business is a liability for both the seller and the buyer. The buyer can inherit whatever historical heritage the business may carry with it, both good and bad. Buyers rarely worry about the good heritage, but they do obsess about the bad. That is where the seller's obligations come into play.

Straight Talk

Even though you think that you are always right, take caution in revealing conjecture as fact. Just because you think it is so does not make it so. That is conjecture. Signed documents, public disclosures, legal actions, or other concrete events are facts. The fact that you talked with someone about something is a fact. Whether their information is reliable or not, is conjecture. Reveal the facts, and temper the conjecture with legal advice from your counsel. Negative conjecture will decrease the value of your business and for no verifiable reason if your conjecture turns out to be false.

Your primary obligation as the seller is to tell the truth about your business. The Golden Rule really makes good business sense under these circumstances. You would feel ripped off if the seller specifically didn't tell you about certain, confirmed aspects of the company that substantially changed the company's future value.

Assume, for example, that you are selling a hamburger stand that has stood on the corner of First and Main streets in your small town for over 20 years. It is a town landmark, which is what the buyers are purchasing. But let's also assume that you were pushed into selling by the confirmed information that the property on either side of you has been sold to an auto dealership and across the street you can expect a new nationally franchised hamburger chain restaurant. This combination, you fear, will reduce your foot traffic and shift current customers to the new competitor, so you decide to sell out.

Notice that the sale of properties and the confirmed plans to build the auto dealership and the nationally franchised burger stand are facts. Documents have been signed, money has exchanged hands, and every expectation is that the deals will proceed as planned.

Your fear about what will happen is *not* fact. It is your fear and conjecture, not a confirmed fact. The only way to know what will happen is to look at the events from a historical perspective. So, what must, and should, you reveal? The facts. The property next door has been purchased by the local car dealership mogul who has told you personally that there are plans to put a luxury car dealership on the site. Also, that the site across the street has been purchased and building plans are confirmed for the restaurant across the street.

You might also offer your assessment of both the positive and negative business possibilities associated with these changes. Traffic might increase due to the added automobile traffic from both the new businesses, and you have the land to install a drive up or more parking. A backlash against the chain could also happen since small towns often don't like national chains putting local businesses out of business. The auto dealership will also triple the local employee count, which could be very good for business, especially since you have always had an excellent relationship with the dealership owners.

The down side is that competition will increase and the local smaller business climate will be replaced with a more commercial/industrial feel. What will that do to business? Nobody knows for sure. Tell the facts, and let the new owners decide for themselves. It could go either way. The seller naturally wants to present it in the most attractive way and the buyer will likely take a pessimistic perspective.

Disclosure is a legal issue. Did you inform the buyers of the facts that are really material to the purchase? If the information was disclosed and the buyers chose to discount its importance, that is their problem not the seller's. Later legal recourse is diminished since the seller cannot be held responsible for bad judgment on the buyer's part.

But if you never told them about these changes, and you knew they were happening, you are now

Hot Tip

Sellers tend to be more optimistic, while buyers are more likely to take the opposite view. Think about disclosure in this light. You want to walk away from the closing clean, with the new buyers knowing everything that needed knowing, and that you fully disclosed what was asked and needed. In this way, if the buyer later comes back complaining, you can honestly say that you were clean at the time of closing.

in a very precarious legal position. The buyer can contend that the intrinsic value of the business was undermined by these future changes and that is why the purchase did not perform up to expectations.

The business might be struggling for reasons other than the local property changes, but if that was not disclosed, the buyers might come after you to compensate them for lost revenue, using the property changes as the justification. Proving them wrong might be expensive, impossible, or both.

Disclosure is a good thing, and recent discussions with an M&A attorney friend of mine indicated that if you have even a doubt about whether to disclose it, you should disclose it. And having it in writing means that there is no possibility of the buyers coming after you later with a "they did not tell us about it" litigation justification.

Keeping Your Corporate Documents Current

This might sound silly to a larger corporation, but you small corporations know what I am talking about in this section. You have corporate obligations to the shareholders and other owners of the corporation. Some of these obligations include:

➤ Having current articles of incorporation and bylaws on file with the state.

➤ Having the corporate name properly registered and protected in the states of operation.

➤ Having minutes of the required stockholder meetings on file in your corporate handbook.

➤ Having minutes on file that record stockholder agreements for every major corporate function. These include moving business locations, changing banks, obtaining credit, selling shares, and other corporate activities.

➤ Having current registered agent information along with the address.

➤ Having all state, local, and federal tax returns filed and current. This includes income, sales, employment, disability, and unemployment taxes also.

Seller Beware

Keeping corporate and other business documents in legal order is critical. I have an M&A attorney friend who told me of a company that was in its final stages of sale only to find out that its state corporate charter had expired five years earlier. This put a stop to the purchase. Ouch!

Larger companies have departments dedicated to making sure that these corporate issues are taken care of and remain in compliance. But smaller corporations are usually so busy performing the daily business activities, that many of these legal issues can get lost in the "I'll get to it later" filing cabinet. You must, as the seller, collate these documents and get them current. This is the least that a buyer can expect; don't you think?

I talked with an attorney who was involved with a company purchase only to find out at closing that the company's articles of incorporation stated that the company expired 10 years before. The company had been operating in violation of its own articles for the last 10 years. You don't want to find yourself in this position.

Legally Covering Yourself When Buying

Let's now take a look at the purchase from the buyer's perspective. Just as the seller is recommended to reveal anything that appears material to the purchase, you are recommended to confirm everything yourself.

Beauty, and truth, is often in the eye of the beholder. Two people can look at the same circumstances and see completely different things. Let's look at the example used in the prior section regarding the auto dealership and its possible negative impact on the new restaurant. This business glass can be either half empty or half full. Let's put a different possible spin on the same situation to show it as an opportunity instead of a problem.

Assume that research on your part reveals that the dealership actually wanted this location because it was close to a hamburger stand since its clientele is expected to be young people who live, eat, and breathe in their cars. In fact, the hamburger stand has a reputation for being a young person hangout, which was part of the location's appeal. The dealership owner wants to test the idea of locating next to a hamburger stand at this location and might then want to replicate it at locations in other local areas towns. The owner resents franchise mentality and will try to route business your way instead of theirs simply to foster a hometown relationship atmosphere.

Is this good news or bad? Is the glass half empty or half full? The seller might hear this same information and not believe it. The buyer might bring a new perspective to the relationship that could turn this into an exciting, multiple location business venture.

So, as the buyer, you should verify this information for yourself. This is good practice and should apply to all major areas of the purchased business. This *due diligence* phase of a business purchase is time consuming and expensive, but absolutely worth it to make sure that you know exactly what you are buying.

You might be thinking that, as the buyer, you have some legal remedy against the seller should the facts, as revealed during negotiations, not turn out as factual. And you might have a legal remedy, but is it worth it? That is a question that will have to be answered after the sale is closed and the future has revealed itself. You are far better served by

Terms of Acquisition

Due Diligence The evaluation process performed by the buyer to verify the underlying, often hidden, aspects of a seller's company. This phase of the acquisition process requires in-depth exposure to typically proprietary company operations and confidential information.

avoiding this unfortunate situation and verifying as many facts and assumptions as possible BEFORE the sale actually closes. This is one instance where pounds of prevention are worth avoiding tons of legal cure.

Financial Commitment by the Buyer

An important point to both buyer and seller is the buyer's financial commitment to purchasing the company. Once the due diligence phase is over, the valuation of the company is determined, and the buyer privately or publicly agrees to the price, he or she should then immediately arrange the required financing. The seller is going to ask for this commitment, just as the seller of a home would ask about the financial worthiness of a homebuyer.

Hot Tip

Notice that having the financing approved after the due diligence stage usually means that the buyer must have involved his or her lenders earlier in the process. In this way, they are already up to speed on the target company, and they can more readily approve the required amounts in time to make a qualified, creditable purchase offer.

As a home seller, you agree to take your home off the market while the buyer obtains financing. This is a risky venture if the buyer is not financially qualified to the level needed to buy the house. You could get to the closing only to find yourself back on the market looking for a new buyer.

The same is true for the buyer of a business, except that the dollars are larger and the financing involved is more complicated. Even more reason to assess the buyer's financial capabilities.

As the buyer, you will have to convince the seller that you can come up with the financing money. You need to either have the money within your own company, or you must have already arranged the required financing with your own creditors. (See Chapter 16, "Financing the Deal," for more information on financing a purchase.)

In Chapter 4, "Staying Legal," you will see the steps that the seller can take to protect himself or herself against the buyer not obtaining financing. As the buyer, you should know that the issue will come up, and you should be prepared to deal with it properly.

Controlling the Negotiations

At this point, you should be getting a clearer picture of the legal complexity associated with the sale/purchase of a business. There is a lot to it, and you just cannot understand the legal implications of every nuance.

For this reason, many buyers and sellers allow their attorneys to perform these negotiations on their behalf. And it really does make a lot of sense for a number of reasons:

1. By not being involved in the minute-to-minute negotiations, you can keep your eye on the overall status of the transaction. This helps to ensure that large, important items are not lost in the details.

2. Your attorney provides a level of objectivity to the negotiations that you, particularly as the seller of a company that you started, will have a difficult time achieving.

3. Your attorney should be an experienced negotiator. He or she should have experience with your type of situation and know what to expect. You do this, at best, occasionally—your attorney does it regularly. Who do you think will be better at it?

4. He or she knows the legal potholes that you will likely only find when you fall into them. That is never a good negotiating tactic.

5. Your attorney can also temper what is, and is not, revealed as part of the negotiations. This will keep you out of legal trouble while still making sure that value is optimized to the seller.

Unless your business transaction is very small, and uncomplicated, you should have an attorney working with you on the sale. You should also have an accountant in the wings to address any financial issues that come up and to round out the team.

Think of yourself as the coach of a football team that just hired a new quarterback (your attorney). This quarterback must know the general guidelines within which he can run plays during the game, but generally, must also have some level of independent decision making. That balance is important to your relationship with the attorney. The clearer you are on what you want out of the negotiations the better chance you have of getting them, simply because your attorney knows where to focus the negotiations.

You can and should expect several things from your attorney:

➤ He or she should have experience with negotiating M&A type of agreements, along with the intricacies of merger financing.

Hot Tip

You control what is offered as part of the negotiations and the overall structure of the deal. Never forget that your attorney is there in an advisory role and that he or she ultimately works for you. Use your attorney's experience and objectivity to your best advantage, but don't let yourself get pushed into a situation that you cannot live with. Ultimately, you and not the attorneys are the one who has to live with the results.

➤ He or she should provide you with a detailed listing of what you can expect.

➤ You should have a written contract with this attorney covering his or her services. Have your own attorney review the contract before signing it.

➤ A budgetary estimate should be included for each item, or at least, each major participation category.

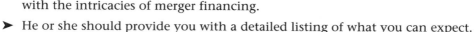

➤ Know that any budgetary estimates assume that no extraordinary items pop up during negotiations.

➤ Typically, the more prepared you are the less it will cost. Why? With attorneys, as with so much else in business, time is money. The more time it takes the more it costs. The more prepared you are the less time it should take and the less it should cost.

➤ Your attorney, along with your accountant, should immediately reveal any possible conflicts of interest between them, your company, and the prospective buyers. If they fail to do this up front and you find out later that they were aware of the conflict at that time, you should fire them on the spot. Any professional knows that this is a fundamental breach of integrity and so should you.

Finding the right attorney is a lot like finding the right doctor. I recommend using referrals as your initial starting point. Ask other business associates and other business owners who have either bought or sold a company for information and referrals. I suggest that you take this experienced owner out to a long lunch and pick his or her brain about anything that he or she is willing to share. Nothing, not even reading this book, can replace a discussion with an experienced buyer and/or seller.

Hot Tip

Be slow to hire an attorney or accountant. These people are strategically very important to your team, and they should not be chosen in haste.

Ask this person for a referral either to their attorney (if things went well) or to another attorney. A personal referral is more valuable than any number of Yellow Page ads, Bar Association flyers, or direct mail pieces. You will be living with, and trusting, your attorney during the course of the preparation, negotiations, closing, and post-closing activities. This has to be someone that you trust; so take the time to pick the right person.

Antitrust Guidelines

Antitrust has nothing to do with "not trusting" someone. This is a governmental term used in determining whether a particular merger/acquisition will cause a shift in the market such that free competition will be constrained. Unless you are Microsoft, Intel, IBM, AT&T, GE, or some other large company, these antitrust issues should not come into play.

Here are some areas in which antitrust laws might come into play for you:

1. Your industry has few competitors and this purchase of a competitor would reduce the number to a level where pricing and product availability would be curtailed, hurting the consumer's right to choose products within a competitive environment.

2. Assume that your company purchases one of its suppliers, who also supplies your competition with key components that are not easily obtained elsewhere. This purchase could have an adverse negative influence on the industry as a whole, reducing competition and hurting the consumer.

3. If the Hart-Scott-Rodino Act's (H-S-R) and the Federal Trade Commission's (FTC) reporting thresholds are exceeded, the proposed acquisition/merger must be reported to the FTC. The general criteria are when one party has sales or assets of over $100 million AND the other party has sales or assets of over $10 million AND a complicated calculation of party values after the transaction. (Yes, that's right. Get with your attorney.)

Unless you are a large company in a small industry, you will likely not have to deal with antitrust issues. And if you are a large company, you likely have your own legal staff who will advise you on your antitrust exposure. I just wanted to include this so that you knew that this can be an issue and that it is worth considering.

Terms of Acquisition

Horizontal Acquisition   Where one competitor acquires another within the same industry.

Vertical Acquisition   Where one company acquires either a supplier or customer creating a strategically unfair alliance that precludes competition.

Employment, Benefit, and Retirement Issues

At the end of the due diligence stage, you should have a detailed discussion about each party's expectations regarding the fair, and legally required, treatment of employees. Here are a few items that should, at a minimum, be discussed:

➤ What are the buyer's intentions and the seller's requirements regarding the retention of existing or acquired personnel?

➤ How will retirement plans be transferred and funded? How will the relative valuation between the two plans be determined?

➤ What will happen to benefit plans after acquisition?

➤ Will health, dental, disability, and life insurance programs be comparably transferred and how?

➤ What type of flexibility do the acquired employees have with respect to investing their own retirement savings? How will this be transferred to the buyer's company?

Buyer Beware

Don't assume that the seller simply wants out and will protect his or her interest at all costs. Most small company sellers are very dedicated to their employees, and they will fight like a parent to protect the rights of those who have been working for them.

Many of these issues are bigger than both of the companies and involve specific legal requirements. Once again, you will need an experienced attorney to walk both buyer and seller through these intricacies.

The SEC Is Always Watching

Any time that you deal with a publicly held company, you should assume that some type of Securities and Exchange Commission (SEC) regulations will be involved. The details are beyond the scope of this chapter and are once again best dealt with by an experienced attorney.

Of importance to a private buyer selling to a public company is that the public buyer will likely have public disclosure requirements. These requirements will affect your company in that what was once a secret is now public information. If you had not informed your employees, customers, or vendors of your intention to sell, they will find out when the prospective acquiring company makes its announcement.

And if you think about it this way, you can understand the SEC's concern.

Assume that the buyer wants to issue new stock to help fund the purchase. This could very well reduce the earnings associated with the existing shares, which could in turn reduce a share's market price. This has a direct impact on the shareholder. If the company intends to acquire debt to pay for the purchase, its earnings could once again be reduced, negatively impacting share prices. The buyer's management and board of directors might think that this is a great idea, but if the shareholders don't support the action, the seller will have problems because the money required to execute the purchase won't be there when needed.

Hot Tip

There are some frequently used exemptions to some SEC filing requirements, but these exemptions are pretty rigorous and should only be assumed applicable with advice of legal counsel.

If the buyer does not have the money and must reveal its intention to purchase your company to get the money from its shareholders and if you are not ready to reveal your intention to sell, you have yourself in a tough situation. Something has to give. You either need to find a creative way to get the buyer out of his or her dilemma or you must prepare yourself for public announcement, by the buyer, of their intention to buy and your intention to sell.

The Least You Need to Know

➤ Full disclosure of the FACTS is the right approach from the seller's perspective.

➤ Verifying all seller FACTS is the right approach from the buyer's perspective.

➤ Find the right attorney and then let him or her do the negotiations.

➤ Under specific circumstance, usually dealing with very large dollar value transactions, antitrust laws might come into play.

➤ Publicly held companies have SEC imposed shareholder disclosure requirements.

Chapter 4

Staying Legal

In This Chapter

➤ The importance of written agreements

➤ The Business Judgement Rule

➤ Sections of a purchase agreement

➤ Negotiating earnout agreements

➤ Basic legal agreement components

"Flip to page 23 and take a look at the wording in paragraph 5," said Joel, an M&A attorney, to his client Jill.

Jill reluctantly flipped through the binder until she got to page 23. She appeared to be reading the page, but she looked pretty disinterested. They had been at this for several hours by this point, and Joel could tell that it was wearing her down.

"What am I looking at?" asked Jill reaching for her fifth cup of espresso. "This seems like stuff we already included elsewhere. And why does it have to be so complicated, anyway? I want to sell; they want to buy. That should be that."

"You have worked for years to get your dress manufacturing business to this point. You plan to retire on the money you receive from the sale. Right?" Jill nodded her head. "This section deals with their repayment provisions, and the special language that they added that allows them to renegotiate the earnout criteria if you fail to do certain things."

"I'll just do them," said Jill. "What is the big deal?"

"What are you supposed to do, specifically? How many action items are there, when are they due, and to what level of performance?" Jill sat for a moment in silence. He couldn't tell if she was stumped or just tired. "Having it all in writing," continued Joel, "is the best way to make sure that you don't forget anything. Can I buy you another cup of coffee?"

If you are like me, you like working with lawyers about as much as you like going to the dentist. However, they are a necessary part of business life, and you will not complete a successful business sale or purchase without legal advice. Keeping track of legal commitments, advice, and contingencies is an integral part of any complicated financing negotiation. Monitoring and paying attention to the legal aspects of the purchase is critically important, although it is often quite dull. Hang in there through this chapter to understand the things you can do that will best ensure that the legal aspects of your sale/acquisition are in proper order.

"Would you write that down, please?"

Doing business requires agreements between people and companies. If you think about it, you really don't sell a product or service. You sell an agreement. You agree to do one thing, and in exchange, the other person agrees to do something in return.

The more detailed that agreement the less likely it will be for future unfulfilled expectations to arise from that agreement. The more informal the agreement the more likely there are to be problems down the road, especially if large dollar amounts are involved since large dollars attract large levels of personal investment. People rarely squabble over $10, but watch them scramble over $100,000. Make that a million dollars or more and you have everyone's undivided attention.

Straight Talk

I like to think of a legal agreement as the written clarification of an understanding between the other party and myself in the agreement. Hopefully, we will never need to pull out the agreement again, except to remind ourselves of our individual commitments. I work hard to maintain the spirit that was there when the agreement was first signed. It is somewhat of a personal failure if I ever need to use the legal agreement as a legal negotiating point. But be clear on this point—what is in the agreement is your ultimate commitment. Don't sign any agreement that contains conditions that you cannot live with, because you are indeed agreeing to live with them, if asked to do so.

There are a few ingredients that must be in every contractual agreement, or the agreement is not considered legally binding:

➤ The contract must specify, in detail, what is covered by the agreement. The more details the better. For example, a product purchase contract should at least specify the product ID/description, price, delivery, and payment terms. If you think about it, this is the minimum information you would need to know to fulfill this purchase/shipping agreement.

➤ There must be a "barter for exchange," which means that one party must give up something in exchange for something given up by the other party.

➤ There must be some type of "consideration" given as part of the barter for exchange. Consideration is a legal term for what you are actually giving up in the transaction. It can be money, stock, material assets, or even a commitment to do, or not do, something.

Notice that a contract is a two-way street. Both parties are expected to negotiate in their own best interest. Neither party can take everything without providing something in return, and what is given must be perceived as having value.

With respect to a company purchase, the typical buyer is interested in buying not only the company but also often some restrictions on the employees/founders. If a founder, for example, gives up the right to start another company for a two-year period after the sale, then he or she should expect to be compensated for that concession. And the seller should be willing to honor the agreement as outlined when signed.

Your attorney is trained to look for all of these little loopholes through which the buyer or seller can move with respect to an agreement. They think about things like:

➤ What happens if one of the parties involved dies?

➤ What remedies should be applied if the radical new technology being purchased later proves not to be viable?

➤ What happens if either party fails to uphold his or her end of the agreement?

➤ What if the Environmental Protection Agency (EPA) files suit regarding a prior company dumping site? Who pays the legal fees and cleanup expenses?

➤ What happens if the merger is not approved by the FTC because of antitrust issues? Who pays for resolution? What if it cannot be resolved?

This list is almost endless, and experienced attorneys are trained to look at all of the various standard and unique particulars that make a contract as comprehensive as possible.

Your attorney works for you and must know what is expected of him or her. Don't automatically accept the attorney's viewpoint as gospel, since he

Hot Tip

Understand that your attorney is a trained professional, but he or she is also fallible and ultimately works for you. It is really tough to sue an attorney for being a bad attorney.

or she might understand the legal aspects of the agreement but not the business aspects. That is your job. Keeping your attorney pointed in the direction of creating a legally binding document that achieves your business goals is an art. It requires time on your part, but it is time well spent. You will have to live with the agreement for a long time.

Typical Buy/Sell Agreement Components

Again, remember the last time you attended a real estate sale closing? Remember all of the documents that you had to sign? That is nothing compared to the number of documents involved with the sale of a business. And add more to that pile if either of the companies is publicly traded, which involves approvals from shareholders before final agreement is allowed.

Here are the basic components of a typical Asset Purchase Agreement. Know that the attorneys will modify these sections, change their order, titles, or even add to them as needed for your particular circumstances.

1. **General Information:** This section outlines the companies involved and their primary business locations.

2. **Sale and Purchase of Assets:** This section outlines the assets covered by this transaction. They can be individual assets, in which case they will be listed in an attachment, or all assets (that is, everything the company owns).

3. **Purchase Price:** This section outlines the money involved, special financing arrangements, and any other information related to paying for the asset purchase. Detailed financing agreement information will be included as attachments to the contract.

4. **Closing:** This section specifies the date, location, and other details associated with the closing itself.

5. **Representations and Warranties:** This section applies to both seller and buyer outlines and details all of the material information aspects of the sale. In essence, the seller states, in writing, that information revealed to that point is true. This section gets very complicated when combined with the indemnification and litigation clauses. BEWARE THIS SECTION and don't skim it or simply defer to your attorney's understanding of it.

6. **Non-Competition:** This section details the restrictions placed on the seller with respect to opening up a new competitive business or going

Seller Beware

Although the Representation and Warranties section is boring, it is also critical that you read and understand its contents. You will sign this document that states your contention that these things are true. It they are not, as presented by the attorney, you might find yourself responsible for unintentional commitments simply because you didn't take the time to read and understand this section.

to work for a competitor. These are hard to enforce since it is really tough to restrict someone from making a living, and sellers should jealously protect their rights in this section.

7. **Representations and Warranties:** This section includes points represented by the buyer to the seller. Remember that buyers also answer to someone, whether it be the SEC, shareholders or other owners. It might include items like approval of shareholders, no legal encumbrances that would restrict the purchase from a buyer standpoint, and/or other items.

8. **Further Agreements:** This section provides a location for the inclusion of any other non-standard agreement requirements. This section can get very long depending on the unique aspects of the agreement.

9. **Conditions Precedent to Closing:** This section outlines the various things that both buyer and seller have agreed to do before closing. Remedies and penalties associated with not meeting these conditions are spelled out in this section. And information related to employment agreements or contingency payments might also be included in this section.

10. **Indemnification; Survival of Representations and Warranties:** This section is really important, and it is often skimmed by buyers and sellers. This can typically become a critically important section if something goes wrong in the future or if something that you alleged as true turns out not to happen. This section can come back to haunt you, and I encourage you to understand it thoroughly, whether you are buying or selling.

11. **Post-Closing Matters:** This section outlines agreed upon actions and conditions that apply to both buyer and seller once the agreements are signed. It could require involvement, or lack of involvement, by the prior management; the rights for sellers to inspect the books if future payments are related to future performance; and remedies should payments not be made as expected.

12. **Risk of Loss:** This section defines who inherits the risk of loss prior to signing the agreement. The need for this section confuses me, but the lawyers think it should be there, so there it is.

13. **Miscellaneous:** This section talks about all the other stuff that wasn't covered elsewhere. Once again, don't skim this section because you are still committing yourself and the company to whatever is contained in this section.

Hot Tip

Err on the side of caution when reviewing and signing agreements. Don't allow yourself to be rushed or intimidated. It is your signature, your word, your credibility, and your money on the line. Take your time and ask for clarification.

14. **Attachments:** This section(s) contain all types of information that are needed to support the contract being signed. It might include financial statements, employment agreements, asset descriptions, the details of special obligations, or other information as applicable. Once again, don't skim the attachments. If it is in the agreement, you are agreeing to it.

After you have signed all kinds of documents, it is tempting to simply treat the rest of the process as automatic. Make sure that you and your attorneys have seen all legal documents prior to closing, and that the closing documents match those provided for prior review. If there are any inconsistencies, this becomes a huge red flag that something might be terribly wrong with this transaction.

More than one buyer or seller has been lulled into a false sense of security only to find out later what they signed did not accurately reflect the intended agreement.

What you sign is what you agree to. It is really difficult to deny that you signed it, and proving malicious intent on the part of the other parties is tough to do.

Board Membership and You

You will see this repeated at other points in the book, but it is an important point for those of you who sit on the board of any corporation. You have a fiduciary, "legal and financial," duty to protect the financial interests of company shareholders. This does not necessarily mean that you must accept the highest bid for a company, but you must at least entertain all offers and give each a fair evaluation.

Terms of Acquisition

Business Judgement Rule   A legal foundation that assumes management and board members operate from a "good faith" basis in making decisions that they feel are best for the company and its shareholders. A conflict of interest situation puts this protection in jeopardy.

Luckily, there is a legal foundation for determining proper execution of those duties. It is called the *Business Judgement Rule*, which works from the legal assumption that all board members and members of management make their business decisions from a good faith perspective. It also assumes that they make decisions that they believe are best for the company and its shareholders.

Managers need to be careful of their position when selling a company. You might have offers from several buyers, each with different strengths and weaknesses. The buyer who plans to subdivide and resell the company might have the highest bid on the table, where the one with the best longer-term benefits to the company might be the lowest. Which should the management choose? This question should definitely be discussed with legal counsel, but the Business Judgement Rule contends that if you have a solid case for the lower offer being of more "value" to shareholders, then taking that offer should not expose board members and managers to litigation.

On the other hand, almost anyone can sue anyone else for almost anything.

Which is the right approach? Trust your judgement. Work from a basis of integrity. Take actions that best increase shareholder wealth and check with experienced legal counsel for guidance if in doubt. The scary part of this is that you could personally be liable for any loss to shareholders that is proven in a courtroom. Now, that is a scary thing that puts the "privilege" of being on a board of directors in a whole new perspective. Doesn't it?

Watch Out for Earnouts

Here is a potential legal nightmare that you should absolutely NOT negotiate on your own. An earnout agreement is one that specifies future payments to the sellers based on the future performance of the sold company. (Basically, it is the same as a contingent future payment agreement discussed in Chapter 16, "Financing the Deal.")

First off, I recommend that sellers avoid these relationships completely unless they remain in control. And this control must allow them to run the company as they see fit, not as someone else dictates. This is particularly true if the earnout proceeds turn out to be a major portion of the business sale proceeds.

If you choose to sign an earnout agreement, make sure that you do it on your terms, not theirs. You want to control the money, people, products, conditions, processes, and other critical business aspects needed for you to achieve your earnout goals. By not protecting critical ingredients, you may set yourself up for failure, which can cost you a lot of time, money, and frustration.

Seller Beware

An earnout agreement is basically a loan that the seller provides the buyer. Verify the financial viability of the buyer and make sure that your future payment is as verified as possible.

Here are a few points to consider if negotiating an earnout agreement:

➤ Set earnout performance goals at reasonable levels. If you have rarely hit the bullseye on your last few tosses, there is no reason to assume this toss will be different. Let rationality, not ego, dictate the goals.

➤ Make sure that the buyer will be able to pay the earnout amounts should you meet your agreed-to goals.

➤ Keep the earnout a smaller portion of the purchase price unless the future rewards are substantial enough to warrant the delayed receipt of purchase money.

➤ Give yourself as much time frame slack as possible to optimize your chances of meeting the goals.

➤ Beware accounting changes, performed by the buying company, that change the financial landscape on which your earnout is based. It would be a litigation prospect if you achieved goals based on the accounting practices in place at the time of the agreement, only to miss them later due to accounting changes over which you had no control.

➤ Talk with your tax advisor about the tax impact of the earnout agreement. It might be treated as today's income, meaning you pay taxes on it today, even though it is not received until a future date.

You entrepreneurs will likely be seduced by the prospect of making more future money on your company purchase by taking on the earnout challenge. This could be a great business move, and only you can make that assessment for your situation. I only suggest that you be smart about laying the foundation today so that you optimize your chances of making those big bucks in the future.

The Least You Need to Know

➤ Get important agreement components in writing.

➤ Use attorneys to negotiate and finalize written contracts.

➤ Understand what is in the agreement because you, and not the attorneys, must live with its consequences.

➤ Sellers and buyers must work with integrity and without conflict of interest, or they open themselves up to potential litigation.

➤ Earnout agreements can be lucrative, but must be strictly negotiated with maximum control retained by the seller.

Chapter 5

The Various Business Arrangements

In This Chapter

➤ Determining the right merger type

➤ Learning buyer and seller motivations

➤ Placing a value on the founders

➤ Avoiding the pitfalls of management agreements

➤ Keeping the shareholders and directors happy

"They are proposing a 2-for-1 merger with a three-year employment agreement for Jenny," said Jenny's CPA. "We nixed the management agreement idea from the get-go. No reason leading with your chin, if you know what I mean?"

Jenny looked at Joyce with a blank stare. She had heard the terminology before, recognized the words, but now clearly understood that she hadn't comprehended much of what Joyce had said. And it all had to do with how much she was being offered for her industrial sewing business.

Joyce continued on to talk about how the buyer had recently undergone a stock split and was performing with a reasonable price-to-earnings ratio. And that it had a reputation for taking care of its employees and the owners of acquired companies.

"The prospective buyers were basically a holding company that looked at its acquisitions as financial targets with minimal strategic synergy. That is why they want you to stick around for a few years until they figure out how we complement the rest of their holdings," continued

Joyce with enthusiasm in her voice, really oblivious to the fact that she had lost Jenny. "What do you think about your having a seat on their board of directors?"

Jenny smiled, sat back in her chair, and looked out the window. Ten years of hard work and customer care involved with building her business came down to a few simple decisions, and she didn't even understand the language involved with that decision. This would have to be changed.

English is an incredible language. It has brought us Hemmingway, Steinbeck, and Robert Frost. It has also brought us tons of jargon, such as asset transfer, stock sale, merger, valuation, and buyout agreement. At some point, you are going to either make an offer to purchase another company or receive such an offer. Understanding the value of the offer is covered in Chapters 15, 16, 20, and 22. In this chapter we present the conceptual foundation upon which the offer's value assessment is based.

Differentiating Mergers and Other Purchase Agreements

It is possible for a company to be sold without it being a merger. A merger involves specific stock-related operations that are not involved when the company purchased is not a corporation.

Terms of Acquisition

Stock The legal device used to determine ownership of a corporation. People or companies that own stock are called shareholders.

Majority Shareholder The person or company that owns most of the outstanding shares in a corporation.

In fact, there are specific reasons for a buyer not to completely merge with another company but instead acquire only a smaller subset of its total assets.

This brings us back to our old friends risk and reward. Remember that a buyer purchases future income benefits, and any associated risk factors tend to decrease the perceived value of the business being purchased. Also, remember that any deal that becomes too complicated also acquires a risk factor of its own, which moves most business people toward transactions with minimal complexity.

Each type of sale/purchase arrangement has its own set of benefits and drawbacks. Which aspects are the most important to the transaction are truly based on the specific transaction and the people involved. Work your way through this section to understand these various purchase/sale arrangements.

Asset Purchase: Buying What You Want

A simple asset purchase is the least complicated of all purchase arrangements. The buyer designates the items that he or she wishes to buy, and the seller agrees to sell them. The seller then passes the items along with their associated liabilities, such as outstanding loans on equipment, to the buyer who assumes their ownership.

Notice that this transaction involves no stock at all, unless the buyer offers stock instead of or in addition to cash as payment for the purchased items.

Notice that the buyer obtains the assets, which are typically equipment or other types of tangible property. It might also include customer lists, proprietary processes, special agreements that have value, performance contracts that can be transferred, copyrights, patents, and other intellectual property. The seller parts with these assets and relinquishes future rights to them in exchange for cash and/or other assets.

Notice that these assets have now been sold at a fair market value, which might be higher than their depreciated book value. Taxes should immediately spring to mind when you see words like that in the same sentence, and your instincts would be right. (See Chapter 20, "Selling Can Be Taxing—Beware," for additional information regarding the tax implications.)

This type of arrangement is often more beneficial to the buyer and less attractive to the seller than a standard stock sale.

Notice that the buyer has made no claim and assumed no liability for any other assets or liabilities associated with the selling company. The selling company is still a solvent, self-sustaining, legal entity that is responsible for its own bills and debts. If it just sold its primary means for earning a living and did not account for its debtors, then the sale was short-sighted; it is not, however, the purchasing company's responsibility.

Notice also that this type of sale requires specific negotiations for each purchased asset, which takes time, money, and personnel, and it might cost the purchasing company more money in the long run.

Hot Tip

Asset purchase plans are the only purchase method available when purchasing a non-corporate company such as a sole proprietorship or partnership, since only corporations can sell stock. The asset purchased might be the entire company for a single price, but the acquisition is still accomplished without any stock purchase.

Stock Purchase: What You Don't See Can Hurt You

When a buyer purchases stock in a company, the buyer becomes a partial owner of that company. This applies to any stock purchase. When the buyer purchases all the stock in a company, he or she becomes its new owner. At that point, all company assets pass to the new owner along with all liens and liabilities.

Notice that this arrangement involves the word *all* and not specific items as seen with the asset purchase arrangement. *All* is not a scary word when dealing with items that you know about, but it can be frightening when dealing with items that you don't know about.

Let's face it, we all wish that the world was a completely honest place and that we knew everything that would happen at any point in time. But it just doesn't always work that way. The sellers might have neglected to tell you about pending actions against the company that had not yet materialized, it might have underpaid its employment taxes for the past year, leaving a debt with the government. Then again, the owners simply might not have known that a prior action on the company's part would give rise to future claims against the company.

For example, there might be litigation against the company that has not yet been filed, and that the owners might not have even known about when you made your purchase. The point is that once you purchase the company's stock, you purchase its assets and its liabilities, along with its legal identity.

If you leave the company as a standalone company, the parent company will not generally be directly liable for any of these unforeseen occurrences. But an unforeseen lawsuit or action by the IRS against the company certainly diminishes its future value, completely throwing your initial projections out the window.

Notice that a stock purchase still keeps the purchased company and its stocks alive as a separate legal entity. This situation changes when two companies merge.

Mergers: Making One Out of Two

The American Heritage Dictionary defines *merge* as "to combine or unite" which is exactly what happens when the stocks of two companies are merged. One of the companies disappears and the stock of only one company remains.

A merger can involve large, medium, or small companies. A larger company can be merged into a smaller one, or vice versa.

For purposes of discussion I will refer to the company being acquired as "target (B)" company, and the acquiring company as "buyer (A)."

There are various types of mergers, however, the most likely types that you will encounter are the forward and reverse merger.

➤ A *forward merger* merges stock from (B) into (A), with only the stock from (A) remaining after the merger. Basically, the acquired company is merged into the buyer's company so that the purchased company essentially disappears.

➤ A *reverse merger* is just the opposite of a forward merger in that the stock from (A) is merged into (B). This means that the stock from the buyer is merged into the stock of the acquired company with only the acquired company's stock remaining after the merge.

A forward merger is pretty obvious, and intuitively it makes sense. The reverse merger, on the other hand, might take a little explaining. There could be any number of reasons for a reverse merger, and one reason is explained here.

Assume that the buying company has a dubious reputation in the industry and is looking to continue its operation while not being hampered by its poor reputation. Purchasing a company with a solid reputation and performing a reverse merger allows the buyer to merge its operations into the purchased company, keeping its assets, employees, customers, and basic operation intact. At the same time it can now function under the good name of the purchased company, which should reap benefits for it into the future.

Notice that if you are the seller in this situation, you want to make sure that you are well compensated for your good reputation since that is the primary asset purchased.

Buyer/Seller Beware

Just because a person can talk fast with the jargon doesn't mean that he or she understands the M&A process. Don't be afraid to ask a few more questions to ensure that this person can not only talk-M&A-talk but also walk-the-walk.

Mergers require a change in stock ownership, which means that a majority of the shareholders must approve the action. For a small, privately held corporation, this is generally not a problem since you are probably negotiating with the owners. For a larger company, this might get complicated and take time, which should be factored into the transaction expectations.

All assets and liabilities transfer from the seller to the buyer when the merger agreement is filed with the proper state authorities, such as the Secretary of State's office. Notice that if the two companies reside in different states, you will have to take certain legal actions to ensure that the desired level of corporate protection is retained within the involved states.

Shareholders in the target company are compensated with shares of stock in the buying company and possibly some cash. Before the merger can occur, both the buyer and seller must come to a valuation determination for each company. From that valuation, an agreement is reached regarding the number of shares of the buying company that will be traded for each share of the purchased company.

Terms of Acquisition

Triangular Merger   A merger involving the target company and a subsidiary corporation of the buyer's corporation.

Take a look at this simple example as a starting point for understanding the merger valuation process.

Assume that the buying company (A) has a stock market value of $5 per share and the target company (B) has a stock value of $10 per share. This means that trading two shares of the buying company (A) for every one share of the target company (B) adequately compensates the shareholders for their ownership interest. They previously owned $10 in a corporation before in the form of one share of (B). After the merger they own $10 of corporate stock in the form of two shares of (A).

The shareholders should be happy with the arrangement since the merged company should have brighter future prospects than (B) had previously on its own, or the merger would not have been desirable to either (A) or (B).

This example is highly simplified, and it won't make you an expert. It is only for you to understand some of the considerations involved when looking at a merger situation.

A Little Cash and a Little Stock

Transactions need not be all cash or all stock. They can also be a combination of the two, which can be beneficial for both parties.

Assume that a company is purchased for $1.5 million and that the purchasing company does not have adequate cash on hand to pay the entire amount. It might, instead, offer $500,000 in cash and $1,000,000 in the buying company's stock.

Straight Talk

Stock ownership offers can appear pretty attractive at first and indeed might turn out to be great investment decisions. But never forget that stock is only worth what someone else is willing, and able, to pay for it. This means that the other person must value the stock at the same general value you expect and you must be able to sell the stock. This might sound obvious, but this stock game gets complicated very quickly and an ounce of caution is recommended.

The seller frees himself or herself from the operation of the company along with any co-signing liabilities that might have been assumed over the years of ownership. He or she also walks away with $500,000 in cash and ownership in a company that both the seller and the buyer hope will be stronger as a result of the acquisition. The future prospects for the stock are bright, making the buyer and seller happy. Furthermore, the buyer avoids a $1 million cash payment and the seller gets to add a substantial amount of money ($500,000) to his or her retirement fund. This is a good deal overall, as long as the stock performs up to expectations, which becomes the seller's primary future concern.

There are tax implications involved with this transaction that affect the net payment received by the seller. (See Chapter 20 for more information regarding taxes.)

Consolidating for Something New and Different

Assume that both the buyer (A) and the seller (B) decide to combine forces as a completely new company. In this case, the stock of (A) and (B) would disappear and a new stock, (C), would be created in the form of a new corporation that represents the combined interests of shareholders from both (A) and (B).

This type of arrangement is called a *consolidation* in that the two share types are consolidated to create a third.

Shareholders in (A) and (B) are compensated by stock in (C) in a ratio determined in a fashion similar to that discussed in mergers. The transactions could involve all stock, all cash, or some combination of the two.

For example, assume that (A) is cash rich, whereas (B) is cash poor but has tremendous technological advantages. Shareholders in (A) might feel that their ready cash reserves, which have no future risk associated with them at all, warrant some type of immediate cash distribution to them as part of the consolidation. (B)'s shareholders are compensated by the shares in (C), but might not deserve the cash distribution simply because they brought little cash to the transaction in the first place.

Board of Director Obligations

All corporations have a board of directors. This board might consist of a single person for a small corporation, or in the case of a company like General Motors, a large number of high-powered executives. The role of the board of directors in general, and its member in particular, is to monitor the overall operation of the organization to ensure that the shareholders asset value (their underlying share worth) is invested in the best possible way.

Common industry terminology talks about the creation of shareholder wealth, and it is the board's job to optimize shareholder wealth creation.

Should the shareholders determine that their stock value is not being optimized because of board decisions, the stockholders can take certain steps to remedy the situation. They can vote in a new board of directors for a start. This does not correct past losses, but it does ensure that future losses are minimized by preventing poor decisions by the same board members. They can also file suit against the board members, which gets a board member into a tricky situation.

Terms of Acquisition

Shareholder Wealth   The underlying value of a share of stock as determined by its assessed market value. Actions that increase market value increase shareholder wealth.

Assume for a moment that you are a board member of publicly traded corporation. Also assume, that two different companies have made offers to purchase your stock. Company (A) is a trustworthy company with a solid reputation and proven track record of taking good care of acquired company assets, personnel, vendors, and customers. Company (A) offers $10 per share for your stock, which the going price for your company the week before the offer was made.

Company (B) offers $12 per share, which is the price per share after the offer became public knowledge. You also know that (B) has never left one of its acquired companies intact, and has indeed sold off the assets and fired the employees from its past two acquisitions.

Which company do you choose? The short term best answer is (B) since it offers the shareholders $2 more per share, or 20 percent more, than the (A) offer which you and all other board members agree offers better long term investment returns. Which one optimized shareholder wealth? It is all a matter of perspective, and the short-term perspective is the safest legal route for shareholders to take. There is little doubt that $12 is larger than $10 and that the shareholders would make more money from the (B) offer. There is risk with the longer-term perspective associated with (A).

Which is the right approach? The board of directors exists to make these determinations, and only later can we assess whether they made the decision that optimized shareholder wealth. Don't forget that the Business Judgment Rule is designed to protect board members who choose the more risky option truly believing that it is the overall best option for the shareholders.

Sell the Company to Its Own Employees

You might find out that the people most familiar with your company are also be the most qualified buyers. Management buyout (MBO) or leveraged buyout (LBO) arrangements allow the employees themselves to purchase the company. A third option is an employee stock ownership plan (ESOP), which allows employees to share in stock ownership as part of a company-wide retirement plan.

Imagine that you are the sole owner of your corporation and decide to sell it for around $10 million. Now picture your senior staff requesting the right to purchase the company for any of a number of reasons including that they don't want to work for any of the current prospective buyers. Your staff will typically not have enough money to purchase your shares, but they might be in a position to arrange $10 million in loan financing to purchase the shares.

Seller Beware

Opening the door to an MBO, LOB, or ESOP arrangement puts your employees in a potential conflict of interest position. If the employees want the employee purchase plan to work out, they have less incentive to work with potential non–employee buyers, which can impede your success in selling or merging with another buyer.

Notice that this financing is going to be heavily based on the financial performance of the company and the guarantees of the management involved. If the company cannot support a $5 million loan, then this MBO option will probably not work out. With an MBO, the management team that arranges the financing will keep up to 30 percent of the equity when the deal is finished as a sort of commission for arranging the deal. If an MBO does not work out, then a LBO is a next possible option where a third party arranges the financing, leaving the management team with between 5 and 10 percent.

An ESOP allows your employees to purchase stock as part of a company retirement plan that invests almost exclusively in company stock. The good news is that all employees are now owners of the company making them, theoretically, more attentive to the company's overall well being. The bad news is that employee retirement benefits could be completely lost if the company takes a major downturn that seriously devalues company stock.

You sell your shares to the ESOP, which obtains its funding from employee payroll contributions. Notice that this plan only works out for companies with large payrolls. There are some tax benefits to you as the seller should you follow the ESOP route.

Take a look at Chapter 23, "When It Is Better Not to Sell," for additional details regarding these three employee purchase plans.

Management Agreements and Why They Should Be Avoided

Have you ever heard of people who purchase a house with a "lease-option" arrangement where they lease the house, while retaining the option to purchase at a future date? Management agreements are essentially the same thing.

When a management agreement is set up, the purchasing company retains the right to purchase the selling company at a future date, but opts to manage the company for a while before actually making the purchase. As the buyer, this provides an opportunity to verify that you are indeed buying what you think you are buying. Kind of like test-driving a car for a month before purchasing it.

The bad news from a seller's perspective is that you can definitely assume that the buyers will find things out about the company during the course of the agreement that they did not know before it started. And you can almost guarantee, the things

Seller Beware

It is almost impossible to set up a useful management agreement without risk to the seller. When the buying personnel become involved in your daily operations, they will definitely learn information about customers, processes, and finances that otherwise would be confidential. If they choose not to purchase at the end of the agreement period, you could have revealed your company secrets and received nothing in return.

that they discover will decrease the value of the company, and the purchase price. They might even find out things that cause them to reconsider, or back out of, the complete purchase.

For this reason, I suggest avoiding management agreements altogether if possible. For the buyers, they also pose the dilemma of sitting on the fence and not simply choosing one side of the other. It ties up your personnel with management activities. Inter-company operations are put into a limbo state since you haven't really made the purchase. Money is also in limbo in that it is both allocated and not allocated at the same time.

Indecision is often detrimental to a business's operation, and management agreements put the purchase into indecision until the period of the agreement expires. For these reason, it is best to avoid them.

On the other hand, if you are a seller with nothing to hide trying to convince a hesitant buyer of your honesty, a management agreement might be the only way to close the deal. As always, you are the only one who can make that determination.

Keeping the Founders Around for a While

As a buyer and as a seller, you have an interest in promoting the future financial prosperity of the company. With smaller companies, the reputation, name, and "goodwill" of the company might be intimately tied with the founders. Larger companies have more employees over which to spread responsibility, meaning that each employee has a smaller impact on the overall business operation. Company "goodwill" is not usually tied to a particular employee except under very unique circumstances.

Straight Talk

If you think about it for a moment, larger companies are typically organized and operated with organizational chart slots with requirements that are filled by people. The people fill slots that are relatively independent of the person filling that slot as long as the basic qualifications are intact. Impersonal, but true.

Smaller companies, on the other hand, are often organized around the people involved since there usually aren't that many people. The organizational chart slots are tailored to match the skills of the people involved.

For example, General Motors might have a position open for an electrical engineer. The company puts an ad in the paper, interviews candidates, and eventually hires someone with the skills needed to fill the position. This person might be one of hundreds of engineers in a given department and, based on that person's specific knowledge, typically can make minimal direct impact on the overall company's performance. As an employee moves higher in the organization or moves into strategic positions within the company, his or her impact will be more profoundly felt, but the mainstream employee works within this diffused framework. If you don't believe me, simply note the popularity of the Dilbert cartoon strip.

Smaller companies have few employees, which makes the impact of each employee more profound. Each employee in a 20-person company comprises 5 percent of the personnel and is typically involved in a much higher level of management decision making than would be possible with a larger company. This is naturally based on the person's specific job responsibility.

Let's now extend this small company scenario to the founders. These are the people who initially created the company and, through their work, dedication, and reputation, grew the company to the point that it can support a 20-person payroll. Their credibility is highly linked to the credibility of the company unless they have specifically worked at hiring excellent employees to whom they have turned over much of the daily operation. This does happen, but it is rare with smaller companies simply because the owners have nurtured their company since day one and they have evolved the operation around their involvement.

There is nothing insidious or wrong with this approach, and it doesn't reflect a conscious scheme on the founders' part to maintain control. It is simply a natural evolution for a successful smaller company.

Now you, the buyer, come along and want to purchase the company. Note that negotiations will probably be made with the founders, who might be completely unaware of their importance to the company. The founders might even downplay their importance. Just know that the likelihood of their being crucial to operations is most often the case. If you let them leave when you purchase the company might put you in the position of owning a company that just lost its most important assets, the founders.

For this reason, it is usually best to keep the founders around for a while, and purchase agreements try to keep the founders with some stock in the new company. This keeps the founders with an incentive to work for the prosperity of the buying company. These seller retention

Hot Tip

Arranging for a portion of a purchase package to include future stock incentives for the selling company's founders is a proven method for keeping their attention in the future. Otherwise, as with most entrepreneurs, their attention will wander onto newer, more exciting pastures.

agreements, sometimes called employment contracts, are usually for two or three years. And they put the selling founders into strategic roles that promote the success of their former company and also optimize their overall contribution to the buying organization.

There are, on the other hand, times when you would want the founders completely out of the picture. If the founder is a strong personality that keeps a lock on the company operations, which might cause substantial conflicts with the management and culture of the buying company, it might be in the buyer's best interest to specifically get the founder out of the picture.

There are also times where your due diligence reveals that customers are not working as fully as possible with the purchased company because of a lack of trust in the current management. This opens opportunities to the buying company since getting rid of the management might increase sales.

As with the purchase/sale of any firm, the devil is in the details and no standard set of recommendations that I can make will apply exactly to your situation. I simply present a few ideas here for your consideration.

The Least You Need to Know

➤ There is no single "right" way to arrange the financial aspects related to the purchase or sale of a company.

➤ Only corporations can perform a stock merger since only corporations are based on shares of stock.

➤ Buyer and seller company valuation is the basis for determining the stock basis during mergers.

➤ Management agreements might be attractive to the buyer but generally work to the detriment of the seller.

➤ The method of transaction financing affects the taxes associated with the transaction.

➤ The advantages and disadvantages of retaining the founders of the purchased company need to be determined on a case–by–case basis.

Part 2
We Have Ways to Make Money Talk

Money has a language all its own. Making it talk in a way that speaks to your particular interests is an art that starts with basic education. Read Part Two and start speaking the language of money.

Chapter 6

The Financials Speak for Themselves

In This Chapter

➤ Learn basic accounting terminology

➤ Understand the importance difference between cash and accrual accounting

➤ Differentiate between income and balances

➤ Determine a company's net worth

➤ Financial statements are art and science combined

"Okay. I see the long face, but I don't understand why," said Jenny to her accountant. "This company has a 25 percent pre-tax income and three months' worth of cash in the bank. What is the problem here?"

"Take at look at the account receivable numbers, and you will understand my disappointment. Notice that the receivable total is around 20 percent of sales?" Jenny shook her head in agreement. "Notice also that their account payable liability is higher than we would like?" Jenny again shook her head. "Now take a look at page 5 of their financial report, note number 4."

There, on page 5, was something that Jenny had missed. The target company had an outstanding receivable to a particular company, and it was having trouble collecting. In fact, this receivable was the total amount shown as a receivable on the balance sheet. The debt had already gone 180 days past due, which was why the payable number had crept higher. Management had made the decision to hold off on vendor payments in an attempt to hold onto some of its cash. Just in case this major customer did not pay. Holding cash in uncertain times is a reasonable business decision on their part, thought Jenny. It just might not be one that she was willing to inherit.

"Good job. You earned your money on this one," said Jenny. "Now what do you think we should do?"

Whether you are buying or selling a business, you must familiarize yourself with the basic financial concepts involved with evaluating a company.

At some point, you are going to have to investigate the financial performance of the target company. Ignorance of basic accounting terminology and principles will leave you at a severe disadvantage. Taking a few minutes to work through, and understand, this chapter will not only improve your financial communications, but will also aid you with understanding many of the topics presented in this book.

General Accounting Terminology

I sometimes think that jargon was invented as a form of job security. Others must trust you when they don't understand what you are talking about. If you have ever tried to order lunch in a Japanese restaurant where nobody spoke English, you are familiar with the concept of trust.

Well, trusting people for your lunch is one thing. Trusting them with your money and the financial well being of your company is something else altogether.

Accountants and attorneys throw numbers and financial jargon around the same as the high-tech people in a computer store do, except in this case they are talking about the underlying worth of the business you are either buying or selling.

Straight Talk

You could live in a foreign country, like Spain, and not speak Spanish. Just imagine how much easier and less stressful it would be if you spoke enough Spanish so that you understood what others were saying and so that others could understand you. The same is true with financial management. You don't need to understand these concepts, but not understanding them puts you at the mercy of those who do.

If you are in a position to either sell or buy a company, then you have already overcome a number of business hurdles. Treat this section as just another hurdle with the fringe benefit of paying dividends for as long as you are in the business world. Now that is a solid return on your time investment.

As you work your way through this chapter, you will find the jargon explained. Push your way through this chapter, but realize that you might need to read it a few times to get the concepts under your belt. A clear understanding of the concepts presented in this chapter will pay off for you throughout the rest of this, and any other, financial or business management book.

Accounting Period Importance

Nothing in our world happens outside of time, and the same is true for business activities. A company sells, produces, and ships products over a period of time. A company spends money in the form of purchases and collects money in the form of income during a specific timeframe.

The period during which this income is obtained and these expenses are incurred is referred to as the company's accounting period. These periods are usually monthly, every three months (quarterly), or yearly (annual). I cannot over emphasize the importance of considering accounting periods. Let me show you why this is true.

Assume that a company shows a profit for a particular three-month period. Also, assume that closer inspection reveals that a major expense item that the company incurred in the past month of the three-month period was actually recorded in the following month, which is outside of the accounting period being investigated. If they had recorded this expense in the third month, as would be expected, then the company would have actually shown a loss for that fiscal quarter. Which is the right way to record the expense? Luckily, there are accounting standards that answer this question.

In general, revenues and expenses must be matched to the timeframe within which they were incurred. If revenues were obtained such that they show up as sales figures within a specific timeframe, then the incurred expenses associated with creating that sales revenue must also be accounted for within that same timeframe. Otherwise, you wind up with an accounting mismatch situation similar to that presented earlier in this section.

In general, companies track their financial performance on a monthly, quarterly, and annual basis, based on their respective fiscal year.

Terms of Acquisition

Revenue Matching The accounting procedure that ensures that sales revenues and associated expenses for a given time period are tracked and recorded so that they appear on financial statements for the same fiscal period.

Fiscal Year The 12-month period during which a company tracks its financial performance. Most companies use a fiscal year that matches the calendar year, but it is not an absolute requirement. For example, the Federal Government has a fiscal year that starts on October 1 and ends on September 30.

Cash or Accrual Basis of Accounting—Ouch!

Hang in there. Before you can begin applying all this newfound knowledge, we have a few more important topics to discuss.

Most sole proprietor businesses think of revenue as when cash is received. They think of an expense as being when a check or cash is actually given for an item or service. And for most people, this is true. This type of accounting is called *cash-basis* accounting. For a business, however, cash-basis accounting is generally not good enough.

Businesses operate on credit, whether credit obtained from a vendor or credit given to a client. Money owed by the company to a vendor is called a payable since you are expected to pay it some time in the future. Money owed to the company by a client is called a receivable, since you expect to receive it at some time in the future.

Notice that money owed to you has not been received yet, so cannot be counted as revenue if you use the *receive the cash* method of revenue tracking. Conversely, money that you agree to pay in the future, although absolutely owed, cannot be treated as an expense if you use the *paid with cash* method of expense tracking since no cash has actually exchanged hands at the moment of the initial agreement.

However, the company still has receivable money coming in and expense payable money going out. Revenue matching requires the expenses and revenues be matched for a given accounting period, so there must be a way of accounting for these receivable and payable items.

There is, and it is called *accrual accounting*. If you think about it, the expenses that you owe build up, or accrue, over a period of time. The same applies to your receivable items. As clients pay their bills, your company's outstanding receivable items are reduced by the amount of payment. As you pay your bills, your outstanding payable items decrease. The accrual basis of accounting matches accrued revenues and expenses so that revenue matching is maintained.

Most companies track their daily operations using an accrual basis of accounting since most companies offer credit to their top customers and receive credit from their vendors.

Income tax returns are often completed on a cash basis of accounting based on the type of business involved, making a conversion between accrual and cash accounting necessary when closing out the fiscal year for tax purposes.

It is important to understand the basis of accounting that was used in the preparation of financial statements. If a company works on a cash-basis of accounting, then the balance sheet/income statement accurately reflects

Hot Tip

Companies with large inventories that operate much of their business on credit might be required by the IRS to file taxes using an accrual method of accounting. Checking with your tax professional on this topic is strongly recommended. This applies whether buying or selling a business. You must know the IRS status either way.

the on-hand financial status of the company at a given period of time. It does not, however, reflect money that the company owes or receivables outstanding that are owed the company, since cash-basis accounting has no way of tracking this unreceived/unpaid cash.

Accrual accounting, on the other hand, includes any unreceived income or unpaid expenses, but shows them as though they have already been paid or received. It is up to the person looking at the statements to understand that the "account receivable" and "account payable" items contained on the balance sheet reflect these pending transactions.

Notice that accrual accounting can make a financially strapped company look good if you are not careful.

For example, the accrual-based income statement might show a large revenue number along with its associated expenses. If a quick look at the balance sheet shows $0 in account receivable, then things look good. However, if you see an account receivable number that is a large percentage of the company's total revenues, then something is probably wrong. If the customer who owes this money is having financial trouble that has delayed its payments, and the target company has not written the receivable off as an uncollectable debt, then you might be looking at a company on the verge of some hard times.

Straight Talk

I have learned over time that there is as much art involved with creating a set of financial statements as science. Always review the underlying assumptions and the fine print associated with any set of financial statements. Always determine if you are dealing with cash or accrual accounting. Always verify any "extraordinary" income or expense items. Always verify the method used by the company for recognizing revenues and expenses.

Don't believe everything you read and don't assume that statements prepared by a CPA or reputable accounting firm are an accurate reflection of the company's condition. Often, they simply use the numbers given to the firm by the company, which is always stated in the six-point type disclaimer.

The payable money is still owed, whether the customer pays or not. If the customer defaults on the note just after you purchase the company, and there is nothing left of the customer to recover for payment of your receivable, you might be the new proud owner of a bankrupt company. Ouch!

Hopefully you are starting to acquire a newfound appreciation for the importance of accounting periods and accounting methods.

Later chapters, such as Chapters 7, "Let the Ratios Be Your Guide," and 14, "To Buy, or Not to Buy …" add more meat to this discussion by tracking examples and providing useful tools for ferreting out the truth.

Financial Statements and Their Use

Almost every financial discussion pertaining to a company starts with the financial statements. Just as your periodic medical checkup presents an overall picture of your general health, the financial statements present an overall picture of a company's general financial health. I will carry this analogy throughout this chapter as a tool for explaining the various financial statements and their significance.

The Balance Sheet

Remember your last health checkup? If not, then you should go get one right away, but that is a topic for another book.

At any rate, your doctor takes your temperature, weight, height, and blood pressure. This information provides a baseline of information that applies to the particular day upon which you had your checkup. It tells nothing about your weight fluctuations during the last six months, whether you had a fever two weeks ago, or any other pertinent information. These are static measurements taken and recorded at a particular point in time.

The financial balance sheet does the same thing. It shows the financial status of the company on a particular day, usually the end of a fiscal period such as a month, quarter, or year.

The balance sheet includes information about a company's accounting value and net worth. It makes intuitive sense that the value of something that you own is obtained by determining the amount of money that an object can be sold for and then subtracting the amount of money owed on the object.

Assume that you own a house worth $150,000, on which you have a mortgage for $100,000. Notice that the net worth or the house is $50,000 ($150,000 minus $100,000). Realtor commissions were omitted from the example for simplicity. Stated another way, when the object is sold and all debts related to that object are paid, you would expect to receive $50,000. This is the general simplified concept associated with determining the net worth of something.

Terms of Acquisition

Fiscal Period   The period of time during which the finances of a company were monitored. It can be for any time period, but generally is assumed to be a month, quarter (three months), or a year.

Fiscal Quarter   A three-month period that existed during a given company's fiscal year, which includes 12 months, or four quarters.

Balance Sheet for Danada Florists, Inc.
At December 31, 20xx

Assets

Cash	12,500	
Accounts Receivable	2,300	
Inventory	2,500	
Equipment	15,400	
Delivery Van	22,500	
Accumulated Depreciation	-4,675	
Total Assets		50,525
Liabilities		
Line of Credit	4,560	
Accounts Payable	1,950	
Credit Cards	3,675	
Van Loan	18,650	
Total Liabilities		28,835
Shareholder's Equity		
Paid In Capital (Stock)	10,000	
Retained Earnings	11,690	
Total Shareholder's Equity		21,690
Total Liabilities + Equity		50,525

It gets a bit more complicated when dealing with a business, but the overall concepts are the same. To determine the net worth of a company you must first determine the value of the things that the company owns, as determined by its accounting records. This is often referred to as the book value of the company's assets.

Terms of Acquisition

Current Assets and Liabilities
Means that the asset can be converted to cash or the liability will be paid off within 12 months.

Depreciation The percentage of the initial purchase price of an asset that it is assumed to devalue in a given year of operation. For example, a piece of equipment might cost $25,000 and have an assumed depreciable accounting life of five years. This means that the equipment devalues, or depreciates, by $5,000 ($25,000/5 years) per year.

Hot Tip

Generally Accepted Accounting Principles (GAAP) are followed by any accountant or financial officer who wants to do his or her job correctly and legally. Make sure that you ask whether GAAP-compliant accounting practices were used in the preparation of the financial statements, and verify who monitored the implementation. If a CPA certified the statements, you can be sure that GAAP guidelines were followed.

Assets depreciate over their assumed useful accounting life. This is a way of allowing the company to deduct a certain amount of an asset's value in the form of an expense item. After all, if the asset is being used, its useful life has been reduced and an operating expense deduction can be claimed. As depreciation adds up from one year to the next, the total amount of *accumulated depreciation* increases.

Determining a company's total asset book value therefore involves determining the initial purchase price of all assets and then subtracting the total depreciation applied to those assets.

Liabilities are a bit more straightforward. The company either owes money or it doesn't. If it owes money, then it should have some accounting means of tracking the liability.

Notice that the net worth of a company is increased by the addition of assets, decreased both by adding liabilities (debts) and by taking a depreciation expense deduction.

The overall relationship among assets, liabilities, and net worth can be displayed as a simple equation, which is the mantra for any accountant:

Assets = Liabilities + Owner's Equity (net worth)

When dealing with individuals, you will hear people refer to their net worth as *owner's equity*. When dealing with a corporation, which can have many shareholders, you will hear people refer to net worth as *shareholder's equity*, which means essentially the same things except applied to many owners.

Notice that this is simply a restating of the earlier relationship we discussed and would mathematically look like this:

Assets – Liabilities = Net Worth

There are many complicated strategies associated with optimizing the balance sheet appearance of a company and many will be discussed throughout the rest of the book. However, a few things are truly independent of the company involved since all U.S. companies must use the same set of accounting rules:

➤ Increasing assets without increasing liabilities will always increase owner's equity.

➤ Increasing liabilities without increasing assets will always decrease owner's equity.

➤ An owner can own a lot of equity and not own any cash if the company's assets are in the form of equipment and other tangible assets and not in the form of cash and accounts receivable.

➤ Owner's equity is obtained by exchanging company stock for assets such as cash or equipment.

➤ It is possible for one company to purchase another and, by merging the stocks (owner's equity), never transfer one nickel of cash from the buyer to the seller. We will talk more about this in later chapters.

Terms of Acquisition

Assets   Items owned by the company that have some value, such as cash, accounts receivable, inventory, buildings, equipment, goodwill, and other tangible or intangible items.

Liabilities   Money owed by the company to some other company or person. Liabilities can include loans for the purchase of equipment or a building, a credit card debt, a bank line of credit, or unpaid payroll taxes. If it is owed to someone, it is a liability.

Owner's equity consists of two major accounting items: paid in capital and retained earnings.

Paid in capital reflects the total amount of money paid by shareholders to purchase company stock. This can be in the form of cash or assets such as equipment. *Retained earnings* are the amount of net income left over from the year that was retained by the company. (See the next section for a detailed discussion about income statements and net income.)

The Income Statement

Anyone who has ever managed a household budget knows that monitoring the amount of money coming in (income) and the amount of money going out (expenses) is important to keeping the bill collectors off of your back.

The income statement provides a standardized way of tracking income and expenses so that anyone can ascertain whether a company is making money, or not.

Income Statement for Danada Florists, Inc.
For Fiscal Period January 1, 20xx to December 31, 20xx

Revenues

Sales	235,500	
Interest Income	4,300	
Total Revenues		239,300
Cost of Sales (COS)		83,755
Gross Margin (Gross Profit)		155,545

Fixed Expenses

Store Rent	24,000	
Utilities	12,000	
Salaries	98,000	
Depreciation	2,800	
Postage	1,600	
Shipping	4,800	
Total Fixed Expenses		143,200
Pre-Tax Income		12,345
Less: Federal Income Tax	<1,852>	
Less: State Income Tax	<370>	
Net Income		10,123
Retained Earnings, Beginning		3,067
Dividends	<1,500>	
Retained Earnings, Ending		11,690

The top of the income statement lists the total incomes the company received from its various sales activities. The income section might also include a section dealing with investment income, should that be one of the company's income activities.

Beneath the sales section of the statement is the Cost of Sales section, which deals with the variable costs associated with the sales numbers shown.

The intention of these two sections is to break down expenses associated directly with generating the sales revenues shown. A person reviewing the financial statements can now determine what percentage of the company's expenses are associated directly with sales revenue generation and what percentage does not change with sales. It is common for a company to become top-heavy, that is, more money is spent on fixed expenses than makes sense for the sales levels. This happens with smaller companies where family members take large salaries to remove profits from the company.

Terms of Acquisition

Variable Cost A cost of doing business that varies directly with the sales level. It might include, for example, paper and ink costs for a newspaper business. The variable cost can be expressed as a dollar figure or as a percentage of sales, depending on the analysis being performed.

Fixed Costs Costs that remain constant and are independent of the sales level. Typical fixed costs include mortgage payments, utilities, executive salaries, and state licensing fees. It can also be expressed as a dollar figure or as a percentage of sales.

As the acquiring company, you might decrease these fixed overhead expenses, thereby moving a company that was previously showing an annual loss into one that shows a profit. And not decrease the sales revenues in the process. A family member could not do this to another family member, but a new owner who is not related can.

Subtracting the cost of sales (or cost of goods sold—COGS) from the sales revenues number leaves the gross margin. This is the amount of money left over to pay the fixed expenses.

Below the gross margin is a listing of the fixed expenses associated with the company. Subtracting the total of fixed expenses from the gross margin leaves the pre-tax profit, or the amount of money that the company made before taxes were taken out.

Subtracting taxes from the pre-tax profit number leaves the net income that the company saw during the accounting period being reviewed.

Shareholder dividends are paid from the net income figure. Moneys paid to shareholders are deducted from the net income figure, with the remaining money being transferred to the balance sheet as retained earnings.

That's right. As if you didn't have enough to worry about in this discussion, I now have money passing between the two financial statements. Well, if you think about it, the two statements have already been passing numbers back and forth. Here are a few examples.

When the company receives a payment from a customer, the check is deposited into the checking account (cash on the balance sheet). It would then show up as income for a company operating on the cash basis of accounting. (We will talk more about this topic later.) When a loan payment of $100 is made, a portion of the $100 goes to interest expense (income statement item), a portion goes to decreasing an existing liability (balance sheet item), and the cash is removed from the checking account (balance sheet).

Hot Tip

Take the time to reread this section until you intuitively understand the examples. Understanding the difference between accrual and cash basis accounting, and its effect on your income statement, will keep you from thinking you have money only to find out later that you have income and no cash.

Terms of Acquisition

Pro-Forma Financial Statements Statements that predict the future based on a combination of historical performance and projected (guesstimated) future performance. Used to project the financial statements of a company as they might appear months, or years into the future. For liability reasons, not often used when selling a company since they might possibly be construed as a commitment of future performance instead of somebody's best guess.

Following are a few major ways that the income statement can be affected by changes in company operations:

➤ Increasing sales increases revenues. If the cost of sales and fixed expenses remain the same, the company will show in increase in net income.

➤ Decreasing the cost of sales, through the addition of equipment or techniques that increase production efficiency while keeping sales and fixed expenses constant, increases net income.

➤ Decreasing fixed expenses while keeping everything else constant increases net income since more of the gross margin is left over after fixed expenses are deducted.

There are an infinite number of things that a company can do to its accounting practices that can make a company appear either more or less healthy that it really is.

Follow through this example to test your understanding. A company decides to install new technology that improves manufacturing efficiencies, which decreases COGS. By keeping the fixed expenses the same and choosing a dividend policy that pays no dividends for a 24-month period, the company increases its cash position in two ways while also increasing its retained earnings. Net worth increases while also improving the book value of the company.

If you got all that, you should congratulate yourself and go have a hot fudge sundae. If not, take a look at these last two sections again and see if it makes more sense the second time around.

The Statement of Cash Flows

If a company reports its financial condition with an accrual-based income statement and balance sheet, then you still need to learn about the actual cash that flowed into and out of the company. Remember that cash is the lifeblood of a company, and the more you know about the cash flow, the more you accurately will understand the overall financial condition of the company.

The *statement of cash flows* is designed to bridge the gap between accrual and cash accounting, so that the person reviewing the statements can understand the way cash moved through the company. I won't cover the details of statement of cash flow preparation since they are routine once the income statement and balance sheets are created. Just know that it exists and that it should be part of your financial evaluation process.

As a seller, know that any credible financial manager assisting a prospective buyer will ask for one, so you might as well have it prepared.

The Least You Need to Know

➤ The balance sheet provides you with a snapshot-in-time view of the company.

➤ The income statement shows revenue inflows and expense outflows during a given accounting period.

➤ Cash basis and accrual basis of accounting decisions can change, on paper, a profitable company to one in trouble, or vice versa.

➤ Always read the fine print of a financial statement, even if you need a magnifying glass and a quart of espresso coffee.

➤ Business lifeblood is cash, and the statement of cash flows should be reviewed carefully.

➤ Beware and study any extraordinary expense or income items shown on the financial statements.

Chapter 7

Let the Ratios Be Your Guide

> ### In This Chapter
>
> ➤ The value of using ratios
>
> ➤ Ratios that highlight overall performance
>
> ➤ Cash liquidity ratio calculations
>
> ➤ Estimate debt usage effectiveness
>
> ➤ Use ratios in conjunction with each other

"This company is going to drive me nuts," said Frank. "I believe in my bones that it is an excellent purchase, but when I look at their financial statement I get concerned."

Frank had been discussing the targeted company's financial statements with his accountant for the past 30 minutes, and had simply become more confused.

The company's level of cash was low for a company its size. Frank knew this just from experience. He believed that there were more people on staff than is needed to support the sales level, and yet, the stock's performance continued to maintain an above average growth rate.

"Perhaps we should perform a ratio analysis on the company and see how it compares with the other companies we are looking at. We could then compare it to the rest of the industry to see how the company stacks up," suggested his accountant.

"Why not," said Frank. He didn't feel comfortable paying top dollar for the stock when he saw conflicting financial information. The truth was out there.

The closer you get to a company, the more difficult it becomes to maintain an objective perspective on it. At some point, you need to step back far enough to determine whether the target company presents the right investment opportunity for you. If you are selling your company, you should know that an experienced financial analyst will perform a ratio analysis on your company and, from that analysis, determine your company's attractiveness. Managing to maintain good ratios might be putting the operational emphasis in the wrong area, but ignoring the ratios altogether is not a good idea either.

This chapter presents an introduction to ratio analysis and outlines the meaning and use of the most commonly used financial ratios.

What Does a Ratio Mean, Anyway?

Life is strange in that you often don't think about some things until they can be compared to another. For example, you might be tall compared to one person but short compared to a NBA basketball player. Heck, there are even some NBA basketball players who are considered short, which is really beyond my comprehension with my 5 foot, 8 inch frame.

My point here is that a number is often just a number until it is compared to another, related number. At that time, the significance of the number is understood.

To say that a company had sales of $800,000 past quarter, doesn't mean much until you know the sales from the prior quarter. Now you know if sales increased or decreased, and you can make a business judgment about the quarterly sales number's significance.

Buyer/Seller Beware

If someone presents you with a financial or operational ratio that you do not understand, don't be afraid to ask about the numeric components of that ratio. After all, the ratio is only as significant as the numbers used in its calculation. If you don't understand the underlying numbers, you won't understand the ratio.

A ratio is used to compare two values, and present them as a single number. Assume, from the prior example, that the prior quarter sales were $700,000. This means that the current quarter shows an increase in sales of $100,000 ($800,000 minus $700,000). From a ratio analysis perspective, you could also say that sales increased to 1.14 times the prior quarter's sales ($800/$700 = 1.14). Stated another way, you could also say that sales increased by 14 percent (1.14–1.0 expressed as a percentage).

You can now compare the company figures to industry figures on a standardized basis. For example, comparing $800,000 and $700,000 to an entire industry can be a complicated process. But comparing a 14 percent quarterly growth rate for a specific company to a percentage growth rate for that company's industry does have management significance.

If the overall industry had a sales growth of 14 percent, then the company is holding its own from a sales growth standpoint. If the industry grew at 20 percent, then some other competitor gained a larger percentage of industry sales growth than the target company gained.

The major benefit of using ratio analysis is that all numbers can be compared from a common basepoint. Percentages do not reflect a raw underlying number. A percentage shows a units-neutral amount that can then be compared to other percentages.

The significance of any ratio is dependent upon the numbers being compared and the relationship between the two numbers.

Understand that the ratios presented in this chapter are common financial ratios that provide an instant comparative view into various aspects of a company's operation. This is not a comprehensive listing of ratios; it does, however, presents those most commonly used. You might find that customized ratios would apply better to a specific company's operations. Although the right combination or ratios and historical trends can highlight a specific company's management aims, it might provide nothing of value for some other company.

How Much Debt Is Too Much?

Few things will push a company, or a personal household, into financial trouble at a faster rate than owing too much money. The question is "How much is too much?"

Ratio analysis supplies a few tools that provide a starting, common basis for debt analysis.

Coverage Ratio

A good place to start with a debt analysis is to determine if the company has enough income to cover the interest due on its loans. When a borrower has problems paying its debts, the first retreat point is to pay only interest on the loan, instead of both principal and interest. The coverage ratio is an analysis tool that provides insight into this important area.

This is a simple ratio that involves only two numbers: the earnings before interest and income tax (EBIT) and the total interest paid on debt (TID, which applies to the company's loans).

The *coverage ratio* (CR) is simply the earnings before income tax divided by the total interest paid on debt. Expressed mathematically, as:

Coverage Ratio = EBIT/TID

Hot Tip

Looking at loans is an excellent place to start any serious financial analysis. If the loans cannot be repaid, then there is a strong chance that the loans will be called by the creditors. This action could put the entire company into financial jeopardy. If a company cannot pay its loans, you have to wonder how much longer it can pay its employees.

Assume that a company has an EBIT of $60,000 and that this same company paid $20,000 in total interest on its debts. These numbers mean that the company has a coverage ratio of $60,000/$20,000 = 3. Is this ratio result too small, too large, or just right? That answer is always a matter of personal investment style and perspective, but maintaining a coverage ratio of 3 is considered a solid minimum. This means that EBIT can drop by two thirds, and the company can still cover the interest on its debts. If the EBIT drops by more than two thirds, the company might default on its loan interest payments causing the entire company to potentially go into default.

This single ratio by itself does not completely define the company, but if this ratio is 1, then it means that this company is barely making its loan interest payments, and any serious downturn in EBIT could put the company in a shaky financial position.

Debt-Equity Ratio

It is also valuable to understand the percentage of a company's net worth that has been allocated to debt. Remember that assets equal liabilities plus owner's equity. If the assets start to equal the liabilities, which could happen if the company borrows a lot of money to pay for the items shown as assets, this will reduce the owner's equity.

Hot Tip

Total Company Debt can be assumed as the Total Liabilities section of the balance sheet. Total Owner's Equity can be assumed as Total Assets minus Total Liabilities.

The Debt-Equity (DE) ratio provides a quick look at the relationship between the amount of debt held by a company and its total owner's equity.

It is a simple ratio:

DE Ratio = Total Company Debt/Total Owner's Equity

Determining the right value for the DE ratio is once again a relative estimation. Once calculated, it should be compared to other firms in the same SIC (Standard Industrial Code). If the targeted company has a lower DE ratio, the target company is holding less debt as compared to its total equity. If the DE ratio is higher, the targeted company is using more debt than equity to finance its operations.

Short-Term Financial Health Analysis

Without enough cash, your targeted company could be out of business before you really get started. Not having enough cash present within the targeted company is not necessarily a reason, by itself, to stop the purchase. However, you should know that you will have to add cash to the company after the purchase should the purchased company does not have enough cash to sustain its operations by itself.

Two common ratios used for cash assessment are the Current Ratio and the Quick Ratio, also called the Acid Test.

Current Ratio Analysis

The current ratio is a simple calculation, once you have a detailed balance sheet in your hands:

Current Ratio = Current Assets/Current Liabilities

This ratio compares the amount of money owed within a 12-month period to the total assets that are assumed to be convertible into cash within that 12-month period, which is assumed all earmarked for paying this debt.

The larger this ratio, the better off the company is with respect to sustaining itself on a short-term basis. At a minimum, this ratio should equal "1" and numbers of "2" or higher are most common for well-run companies.

Notice that the inventory is part of the current assets along with prepaid expenses. It is rare that you can convert inventory into cash at 100 percent of its book value, which makes the Current Ratio analysis optimistic.

Terms of Acquisition

Current Assets These are assets that can be converted into cash within a 12–month period.

Current Liabilities These are debts that must be paid off within a 12–month period.

Quick Ratio (Acid Test) Calculation

Pulling inventory and prepaid expenses out of the current ratio calculation provides a clear picture of the ready cash currently available to this company. The Quick Ratio does just that:

Quick Ratio = (Current Assets – Inventory – Prepaid Expenses)/Current Liabilities

The numerator (top part) of this equation will typically consist of the cash, account receivable, and other readily convertible assets, and will be smaller than the numerator used for the Current Ratio. As a result, you should expect the Quick Ratio to be a smaller number than the Current Ratio, but it also represents a more pessimistic view of the company's ability to pay its own short-term debts.

It is not uncommon for a Quick Ratio to be under 1, with numbers between 0.8 and 1.0 most common. Numbers lower than 0.8 might indicate that the company is running short on its available cash, which could create a problem for you soon after the purchase. Performing a Quick Ratio analysis over a period of time that extends back 12 to 24 months provides a trend of the company's cash position. If the trend is upward, you might not have a serious problem on your hands. If downward, there might be hidden problems with this company from a cash flow standpoint. This is a little like buying a racehorse only to find that it has an incurable blood disease. At the

Terms of Acquisition

Inventories Items held for the generation of income that could be either finished products that are ready for sale, or the components involved in the manufacture of finished goods.

Prepaid Expenses Expense items paid in advance of when they are actually consumed in the revenue-earning process, such as insurance, supplies, taxes or credit balances with vendors.

risk of sounding heartless, you might not want to inherit these problems, or at least want to charge the sellers for the increased risk associated with purchasing a cash-poor company.

Radical changes in Current and Quick Ratios within a short period of time (three to six months) are cause for interest and closer scrutiny on your part.

How Quickly Do Customers Pay?

Next to cash as the company's lifeblood is the promptness with which current customers pay their outstanding debts, or Account Receivable. The Average Collection Period calculation provides a snapshot analysis of the overall company's credit collection performance:

Average Collection Period = Accounts Receivable/ (Sales/365 days)

This is an important number that is certainly worth calculating, both as a management criteria for your own company or when analyzing the performance of another. It shows the current amount of Accounts Receivable divided by the average sales that occur on a specific day of the business year. The result of this calculation is an estimate of how long it takes to collect money from credit customers.

But, there are some assumptions associated with this number that are worth discussing because they determine the effectiveness of this ratio.

Notice that the Account Receivable number used is that present on the Balance Sheet on the day of the analysis. This number might be uncharacteristically high or low for the company in question, so verifying the status of the account receivable number as it compares to normal operation is a good idea.

Also notice that the denominator (the bottom part of the equation) is an average of sales throughout the entire year. This presents a possibility of comparing apples and oranges, and let me explain why.

The basic assumption of the denominator is that sales occurred evenly throughout the year, where the numerator assumes a specific point in time. If sales truly are consistent throughout the year, then this ratio provides an accurate assessment of the receivable collection period. If the company just experienced a huge burst in sales over the past 30 days, then this number will be artificially high. Why? Because the denominator will average out the recent burst over an entire year of sales, reducing the recent sales impact, while the numerator will substantially consist of recent sales activities which consists primarily of the large 30-day sales burst, in accordance with the example.

Straight Talk

As part of any company analysis, you should verify the Average Collection Period with the company's standard credit policy. If the company policy sets net 30 day terms, and the company has an average collection period of 20 days, life is good, and the existing customer base pays earlier than expected, probably to take advantage of discounts for early payment. If the Average Collection Period is 60 days or more, you just might have a problem that could become your problem if you continued with the purchase.

If sales have been low over the past 30 days, as compared to the rest of the year, then this number will be artificially low. Why? For the opposite reasons presented in the previous paragraph.

Also notice that the denominator will include cash and credit sales if it is taken directly from the income statement. To determine the actual credit collection period, the denominator should only include credit sales with cash sales being excluded. Total Sales is used if there isn't a credible breakdown of credit and cash sales, although you should understand that using Total Sales affects the number calculated.

Determining Inventory Usage Efficiency

Have you got stuff in your basement that you look at, realize that it takes up space, and can't even remember the last time you looked at it? You probably said to yourself, "I need to get rid of some of this old stuff that just isn't useful any more." Okay. Maybe I'm the only person this has ever happened to, but bear with me.

Your frustration with having all that space occupied by stuff you cannot use is shared by companies that have too much inventory as part of their overall operation.

A manufacturing company must have some type of raw materials and/or finished goods inventory to generate sales revenue. If the company purchases too much inventory in comparison to its needs, it will have money tied up in inventory that it cannot turn into sales revenue. In essence, the inventory money has been spent and is not generating any income for the company.

If a company purchases too much inventory, then it is wasting its money on unused inventory. If it purchases too little, then it might have product shortages because of the inability to manufacture the customer-demanded items.

Determining the optimal inventory level is an art form, but you can use the inventory turnover ratio as a starting point.

Inventory Turnover = Cost of Good Sold/Inventory

Note that the cost of goods sold is a value derived from the income statement and the inventory number is taken from the balance sheet. Also notice that you are only looking at the costs associated with creating a product and the cost of the inventory currently on hand.

The proper value of the Inventory Turnover Ratio will vary from one industry to another, but you should find commonality among companies within the same industry.

Hot Tip

As a starting point, assume that the Inventory Turnover Ratio should be at least 4, with a higher number indicating that the company turns over its inventory on a more efficient basis. This is usually good news because it means that the company's assets are not excessively tied up in inventory.

This ratio has limited meaning for a company that produces a "service" instead of a "product" because inventory is usually very small for a services firm.

The Cost of Doing Business

It is always a good idea to take a look at the overall company performance while also looking at the details. And a good place to start is determining the amount of each sale dollar that is retained as income at the end of the business day.

Straight Talk

Finding valid comparative financial ratios will require a little research on your part. Always try to find ratios for the industry that most closely matches that of the target company. If possible, find the ratios that apply to the targeted company's closest competitors, if that information is available.

Annual reports are an excellent starting place for any publicly traded company. Trade associations will publish information for their specific industry. The government also tracks information on a Standard Industrial Code (SIC) basis. Financial or investment services might also have similar information you can access. Dun & Bradstreet also tracks this information, if provided by the companies. Finally, check with your library's research department to see what they can find out for you.

Net Profit Margin

We have discussed net income in prior sections, but we really didn't look at a way of determining whether the amount of net income retained is right for the company in question.

The Net Profit Margin ratio provides a simple yet effective way of determining the profitability of one company with respect to other companies within the same industry or in other industries.

This calculation is also a simple one:

> Net Profit Margin = Net Income After Tax/Net Sales

This number will appear as a ratio, which is always less than one and is usually expressed as a percentage.

Assume that a company has $1 million in net sales, and $150,000 in net income after tax. The net profit margin is then calculated as 150,000/1,000,000 = .15 or 15 percent.

Is 15 percent good or bad? This depends on the industry and other related factors. For some industries, a 5 percent profit margin is considered excellent where others would pack up their bags and go home with a 5 percent profit margin. Consulting companies might show profit margins of 20 percent or higher.

Other Relevant Operational Ratios

As you get deeper into a company's operation, you will want to learn more about the management's philosophy. Here are a few ratios that will help you get a starting point regarding the current management's areas of emphasis. All these ratios should be expressed as a percentage after being calculated. After they are calculated, these percentages can be compared to others in the industry to get an assessment of how the target company compares to others in a similar situation.

Calculating the percentage of a sale revenue dollars that is spent on sales and marketing activities tells you if the company is under or over spending its sales and marketing dollars.

> Marketing Percentage Cost = Total Sales and Marketing Costs/Total Sales

If the company is in a technology environment, research and development (R&D) is an important investment area. Calculating the percentage of

Buyer/Seller Beware

Avoid the trap of making all management decisions based on ratios and financial numbers. I prefer to use them as pointers to other potential problems that might otherwise remain hidden. Without the ratios, you make decisions strictly on intuition. Deciding strictly "by the numbers" runs the risk of oversimplifying a complex business problem. Intuition, experience, and solid ratio analysis is the optimal combination.

sales dedicated to R&D tells you the level of importance attached to R&D by this company.

Percentage R&D Expense = Total R&D Expenses/Total Sales

This number might be as high as 10 percent or higher for advanced technology companies, and might be as low as 1 to 2 percent for companies in less dynamic environments. If your target company spends a lot on R&D, but has few patents or other proprietary technologies to show for it, then something might be wrong. If the company underinvests in R&D as compared to others in the industry, then it might lag others with respect to new technological developments. This lag might pose problems for you a few years after your purchase.

Calculating the percentage of sales that go to covering the cost of sales is a good indicator of the profits associated with sales. A high percentage cost of sales means that the company might not be focusing adequate attention on optimizing the production of the goods and/or services that are ultimately sold.

Percentage Cost of Sales = Cost of Sales/Total Sales

It is common to break down the cost of sales analysis by market or product segment to determine the areas of high and low profitability.

A final operational percentage (ratio) calculation I recommend is one that determines the percentage of sales used to cover fixed expenses.

Percentage Fixed Expenses = Total Fixed Expenses/ Total Sales

If this number is too high as compared to others in the industry, you might find that the company has lost sight of its revenue generating activities. It might have too many employees, too much equipment, or it might have spent a lot of time and money on infrastructure, and not paid enough attention to creating sales. Once again, this number by itself doesn't mean anything, but it surely indicates that more attention should be paid to how fixed expenses are allocated.

Hot Tip

Remember from Chapter 6, "The Financials Speak for Themselves," that subtracting the cost of sales from the net sales provides you with the gross margin. Dividing the gross margin by the total sales provides you with the percentage gross margin for the company in question. This percentage is calculated and compared to others in the industry, and varies widely among industries. If the percentage gross margin number is low, then the company has less money left over to support fixed expenses that must be spent just to keep the doors open.

Rating the Stock Performance

As a shareholder, you always want to know how your stock investment is performing. This section presents two common evaluation tools that provide some insight on the overall performance, or perception of future performance, associated with a company's stock.

The Book Return on Equity calculation compares the amount of net income reported by the company to total equity investment made by shareholders to create that net income.

Book Return on Equity = Net Income/Owner's Equity

Assume that a company shows a net after tax income of $150,000 and has an Owner's Equity (as shown by the balance sheet) of $1,000,000. The Book Return on Equity is 150,000/1,000,000 (that is, .15 or 15 percent). This 15 percent might be good or bad depending on other possible investment opportunities. If the overall investment climate can provide a 20 percent return on an investment, then 15 percent might be low. If, on the other hand, the best alternative investment is in the 8 percent range, then 15 percent looks great. Once again, comparing this ratio to others in the industry gives you an indication of how this company relates to others in a similar situation.

Those of you who are invested in stocks have undoubtedly heard about the price-to-earning (PE) ratio. This number compares the current market price of a stock to its earnings over the prior 12-month period.

PE Ratio = Stock Price/(12-month Earnings/ Number of Issued Shares)

This number is bantered around a great deal, and it is actually simple to understand.

If a stock is selling for $50 a share, and its earnings over the preceding 12 months is $5, then it has a PE ratio of 50/5=10. This means that, should the earnings continue at the same $5 per year rate, the earnings gained over a 10-year period will equal the current stock price. Earnings that decrease will increase the time period required to match the stock price if the stock price remains the same. Earnings that increase will decrease this period should the stock price remain the same.

In reality, the stock price will typically vary with the earnings reported to keep the stock within a specific PE ratio range. The baseline used to determine the right PE ratio is determined by the overall industry average for the company under investigation.

Buyer/Seller Beware

The executive management team of a publicly held company is often compensated based on the increase in stock price, which is intimately linked to earnings and the PE ratio as compared to the rest of the market. More than one company has been put into a compromised financial condition simply by having a management team that managed to optimize stock price and not to optimize longer-term financial health.

A Word of Caution Regarding Ratio Analysis

One ratio does not a company determine. A company with a low quick ratio might also have a low debt-equity ratio keeping debt at a lower level because cash is used to finance operations. Less cash with lower debt might be the right approach for this company. A low quick-ratio, a high debt-equity ratio, a low inventory turnover ratio, and a long average collection period indicate a company in need of financial management correction.

So, a single ratio will not determine the health of a company, just as measuring only the heartbeat rate does not, by itself, determine a person's health. Looking at the ratios presented here until you see an overall picture forming is always a sound procedure.

The Least You Need to Know

➤ Ratios are objective numbers that can be easily compared among companies and industries.

➤ The liquidity ratios provide an easy snapshot into the cash condition of a company.

➤ The equity ratios give insight into the investment returns related to the target company as compared to other investments.

➤ Operational ratios highlight the effectiveness of daily operation.

➤ No single ratio determines the company's financial condition although it can indicate areas in need of further investigation.

Chapter 8

Making It All Less Taxing

In This Chapter

➤ Understanding capital gains and taxes

➤ Selling assets instead of the whole company

➤ Selling the whole company instead of just assets

➤ Special small corporation tax exclusion rules

➤ Comparing S and C corporation sales

"I'm not sure that I want to give them this much cash as part of the deal," said Mike to his financial officer.

"It is tough not to," responded the CFO. "The president and two members of his staff just acquired their stock within the last six months. So they won't qualify for the capital gains rates for another six months. They have to have some cash to pay their taxes."

Mike sat back in his chair. There had to be a way to structure this deal so that he could pay a lower price for the company, put in less cash, and keep the management interested for a year or two after the purchase was finally completed.

Mike raised his hand to get the CFO's attention. "What if we did something like this? What if we raised our offer price by 5 percent, but paid only half the cash amount we initially proposed followed by the balance in stock, dispersed over a two-year period. This way we get to keep our cash, they get a higher sale price, and they get to take advantage of the capital gains holdings. What do you think?"

The CFO looked up from his calculator and smiled. This was always a good sign coming from a CFO.

Merger and acquisition deals are only limited by the imagination of the participants. And we all can be pretty creative when it comes to not paying the government any more money in taxes than absolutely necessary.

More than one of us has driven from one side of town to the other simply to take advantage of a special sale or other bargain. Thinking about taxes early in the sale/purchase game can decrease the amount of taxes that the seller must pay by 15 percent or more. Not thinking about taxes can put a seller into a financial situation where he or she has sold the company, incurred a huge cash tax bill, and cannot sell any stock to pay the bill. Not a pretty picture. Both buyers and sellers should read through this chapter and start orienting their thinking toward the tax implications of the transaction.

The Overall Impact of Taxes

Uncle Sam is always there making sure that he gets his, and possibly, your fair share of any money transaction deal. Purchasing a company is no different.

On the surface, you would think that taxes would only affect the seller, since he or she is the one receiving money. Not true. You, as the buyer, also have tax issues that deserve consideration, or you might end up paying more for the company than you expected once the final tax bills come due.

For example, assume that you purchase assets from a company, instead of performing a stock purchase or merger. The assets have a market value that is fixed at the time of your purchase, and any previous depreciation becomes history associated with the old company. This historical depreciation does not pass onto, or apply, to your company.

Hot Tip

Asset purchases allow the purchasing company to define its own depreciation expense policies which is advantageous to the buyer. I always like to define my own policies instead of inheriting those handed down from others.

Assume, on the other hand, that the buyer purchases the target company's stock. This action transfers asset ownership to the purchasing company simply because the stock represents company ownership and purchasing the stock is also purchasing everything owned by that stock. The previously existing accounting basis of the asset is transferred at its existing depreciated value and not at its existing market value, which would be the case if the asset had been acquired as an asset purchase.

Which of these situations is most advantageous? It all depends on the goals of the buyer and seller. An asset that transfers at a higher accounting value, as is often seen with an asset purchase, provides greater future depreciation expense deduction opportunities. These larger expense deductions decrease the taxable income seen by the purchasing company. If the purchasing company is privately held, decreasing taxable income as much as possible is usually the desired financial course.

On the other hand, a publicly traded company might want to show as much income as possible so that earnings per share look as high as possible. In this case, transferring the asset at a lower basis, which means smaller depreciation expenses, might be the preferred approach, making a stock purchase more attractive.

It is even possible to play with the way the purchase price for a company is allocated over the various aspects of the company. Assume that a company sells for $500,000 and has an inventory book value of $50,000. Also assume that goodwill transfers as part of the transaction. How much of the $500,000 should be considered goodwill and how much inventory. If the buying company wants to increase its income for the year, it will want to increase goodwill and decrease the valuation placed on the inventory. Why?

Decreasing the inventory value decreases cost of goods sold, which, subsequently, increases the gross margin on products sold. This has the accounting effect of increasing net income. In addition, goodwill can be depreciated over a larger number of years, which allows for a smaller depreciation expense, and also increases the net income. The overall $500,000 remains the same, but the way in which the purchase price is allocated will affect the income realized from the purchased company during the next fiscal period.

Terms of Acquisition

Goodwill   The value attached to the good name of a company. Just having the company name associated with an organization is worth something, and that value is tracked as goodwill.

If a company's management is compensated based on net income, the management has an incentive to optimize the purchase decisions so that net income is increased. Aggressively depreciating assets increases expenses; this decreases net income, which is counter productive to the management's aim. Therefore, the management will take financial and accounting steps to decrease expenses and increase net income, while still paying $500,000 for the target company.

Much of life shows us that beauty is in the eye of the beholder, and the same applies to business purchases.

Sales Tax May Be Charged on Asset Purchases

Just when you thought that you were aware of all the taxes involved, you are hit with another potential tax. If you purchase an item at the store, you would expect to pay state sales tax on it unless it somehow was exempt or if your particular state does not have a sales tax.

Any assets that you purchase from another company might very well be subject to sales tax, and you should verify this with your accountant before making any final proposals. This could add to the asset cost to the tune of 4 to 8 percent in sales tax payments for covered assets.

Purchasing the company stock, or merging the companies, avoids the sales tax issue since no assets were sold as separate items.

Differing Tax Perspectives

As with so many other aspects of buying and selling businesses, the buyers and sellers have related but different motivations. Both parties will generally want to minimize the amount of money that is paid in taxes, but other aspects of the transaction might supersede the tax minimization desire. A simple example of that was shown in a previous section. A publicly traded company might be willing to structure the deal where it paid more in taxes so that it can show a larger net income at the end of the fiscal accounting period.

There are ways to structure the overall buying and selling so that taxes are avoided altogether, but this requires both buyer and seller to work with each other.

Most sellers attempt to minimize the amount of tax that they must pay on the sale price of their business. This can be done in any of a number of ways, but the most common methods are to:

Buyer/Seller Beware

Beware the tendency to spend money simply to decrease taxes. Remember that spending a dollar only saves you a few cents in tax payments, and who would spend a dollar to make only 50 cents? Manage your company so that it remains financially sound and then optimize for tax reductions. Spending yourself into bankruptcy to avoid taxes doesn't make much sense to me.

➤ Work to classify as much of the income from the sale as capital gain, so that it qualifies for more favorable tax treatment.

➤ Whenever possible, avoid the pitfalls of double taxation, where income is taxed at both the corporate and the personal level.

➤ Make sure that enough cash is secured from the sale to pay for any taxes that will be assessed. Otherwise a high sale price could strip the seller of cash reserves while making him or her a wealthy person … on paper anyway.

➤ Put off tax payments into the future by deferring the receipt of stocks or other payments, so that tax is not due until that future date, which might also arrive with a lower tax bracket. This tactic is also used when a waiting period is needed to have sold stocks qualify for capital gains taxation treatment.

Buyers really don't have many options at their disposal with respect to minimizing their tax bill other than playing with the various valuation-apportionment techniques discussed at various places in this chapter. In essence, the buyer wants to purchase the company with as few encumbrances as possible, for the lowest price, and in such as way that looks beneficial for the purchasing company's financial reporting goals. The buyers might also want to ensure future participation on the part of the selling company's management, which might make a stock transfer transaction that occurs over a period of a few years an attractive arrangement.

Taxable Transactions

Any purchase that involves the exchange of cash, promissory notes, or other liquid-type of assets will generally be considered a taxable transaction by the Internal Revenue Service (IRS). This means that the seller will have to pay taxes as a result of the transaction.

The seller might not object to this since this usually means that he or she gets money up-front and does not have to worry about future payments to receive the full sale price amount.

If Company B purchases all of Company A's stock, then A's shareholders will have to report the gain received on the sale of their stock. Depending on the duration of holding, from a tax standpoint, this might be treated as a capital gain or as standard income. The benefit to shareholders who have held the stock for more than 12 months is that the gain is subject to a maximum capital gain tax rate of 10 percent for those in a 15 percent regular tax bracket and 20 percent for everyone else. Notice that this rate is lower than the applicable tax rate for standard income, which makes this option attractive to most investors.

If the seller of the company is also its founder and the company is more than one year old, all of the founder's stock is subject to the capital gain tax rate.

Hot Tip

Sellers should remember that any loss currently carried over from previous tax years can help the buyer if the entire company is acquired. That loss may become a deductible expense to the buyer once the transaction is completed. That prior loss could be worth something, so don't just throw it in without getting something in return.

Here is where things get really interesting from a tax standpoint. Suppose that Corporation A sells its assets to Company B, but not its stock, and then chooses to liquidate—disbursing all remaining assets, cash and materials, to the shareholders. Moneys received in exchange for the sale may be subject to double taxation.

When A sells an asset to B, it passes at "fair market value," instead of at its depreciated "book value." The difference between fair market value and book value is treated as income, or gain, for A. If the asset was held for more than 12 months, the gain is subject to capital gain taxes. Otherwise, it is subject to applicable regular income taxes. In either case, A must pay taxes on the sale transaction.

Company A is now liquidated, distributing all assets to shareholders in accordance with their respective percentage of ownership in the company. These liquidated assets are now taxable to the shareholders, who must report this income on their returns. If the stock was held for more than 12 months, tax is assessed at the capital gain rate.

Notice that this could amount to as much as a 59 percent tax rate on the overall transaction. A 39 percent capital gain rate could be applied to the proceeds of the initial asset sale within the corporation, and then another 20 percent tax rate could be applied to the corporation liquidation phase. If the shareholders had simply sold their shares directly and their holding period qualified for capital gains, the total tax bill would be only a single application of the 20 percent capital gains tax.

Straight Talk

A buyer might use a double taxation situation to his or her advantage. The buyer might not want to purchase the company stock for any number of reasons including a belief that the stock price is too high. By agreeing to purchase the stock instead of purchasing individual assets, the buyer could negotiate a lower stock purchase price using the avoided double taxation as the seller's incentive to accept the lower price.

Imagine the reality of selling individual assets instead of selling the whole company as a single entity. Each asset's fair market value must be determined. Its internal book value must be determined. Any liens must be resolved along with applicable ownership titles. All buyer-related tax accounting procedures related to tracking of the asset's applicable gain or loss resulting from the transaction must also be tracked.

Selling the stock, along with the entire company, is a much simpler process from the seller's perspective, but holds liabilities for the buyer for which the buying company will want to be compensated.

Stock Transfers Might Be Tax-Free Money

Notice that the last section involved the transfer of cash or other relatively liquid assets to the sellers in exchange for assets, stock, or both. These types of transfers involve some type of taxable gain to the sellers.

Purchases that involve the transfer of stock from the buyer to seller might be tax free if transferred in compliance with IRS Code Section 368 requirements. There are seven basic Section 368 transaction types, A through G. However, the three that pertain to acquisitions are A, B, and C. Each has its own set of requirements to ensure that the transfer is tax-free. Verify with your tax professional that your proposed transaction meets the requirements.

M&A accountants talk about the difference between a *Purchase* and a *Pooling of Interests,* so a few words on this topic is worthwhile. The purchase method is just what it sounds like—a purchase of one company by another. The purchase price paid is allocated over the various business assets purchased and the transaction is completed. Assets are stepped up to fair market value. If the entire company is purchased, the difference between the cost of the assets purchased and the total price paid for the company is recorded as goodwill, which is also depreciable.

Pooling of interests involves pooling, or merging, the two business entities into one. Assets and liabilities transfer to the buying company at book value with no step-up on asset basis. Once pooled, the two companies act as one, that is, as if the acquired company never existed.

You sellers may very well find this one paragraph worth the entire price of this book. You should be very careful when looking at a stock-only transaction. *Make sure that there are no clauses that keep you from being able to sell the stock you are given as part of the purchase.* If the purchasing company is not publicly traded and all you receive is stock in the purchasing company, how are you supposed to turn that stock into money?

Even if the company is publicly traded, there might be restrictions placed on how, when, and how much of your stock you can sell at any point in time. It would be a shame to sell your company for a few million dollars in stock, to be liable for the capital gains received on the shares, only to find out that you cannot sell the stock. It happens.

Hot Tip

A tax-free exchange is not possible unless the seller accepts at least 50 percent of the purchase price in buyer stock. Whatever portion of the purchase price payment is received over the 50 percent stock threshold is subject to tax. The only way to avoid taxes completely is to accept 100 percent of the sale price in buyer stock.

Seller Beware

If you are a seller and you receive stock as part of the transaction, make sure that you can sell that stock. Otherwise, you could find yourself no longer the owner of your company (wealthy on paper due to the stock but not in reality) and then have to pay a lot of cash to cover the capital gains on the stock you received.

Comparing C and S Corporations

You might be one of those business owners who decided to transact business as an S corporation, which obviously must be allowed in your state or the option would not be available to you.

There are some differences with respect to how the income obtained from the sale of assets of an S corporation is treated as compared to a C corporation.

For starters, there is no possibility of double-taxation since the S corporation does not pay taxes in the first place. All income is passed, on a proportional basis, to all shareholders, who then pay taxes at their respective personal rates.

Assets that have been held for more than one year and that are then sold for a gain are taxed on the shareholder's return at the appropriate long-term capital gains rate. However, Cash and Accounts Receivable are treated differently. These two asset items are transferred, and taxed, as ordinary income since they are not assumed to ever have a 12-month holding period.

Good News for Small Business Corporations

Now here is a break that you want to know about if you are selling a "qualified small business," which refers to a C corporation with assets that do not exceed $50 million. This corporation must transact business as a manufacturer, retailer, or wholesaler. The stock must have been issued to the shareholders after August 10, 1993, and it must have been held for five years.

The good news is that Section 1202 of the Internal Revenue Code says that you pay capital gain tax on only 50 percent of the long-term capital gain. There are limits on this exclusion that you should definitely review with your tax professional, but saving this much tax expense is certainly worth looking into.

The Least You Need to Know

➤ There are basically two types of ways to handle the purchase of a business: acquisitions and pooling of interests. Each transaction falls into one of these categories.

➤ Buyers usually want to structure the deal so that they maximize the income reporting by their company as shown on the financial statements.

➤ Sellers want to structure deals so that as much as possible of the sale price is taxed at capital gain rates.

➤ If stock is part of the purchase agreement, make sure that there is a way for you as the seller to convert that stock into money.

➤ Asset sales may cause double taxation for C corporations if the corporation liquidates after selling its assets.

➤ S corporations have different rules from C corporations.

Part 3
Checking Out a Target Business

You have to find and pre-qualify a business before you can really get serious about buying it. Part Three gets you started in the right direction to find the target company that is right for your acquisition objectives.

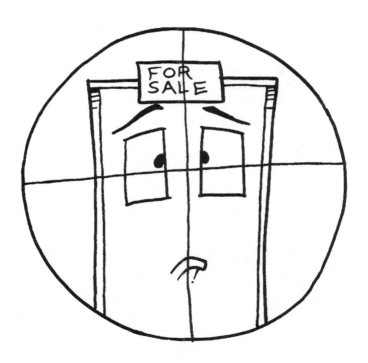

Chapter 9

Top-Level View of the Proposed Acquisition

In This Chapter

➤ Verifying the items and services that the company sells

➤ Verifying the legality of patents, trademarks, and copyrights

➤ Making sure you are dealing with the owners and decision makers

➤ Protecting yourself from tax, legal, and insurance claims

➤ Verifying intellectual property assets

Before he went any further, Jerry wanted to make sure that the basic business aspects of the deal were intact. As he sat and pictured himself making decisions about the company that he was planning to purchase, more questions came to his mind.

Who are the company's major customers? Are there many of them or does the business depend on just a few key customers? Can this company's distribution channel handle the addition of the products from the company that Jerry currently owns? How fierce is the competition in this part of the country?

These were all good questions, and ones to which he currently had no answers. But he needed these answers before he could move any further with the negotiations. There had to be a way to break this stalemate, and soon, or the entire positive momentum he had created to this point could be lost. What to do?

There is a point in any purchase when you have to move your investigation to the next level of detail. Your initial survey identified the target company as a viable acquisition candidate, but your early information is almost never enough to put a credible range on the finances involved with the purchase.

Obtaining this detailed information is as much art as business science, and the best approaches blend the two. Much of the public information can be obtained by extrapolating what is known about a company or industry into the unknown areas in question. Obtaining the specifics of the company and its position within its marketplace can be an art form where the beauty is in the style, manner, and credibility of the buyers and sellers. You must obtain this information from the buyer, purchase the information from a third party, or find other methods of determination. Otherwise, any future financial projections will be based on unsubstantiated conjecture as opposed to educated guesses. Which would you prefer?

What Does the Company Sell?

Buyer beware is good advice for any consumer, and it is particularly sound when it comes to purchasing a business. The reality is that the sellers probably will not reveal everything there is to know about the company you are purchasing. It might happen as a result of deception, but more likely, it results from innocent omission.

It sometimes happens that the sellers are simply so close to the company that things that would be of interest to you are simply "the way it is" for the sellers, and not worth mentioning.

Hot Tip

The success or failure of a company is usually based on a combination of unique things that make this company different from all others. Investigate the pieces, but always keep your eye on the unique combinations that might spell success.

Oddly enough, companies often do not see their own operation as well as an outsider might see it. Any consultant will tell you the same thing. This is the essence of the justification for using consulting services instead of using internal people to perform the same work.

Think about a bookstore for example. With large book stores dominating the market, the small bookstore must stay on its toes to stay in business.

If a local bookstore sees itself primarily as a provider of books, then it will probably struggle to maintain a consistent clientele. If, on the other hand, the store sees itself as a book store/social center where local people can congregate to catch up with each other and talk about their latest reading find, you have a recipe for repeat client visits. Clearly, the books must be there, but books without atmosphere might not be enough.

So what does this bookstore sell? Books? Or a total literary experience? I maintain that the more successful bookstores provide some special products or services that cater to the people who live in the local community.

As another example, there is a bookstore in the western Chicago suburbs that provides the best collection of technical books I have ever seen. If I am looking for a book on technical subjects, such as computers, programming, the Internet, or other advanced technology areas, I go there first. I pay full price for the books, but I know that if a book on a specific topic is to be had, this bookstore has it.

It turns out that this bookstore has a dedicated clientele that attend workshops, author signings, and other special events. They even communicate with each other about projects, jobs, fairs, and other human-interest subjects. Clearly, this bookstore provides more than just books.

If you were to buy this business and shift the focus from technical books to general topic books, there is a reasonable likelihood that you would lose a percentage of your existing clientele. Customers are a business's most important asset, and shifting a business's focus without paying close attention to the aspects perceived as valuable to the customers could cost you in the long run.

Notice that this discussion deals with more than the assets of the company, such as inventory, products, equipment, and buildings. It deals with the intangible aspects of the company that might be the difference between this company and others, which are comparably equipped, but don't thrive as well. A careful review of the overall company operation is needed to fully understand what you are buying that is over and above those things listed on the balance sheet.

How Healthy Is the Company Financially?

We are going to spend several chapters looking at the financial aspects of a company to determine, from the numbers, the state of its overall health.

Just remember a few general points as you look at some of the details presented in Chapters 6, 7, 8, 16, and 19:

➤ A growing company needs an adequate financial capacity to pay for that growth. Growth is not free, and rapid growth has put more than one company out of business.

➤ A shrinking company might deplete its cash reserves in a short period of time. Make sure that any financial assessments you make today incorporate projected negative cash flows into the future, up to the point of purchase.

➤ Shrinking companies also borrow to fund their operation through the lean times. Make sure that the company hasn't borrowed itself into an unrecoverable position.

Buyer Beware

Don't take the seller's version of what made them successful at face value. The seller might not even know the unique combination of people, products, luck, timing, or other characteristics that truly made them succeed where others might have failed.

➤ In essence, whether in a growing or shrinking marketplace, you want to make sure that you either have adequate cash reserves on hand or have access to credit. Cash is like oxygen to a business, and without cash the business won't last for long.

Amazing as this might sound to many of you, and contrary to the advice of some accountants, the value of a company is not based solely on its financial statements. A company's value should be heavily based on its perceived future performance levels, which are far less certain. Taking the time to determine required cash levels forces you to project the future, which in turn requires you to perform a reality check on the proposed target company. If it passes the cash requirement test, you just might have a company worth pursuing. If not, make sure that the purchase price reflects the additional risk that you are taking by purchasing a cash-poor company.

You will find me coming back to the relationship between risk and reward several times throughout this book, which might give you some indication of its importance.

Hot Tip

If you do not properly assess the risks associated with an investment, you will have a difficult time properly assessing the financial return required to make the purchase viable.

Your starting point is always the financial reports. If the selling company has a difficult time presenting you with financial reports that are, to some reasonable degree, objectively verified and accurate, then you should have questions about other things that you have been told. After all, a primary reason for a business's existence is to make money, and if the management hasn't done a solid job of verifying their financial performance, you have to wonder about their level of attention to less critical items.

If possible, get your hands on financial statements from the past five years, so that you can determine either positive or negative trends.

Should you see a company that has been consistently in a cash poor position for all of its prior years, suddenly showing a surplus of cash on the current balance sheet, something different must have recently happened. It is worth the question to find out what has changed.

Should you see a company that consistently increases its owner's equity, and a dip in the past few years, you should also ask the current owners for their assessment of why this happened.

Any general changes in financial condition, whether good or bad, are areas of interest. Notice that I used the word "interest" and not concern since concern implies that something is wrong, which may not be the case. Don't treat the questioning as an inquisition, but simply as one businessperson talking to another. You will probably find better cooperation and better answers.

Who Really Owns the Company?

Do you believe everything that you hear? Probably not, or you wouldn't have made it far enough in your business life to need a book like this one.

The same is true regarding company ownership. Just because someone manages a company doesn't mean that they have any ownership rights to the company. Just because someone's title is president or chief executive officer doesn't mean that he or she is an owner.

On the flip side, just because a person doesn't have an executive title doesn't mean that he and she is not an owner. Some owners realize that they are not executive management material and hire professionals to run the company. The owners have their say at the board meetings where their voting rights are exercised.

Make sure that you determine the legal structure of the company. This means determining if the company is a sole proprietorship, partnership, C corporation, or S corporation, among others. In addition, find out the home state for the corporation, and determine who is the registered agent of the corporation. This information is public record, and it should be available from almost any Secretary of State's office.

It is important that you clearly determine who owns the target company and the level of consensus present among the owners regarding the pending sale. It is often helpful to find out details regarding the board of directors, since they are the ones who will ultimately approve the sale of the corporation. Determine whether they are owners, their percentage of ownership, how long they have been on the board, and any other company with which they serve in a board member capacity.

Hot Tip

If the company is registered as an S corporation, it can have no more than 75 shareholders.

Publicly held corporations must disclose their overall stock ownership situation in their annual reports. From these reports, you can determine what percentage of the company is held by the general public and what percentage is in the hands of a few shareholders. This concentrated stock ownership situation often occurs when a company started out as a privately held corporation that then makes a public stock offering. A certain percentage of the stock is held by the original owners with the balance sold as part of an initial stock offering (IPO).

Obtaining a copy of the latest annual or quarterly report to shareholders is usually simple. Call the shareholder relations office of the corporation and request one. If they require that you be a shareholder before they will release one, then buy a single share of stock and then request the report. Generally, they will send you one even if you are not a shareholder since the report should entice you to become a shareholder.

Privately held corporations are under no obligation to reveal ownership information, but you would be remiss if you did not clearly understand who owns what and their sentiments regarding the possible sale. You, as the buyer, will inherit dealing with these owners. The least you deserve to know is who they are and how much of a problem they might be in the future.

Who Really Runs the Company?

On the non-ownership side, make sure that you learn about the employees so that you can determine who actually runs the company. Often, the executive management team calls the operational shots, but quite often, they implement policies determined by people with lesser titles. Even more interesting to me are the executives who hire their own confidantes to work as managers within their company. These people might have worked with the executive for years, and they might be fully trusted by the executive management team.

You might think that the president is making her decision with feedback from the other members of the executive team, only to later learn that a mid-level manager is the one bending her ear.

Straight Talk

I worked at a company for several years where many of the management decisions were ultimately made by the president, but they were made with advice from one of the mid–level managers. They had worked together for around 10 years, and the president had come to rely on this particular manager's judgment. I kept making the mistake of working through the executive staff, and was often frustrated by the lack of success. Once I learned of their working/personal history, I shifted to working with the mid–level manager who, by the way, I liked and respected. After that, I found that I was heard more frequently and that some of my ideas found their way into reality.

Don't be surprised to find out, especially for smaller companies, that mid-level managers are actually calling the shots both on a daily basis and also on major strategic decisions.

What Is the Company's Intellectual Capital?

Intellectual capital is a particularly important area of consideration, especially in today's high technology business environment. *Intellectual capital* (property) might include software programs, Internet Web site locations, trademarks, business processes, certifications, special processes, and other non-tangible items that are of value to the company.

Placing a value on trademarks, copyrights, and patents is an interesting topic that is beyond the scope of this section. The intention here is to ensure that you consider these types of items when investigating a potential acquisition target. A few questions regarding intellectual property items might open a completely new perspective to the company that you are looking to acquire.

Terms of Acquisition

Intellectual Property (Capital) Asset items owned by a company that are not tangible in nature, like equipment, but still have commercial value. Typically these properties involve legal protections, such as seen with patents, trademarks, and copyrights.

If you get serious about purchasing the company and its intellectual property, you should make sure that the items are truly owned by the company, and that they can legally be transferred with the sale. You will also want to verify their remaining useful life. Paying a lot for a patent that expires in a few years might not make financial sense, while purchasing one early in its useable life makes it more valuable to both you and the seller. This section won't make you an intellectual property attorney, but it will provide you with a basic understanding of intellectual property protection.

Important Trademark Highlights

A trademark is the name of a product or service that is sold by a particular company. For example, anything with Ford on it is associated with the automobile manufacturer and, by association, receives all the positive and negative points associated with Ford. Ford is a registered trademark of the Ford Motor Company, and any other company else who tries to transact business using Ford as part of its product name might very well find itself being sued by Ford Motor Company. Just having the name "Ford" associated with a product or service provides credibility that, unless authorized by Ford Motor Company, might represent an unfair usage by a non-Ford company. And if that company does a poor job of designing its products or services, Ford Motor Company might be negatively impacted, which could hurt them as a whole.

For this reason, large companies dedicate entire departments to monitoring, preserving, and enhancing *brand equity*.

For example, Pepsi has teams that travel to Pepsi suppliers who sell only Pepsi and not Coke. These people then place an order for something like a "hot dog and a Coke." If the counter person simply takes the order and provides a Pepsi instead of a Coke, without letting the customer know that it is Pepsi and not Coke, the retailer can lose its license to sell Pepsi.

If you think about it from Pepsi's perspective, their brand name is being diminished since their product is being sold as a Coke product. The counter person must say something like "Is Pepsi okay?" to remain in compliance with the Pepsi requirements.

Terms of Acquisition

Brand Equity   The asset value associated with a particular trade-marked name, such as Ford, Coca-Cola, Yahoo!, or Kleenex. Increasing the perceived market value of products bearing the brand name increases its brand equity.

Service Mark   This is similar to a trademark except related to a service procedure instead of a particular product. This term is commonly used by service organizations, such as consulting, accounting, and training companies.

There are complexities associated with determining when legal trademark ownership starts, but the most definite proof of ownership is to have a Trademark Registration with the United States Patent and Trademark Office. A formal registration procedure is required to register a trademark, but from the point of registration forward, you, the owner, have the legal right to stop others from using the trademark and can recover damages in a lawsuit.

Once again, go to one of the Federal Repositories for details associated with trademark registration, but make sure that you verify ownership with the target company's management or you might not be purchasing the expected level of legal trademark protection.

Important Copyright Highlights

A copyright is used to protect the expression of something such as a book, magazine article, screenplay, or advertising. Assume, for example, that the target company has a specific trademark that is widely know as associated with the company. The company might have produced a manual that provides general brand equity management tips along with specific instructions on using the company's brand itself.

Note that the trademark is protected under its trademark registration, and the manual, as a written expression of company policy, is protected under copyright law. If a company uses a particular trademark in conjunction with specific associated text, both trademark and copyright protection law would be involved.

Hot Tip

It is a good idea to talk to a copy-right attorney when determining the effective date at which something is really copyrighted, since the details often get confusing.

Copyrights obtained by persons after 1977 are protected for 50 years past the life of the author. For employees of companies that perform the copyrighted activity on behalf of their employer, the copyright lasts for 75 years from the date of publication or 100 years from the date of creation, whichever comes first.

In general, however, as soon as something is published, it is copyrighted whether a formal copyright has been recorded or not. To protect your litigation rights, the work should always be formally copyrighted with the United States Copyright Office. The procedure is simple and inexpensive.

Verifying the formal copyrights of the targeted company to any works included in the sale is an important process. Once again, check with any Federal Repository for additional information and the required forms.

Important Patent Highlights

Patents are obtained by people or companies that have a better device, design, or process that is substantially unique enough to be considered novel or non-obvious.

Patents are expensive and time-consuming animals that many smaller companies do not pursue, often to their own regret. A typical patent might cost $20,000 or more and take several years to record. In addition, from the point that the patent is recorded, it becomes public knowledge meaning that all of your competitors also know what you know about your patented product or process. For this reason alone, many companies do not pursue a patent.

On the other hand, if another company produces a product similar, or even identical, to yours and you do not have legal protection, the winner will be determined by the marketplace and not in the courtroom.

Patents are issued by the United States Patent and Trademark Office, and have terms of 17 years, after which the idea becomes unprotected. That might seem like a long time, but more than one company has been successful for 17 years based on patent protection only to find its own success used against it as others copied the idea and competed at a lower price.

Are There Any Tax, Insurance, or Legal Actions Pending?

We live in a litigation-oriented society. Almost every business has to deal with the legal profession in one way or another. If we are lucky, we simply use attorneys to ensure the legality of our agreements and standard business matters. Unfortunately, some companies find themselves the target of a lawsuit that might put the company out of business if lost.

For example, assume that you are in the process of purchasing a toy manufacturer, and then you find out that there is a pending class-action lawsuit against the company based on a toy that it marketed several years before. Depending on the type of suit, its validity, and the type of damages sought, this suit alone might turn a solid investment into one fraught with liability and uncertainty.

A simple call to the target company's local Better Business Bureau, Chamber of Commerce, or business licensing office will provide you with general information about the target company. If there are a number of unresolved complaints against the company, and it deals with the general public, then you should question the selling management about their resolution and what brought them to that situation the first place.

Straight Talk

Pending litigation works both ways. It is possible that the company has pending litigation against another entity whether it be a person or another company. If won, the litigation proceeds might provide the company with a cash infusion that could spur it on to another level. Once again, the future is always uncertain, but the possibility of winning a suit along with its judgments might turn a questionable deal into a risk worth taking.

Also, don't forget to verify the status of pending employee suits whether for personnel-related or injury-related claims. These can also be expensive if lost, and you should be informed about these risks before signing your purchase checks or transferring stock.

Nobody escapes Uncle Sam and payroll taxes. Receive written verification of payroll tax payment status and ask whether all past state, federal, and sales taxes have been paid. The company has a fiduciary responsibility to pay these taxes in a timely manner or receive huge penalties. You don't want to inherit the expensive fallout from someone else's carelessness.

The Least You Need to Know

➤ The relationship between the company's market segment growth and the overall economy's growth is important and worth determining.

➤ Executive managers might not be the decision-makers in the target company; just as, executive managers might not be the owners.

➤ Litigation, whether active, pending, or threatened, will affect the financial assessment and must be included in any financial negotiations.

➤ The value of intellectual property is subjective, but must be considered when purchasing a company. This is particularly true for advanced technology companies.

➤ If you look closely, you might find that a large portion of a company's worth is in its processes and other internal procedures that might not show up as valued assets on the financial statements.

Chapter 10

What Is Their Market?

In This Chapter

➤ Analyzing the customer base

➤ Protecting yourself with distribution agreements

➤ The importance of a company's marketing position

➤ Assessing a company's overall market health

➤ Going international with your eyes open

Although the proof was there on his desk, Mick still couldn't believe his eyes. His accountant had just presented him with a letter received from a German law firm stating that his client had just gone out of business.

This news by itself was bad enough. The really bad news was that his German distributor, which composed around 20 percent of his company's overall revenues, was more than 80 percent dependent on this now defunct German company. In short, Mick had not only lost 20 percent of his revenues, but had lost his German distributor as well because the distributor just didn't have the financial reserves needed to weather the loss of this major customer's outstanding accounts receivable.

Mick intended to look at the possibility of buying the German distributor, but just didn't think that his company had the money to make the purchase. Moreover, he really knew nothing about Germany's markets anyway, which is why they used a distributor in the first place.

The details of this distributor-customer relationship had slipped through the cracks of the initial assessment of his recently acquired company. The mistake had just cost him big money. He would never make this mistake again.

Owning a company that does not have a viable market or stable customers is like throwing a party that nobody wants to come to. You spend the time, effort, and energy preparing to sell your products or services only to find out that nobody can use them.

You are generally aware of your own company's sales and marketing shortcomings and understand how they affect operation. It is also important to uncover those deficiencies and strengths in a proposed acquisition target company.

This chapter deals with the overall marketing issues that will largely determine the sales and marketing environment within which you will live after the acquisition is completed.

Defining the Company's Marketing Position

A company's market position determines its marketing "identity" with respect to its competition and buyers. Think of a market position as the next thing that a consumer thinks of when thinking about the company.

For example, McDonalds would have a market something like "providing fast food, primarily hamburgers, easily purchased by people traveling from one location to another."

Wal-Mart would have a market position of being a "provider of a wide array of consumer items at a low price."

Straight Talk

Don't underestimate the value of overall market performance when assessing a company or its market segment. It is easy to make a living as a moderate building contractor when the overall economy is booming and customers need houses and commercial property built. In this case, just being in the right place at the right time is enough to make a living, or more. Surviving, or thriving, in a marketplace downturn requires effective management and an overall edge. If your target company shows a reasonable rate of return in a thriving market, don't take it at face value. Dig a little deeper to learn more about operations. If the marketplace takes a downturn and the company is poorly managed, the target company might be a marketplace casualty.

So, you wouldn't go to McDonalds for a fine Italian dinner just like you would not go to Wal-Mart to purchase fine leather living room furniture. Market positioning determines a company's operational perspective while also defining its customer base. People must first associate the company with the product or service they plan to purchase. If the buyers of the targeted company decide to offer products or service that are not in compliance with the current positioning of the company, they might find themselves creating a new market instead of taking optimal advantage of the one that naturally came with the purchase.

How Healthy Is Their Market?

No company exists in a vacuum, even the largest ones like IBM and General Electric. All companies have markets and customers who comprise them. If the markets and customers are doing well, decent companies also tend to do well. If markets take a downward turn, only the best run and prepared companies thrive.

How do you determine the strength of the marketplace and what is considered "good" performance? Try these as starting places.

If you are looking at a company that is subject to governmental regulation, looking around will most likely reveal government reports on the industry as a whole, and possibly your company in particular. The library is an excellent place to start looking for these reports. If your local library doesn't have one, ask for the location of the closest Federal Repository. These usually store copies of governmental documents. After all, our tax dollars paid for the reports in the first place, so you might as well take advantage of them.

If the Federal Government does not regulate the industry, it might be regulated by a local state agency like the Public Utility Commission. If so, you should try the agency for any publicly available industry reports. This could save you time and money, and provide you with information that is relatively unbiased because it comes from a supposedly neutral source.

Even if the industry is not regulated, there is almost always an association or trade group that has done a study on this industry. Looking in newspapers or trade publications might present you with a summary and might also provide you with a reference to the study itself.

Terms of Acquisition

Growing Market   A market that has total revenues that increase from one year to the next, preferably over a five-year period or so.

Market Share   The percentage of total market-segment revenues attributed to the target company's sales activities.

Standard Industrial Code (SIC)   A numbering system used to categorize companies by their primary business activities. Helpful in comparing companies from the same industry because they can be grouped by SIC.

Knowledge is power, and information can lead you in the direction of that knowledge. Putting the right industry information into the hands of experienced marketing people will provide you with an excellent snapshot of the industry and your target company's position in that market.

There are market research firms that specialize in finding the answers to questions like those presented in this section. It might be worth the money to have them check it out for you.

Here are a few observations regarding industries and their marketplaces:

➤ A growing market is always good news, but also indicates that other new companies will be future competition. Hot markets are magnets for new entrepreneurial or intrapreneurial activities.

➤ Shrinking markets are almost always bad news. The markets might be shrinking from an overall shrinking of the general economy, or they might be shrinking from specific market-segment activities such as legislation.

➤ If your target company has a growing market share in a growing market, you are possibly holding onto a tiger's tail. Hang on and enjoy the ride, but remember that the ride won't last forever.

➤ If your target company has a shrinking market share in a shrinking market, you should think twice, or even three times, before finalizing the purchase. Make sure that your valuation process accounts for these two very important points.

➤ If your target company has an increasing market share in a shrinking market, this generally means that they are absorbing business from customers whose prior vendor became a victim of the poor market conditions. This speaks well for the target company, but still raises concerns about the overall market.

➤ If your target company has a shrinking market share in a growing market, there is something wrong and you need to keep looking until you find it.

I suggest that you also compare the market segment growth to the overall growth of the economy, which fluctuates from year to year. This number is available in the *Wall Street Journal* or any number of other financial publications, including many local newspapers. Every quarter, the government releases overall economy growth rates. If they are not in your paper, ask your

Buyer Beware

Just because a market is growing doesn't mean that it is the best place to put your money. It only means that the overall market segment sales are increasing, which could be the result of overall market expansion or simply the result of inflation which naturally increases the dollars sold from one year to the next. Understanding the reasons for the increased sales is important to understanding the market itself.

local library's reference desk for help in getting that number. Remember that if it is listed as a quarterly figure, you need to multiply it by four to find an estimated annual rate, if not provided as a prior 12-months historical record.

If the overall economy is growing at a 4.5 percent annual rate, and your industry segment is growing at 9 percent, you are looking at an industry growing at twice the national average. If, on the other hand, your industry is growing at 1 percent, you are looking at an industry performing at one fourth the national average, which means something is wrong in that industry. Once again, you need to keep digging until you find out why the industry is not keeping pace with the national growth averages.

Who Are Their Customers?

You can learn a lot about a company by fully understanding its customer base. Customers know your company better than anyone else including many of the employees. Customers have typically seen the company on both its good and bad days, and have assessed the company's overall status. That they are still customers says a lot about the company in and of itself. If the entire customer base is new with few repeat customers, that leads you in another direction where you might not otherwise have looked.

Getting detailed customer information is often difficult because a customer list is a company's most prized possession and not usually shared with anyone outside of the immediate company.

It is possible, on the other hand, to obtain a general customer list that allows you to assess the overall characteristics of the customer base. In the early stages, you don't need to know the precise customers because you will find that information useful only when you get into finer levels of detail. In the early stages you are looking for general information; this should include the following points at a minimum:

➤ How many customers does the company consider inactive and active?

➤ What percentage of the total customer list is currently active?

➤ How are the customers divided with respect to size (revenues) and geography?

➤ What products or services are primarily purchased by the customers, broken down by both sales revenue and units purchased?

➤ Are purchases seasonal?

Seller Beware

Sellers should save the sharing of the customer list for later in the sale process. Make sure that the buyers are really interested before sharing the details of your customer list, and even then, only under an agreement of non-disclosure that clearly defines proper usage of that list. When dealing with a customer list, a little paranoia might be in order; the "buyer" might actually be a competitor.

➤ How do the customers break down with respect to length of time that they have been customers? I suggest you correlate this customer list by standard purchase intervals so that you can determine repeat customer information.

➤ Which products are purchased by the various segments created in the earlier steps?

➤ What types of payment terms are offered customers? What is the standard collection period for customers, based on an aging report?

➤ Try to find out any information regarding the percentage of customer purchases that are made through the company instead of one of its competitors.

➤ How are customers typically sold the company products or services? Are they sold directly from the company, through sales representatives, distributors, over the Internet, or other means?

Notice that this information tells you about the company's overall customer base while not revealing any specific customer information. Naturally, if you are purchasing a company from a small industry segment you should be able to surmise the identity of the major customers although you still might not know the specific contact-person information.

Straight Talk

Don't underestimate the value of a specific person's name within a customer account. This is particularly true for larger organizations. It is one thing to call General Motors's main information number to find the right contact for a product or service. It is another thing completely to call a specific person who is already favorably inclined toward using your products or services.

You should now know the percentage of customers who represent repeat business. You should also know how long they have been customers, whether the company is expanding its market presence (based on new customers to repeat customers), the products that sell the best, and the market segments into which the company has had the most sales success.

If you find that a large percentage of the company sales is to a small number of customers, which is often the case, then you should make a point of getting detailed account status information regarding these particular accounts. Should a few large customers disappear after you purchase the company, you could be left as the owner of a company with a large debt and many small customers. All future financial projections would be off in the wrong direction if you found yourself in this unfortunate situation.

If you are buying an established company with few repeat customers, you should ask why. This is highly unusual, and it could mean past customer problems.

If you see a spurt of new business that comes from new customers, you should ask why and determine the management motivations for shifting the company focus.

If you find a large number of products or services offered by the company and determine that only a few of these products compose a large percentage of company revenues, you should ask the reason for maintaining the large product/service base. They might have simply overlooked the issue or there might be a strategic reason to keeping the appearance of a large product/service base.

If you find that the customers are geographically located near the company, you should investigate management's reason for this situation. This is particularly important if your company is located in another geographic location, and you expected to cross sell your existing customers with the acquired company's product or service.

The sales channel is very important, especially if you plan to sell your products through the acquired company's sales/marketing network. Understanding the primary sales channels and their applicability to your offerings is of critical importance if you expect later synergy between the acquired marketing channel and your existing products and services.

This information allows you to assess the value of the overall customer base. If you are still comfortable with the company after your initial customer assessment, you should be able to talk the seller into providing more-detailed information regarding the specific major customers.

Who Is Their Competition?

The company's competition will become your competition if you actually buy the company. In addition to learning about customers, learning about the competition can tell you a great deal about the company.

If the company competes effectively with other high-quality companies, then you know something positive about your acquisition target. It is hard to survive against excellent competition unless you are doing something right.

Find out if there is a personal or professional relationship between the management and/or ownership of the target company and any

Terms of Acquisition

Purchase Phase The length of time between purchases. For large capital equipment, this might be a very long time, where commodity products such as sugar might have a short purchase phase.

Active Customer A customer that has purchased within a timeframe defined by two or three purchase phases.

111

industry competition. It is always better to know this information before you buy rather than to find the person you bought from working for your harshest competition.

The following are a few questions that represent the minimum information that should be asked regarding competition:

➤ What does the competition do better or worse than the target company?

➤ What are the ages of the competition and does the target company share customers with other competitors?

➤ Are there employees of competitors who used to work for the targeted company?

➤ What are the relative sizes of the competition compared to the targeted company?

➤ Are any of the competitors participating in the purchase of the targeted company? If so, how much proprietary information was disclosed as part of the procedure?

➤ Ask the existing management about the strengths and weaknesses of the competition.

In no way should you feel restricted to only these questions. The more you know about the competition, the more you know about the target company and the marketplace it faces on a daily basis.

Distribution Channels and Standing Agreements

A company cannot provide its products or services to customers if prospective customers don't know that the company exists.

It is the role of the sales and marketing departments to ensure that an adequate number of prospective buyers know about the company, understand the company's offerings, and will eventually part with money while making a purchase.

Hot Tip

Clearly understanding the products or services that a company sells, and how they are sold to customers, is a mandatory first step in understanding the marketing and sales mindset of the target company.

Companies provide these marketing and sales services through any number of different channels, which generally fall into one of several categories:

➤ **Direct Sales:** Where sales are transacted directly between the company and its customers. A retail store or restaurant is an example of a direct sales operation.

➤ **Distributor Sales:** An intermediary company that purchases products from the company and then sells those products either directly to customers or to additional intermediaries. Distributors typically purchase large quantities of product in exchange for substantially reduced pricing.

➤ **Manufacturer Representatives:** Sales oriented companies that handle the sales aspects of a customer transaction in exchange for a percentage commission based on the total sales dollars. Reps do not typically stock inventory and rarely purchase products or services from the company. They instead represent the company when selling to customers, replacing or supplementing a company's direct sales force.

➤ **Online Sales:** Sales transacted electronically, usually over the Internet. Customers visit a Web site, determine the products or services that they wish to purchase and then arrange for payment and delivery electronically. Amazon.com is an example of a company providing online sales capabilities.

➤ **Mail Order:** Sales activities that happen as a result of a catalog or other flyer mailed to the prospective customer, who then makes the purchase decision and the actual purchase via the mail.

Most modern companies use a combination of sales channels. Different sales channels might be used for different products or services provided by the same company. For example, a technical product might be sold through a distributor who provides a high level of customer-oriented technical support. On the other hand, an instruction book might be sold online because the sale transaction is routine and easily managed.

A restaurant might use direct sales in its retail location, but might sell its foods in frozen form through distribution channels to grocery stores.

Of particular interest to you as a prospective buyer of the company is its relationship to distributors. More than one company will show robust sales and profits, but neglect to recognize a serious strategic flaw in its distribution operation.

If the company sees a large percentage of its sales through a particular distribution channel, and something were to happen to that channel, the company could find itself out of business. It usually takes several months, at a minimum, to set up a sales program. In my experience, changing distribution channels or sales methods is a 6- to 12-month process that should not be taken lightly.

Buyer Beware

It is always a good idea to verify the relationship between the principal owners of the target company and the international companies with which it does business. It is common for relatives or close friends from different countries to work with each other as a way of minimizing the risks. These relationships might not smoothly transfer to you as the new owner. Internationally binding agreements are only a starting point, and enforcing them in a foreign country can be an expensive, frustrating, time consuming, and sometimes fruitless process. First verify the intent, then verify the agreement.

Should you find that the target company is highly dependent upon the success of one of its distributors, then you must verify the legal relationship between the company and the distributor. You must also verify the future prospects of the distributor, because the demise of that distributor might also signal the demise of the target company, unless it has sufficient cash reserves to weather a radical shift in marketing channels.

You also want to check out the legal agreements that exist between the two companies. If the agreements have reasonable financial terms and provide a high level of future continuity, then the future risk is minimal. If, on the other hand, you find out that the two companies have a historically contentious relationship and that the contracts are up for renewal in a few months, you must learn enough about the relationship to assess the future level of exposure.

Most importantly, don't assume that the products or services will sell themselves after your purchase just as they did before the purchase. Your purchasing the company will change things, hopefully for the better. If your purchasing the company will have a negative effect on future distribution-channel relationships, then you want to find this out before the purchase is finalized.

International Business Implications

Everything that I mentioned in the prior section regarding distribution channels applies two-fold when working internationally. The intricacies associated with international marketing and sales cannot be exaggerated. There are United States laws to contend with. There are laws and local customs in the foreign country to consider. There are payment and intellectual property rights status issues to review. In short, doing business internationally is a complicated, exciting, potentially lucrative, but risky venture.

You should also clearly understand the level of international financial activity associated with the target company and assess its likelihood of continuance into the future after your purchase.

The Least You Need to Know

➤ Market positioning determines the marketing philosophy of a company. Understand it and you will better understand the company.

➤ Purchasing a growing company in an expanding market is almost always a good thing, which usually comes with a premium price tag attached.

➤ The customers are the lifeblood of a company. You must acquire a detailed understanding of the customer base to clearly understand a company's marketing operation.

➤ Distribution and sales agreements are a critical part of a company's business operation, and must be examined in detail.

➤ International businesses are exciting and full of opportunity, but also full of potential risks. Taking the time to evaluate the players and financials will minimize the possibility of unexpected future surprises.

Chapter 11

What Do They REALLY Have of Value?

In This Chapter

➤ A closer look at company key products

➤ Comparing internal development to acquisition

➤ Evaluating special customer and vendor agreements

➤ Placing a value on intellectual property

➤ Understanding company marketing strategy

"These guys are going to drive me nuts. Every time we turn around, they add something new to the negotiations. They act like they are the ones with the money, not us," squawked Dennis, the president of a manufacturing company. "I'm almost to the point that we should just start our own division and stop this nonsense altogether."

Mindy, Dennis's CFO, listened in silence. This was always a good time to sit and watch. At some point, he would calm down and ask for her opinion, which she had come to learn he really wanted and valued.

"Okay. I'm done with my tirade. What do you think? Is it worth continuing with this purchase, or should we drop it and move on?" he finally asked.

"As you well know, we ran the numbers comparing the costs of our internally developing these skills or buying them. These guys are asking for a price that is roughly in the same ballpark as our internal estimates." Mindy let that sink in for a moment. "We both agree that it would take us three years, or so, to bring a product to market and then another few years to create the

name recognition. These guys already have both for the same cost as our internal development efforts."

"So, you are telling me that buying costs the same amount of money, gets us into the market quicker, and has less uncertainty. Is that all?"

"Well, no. They also might have another prospective buyer."

Now, that got his attention.

An essential aspect of any large ticket purchase is knowing *what,* in fact, you are buying or selling. Usually, the items being sold are representative of something else, and it takes time, attention, and some intuition to get a handle on the items really being transacted. Work your way through this chapter to add more substance to your understanding of the intangible aspects of a company that translate into real dollars during negotiations.

What Does the Company Really Sell?

We touched on this idea of finding a company's core products in Chapter 9, "Top Level View of the Proposed Acquisition." In this section, I want to add a little more meat to the discussion by looking at the differences between what a company advertises as its products and services and what has really made it successful.

There are countless examples of companies that seem to offer one thing, but succeed by offering something less obvious.

Straight Talk

Advertising is for the world outside of your company. It is designed to create a mental impression and awareness about your company, its products, and services. Know that you put the most positive spin on something in your ads, which may not completely accurately reflect your own internally determined situation. Treat advertising and public relations information as a starting point as opposed to the absolute truth.

American Express has done this for years. They appear to offer a credit card service, but closer investigation reveals some interesting facts. They charge no interest on their card purchases, charge an annual fee when others are offering no-fee cards, charge the retailers a higher fee for accepting AMEX's card, and yet still prosper. When conventional business logic would indicate that this company would be on the verge of extinction, it keeps flourishing. I have an American Express card, I would never travel outside of the U.S. without it, and my story is probably not unique.

This company offers credit services, but what it really sells is security and insurance.

First, there is no pre-set credit limit like those included with other standard cards. This means that you won't be checking into a hotel at 3:00 A.M. after having traveled all day only to have your credit card denied due to a credit limit problem. This has happened to me using VISA cards, even when the cards were current. I used the VISA initially to get some type of bonus points, but when the charge was denied due to my being over my limit, I was stuck. I called VISA, who flatly turned me down for assistance for the night, and I vowed at that moment never to carry that particular VISA card again.

I then pulled out my American Express card and charged the night. No problems. No hassles. I slept like a baby even though my charges on that card were higher than usual due to an unexpectedly active travel schedule.

Something similar happened when all of my belongings were stolen in Barcelona, Spain, on a Sunday. The two VISA cards I had flatly turned me down for any type of assistance. However, American Express transferred me immediately to an operator in England who not only got my travelers checks reissued but also made arrangements to get my airline tickets, passport, EurailPass, and some cash reinstated.

This is not meant as a promotion piece for American Express, but I really want you to see why I, and so many others, carry the American Express card. It is security. "Don't leave home without it." American Express clearly understands its market and caters to it in a professional, direct yet familiar manner.

If a company purchases American Express, it has to understand this critical aspect of the business model. It may look like a credit card company, but it is really a security company that offers credit card services. Cutting back on the services that make the AMEX card valuable will make it look just like any other card. This puts them into a commodity market as opposed to a specialty market where distinction commands a more demanding customer, but also commands a higher selling price.

Straight Talk

There is a common business case used in MBA school about a company that manufactures and sells drill bits. If it sees itself as a drill bit manufacturer, it will spend its time concentrating on better ways to design, manufacture, and sell drill bits. If it sees itself as a company that assists its customers in the creation of holes, it opens itself up to a wide variety of other possible business ventures, such as lasers. You don't get a diploma from this little story, but you should now be getting the picture.

The only way to get a clear picture of what has made a company successful is to take the time to do some research.

➤ An advertising and literature search will get you started.

➤ Investigate industry publications for an assessment of the company.

➤ Look to the annual report if it is a publicly traded company.

➤ Talk to the company's customers, and take the time to ask detailed questions and listen to their responses.

➤ Talk to the company's vendors; you might be amazed the things you can learn.

➤ If the company has been through multiple owners, you might want to talk with some of the prior owners if possible. These folks might be under non-disclosure agreements, so don't be offended or surprised if they will not talk to you. It never hurts to ask.

Once you know what the company really sells, you can assess your ability to capitalize on its prior success. Will your company be able to maintain the level of required excellence set by the prior owners? Did the prior ownership completely miss the point and open a huge opportunity for you and your company to provide the existing customers with a better approach? Will this turn into untapped revenues for you as the new owner, or is there something you missed that only the current ownership knows?

What Do Their Customers Really Buy?

The other part of the equation involves the customers themselves. What is it that they think they are buying?

Again, it may sound strange, but companies often don't know why customers use their products or services over one of their competitors.

I have landed many a deal against much larger competitors simply by listening to the customer, and offering what he or she wanted.

One danger associated with buying a smaller company is that some people buy from a company simply because it is locally owned. Once it transfers ownership to a larger national company, you might find that some of the prior clientele shift to another local vendor. This may or may not affect your purchase decision, but you are better served knowing these things in advance instead of being caught off guard.

Hot Tip

Learning to listen, instead of talk, is probably the hardest skill to master for anybody. It is arguably the most important skill for almost any successful sales person and incredibly important for the rest of us.

Premium or Commodity Priced Products or Services

This is another important topic that was covered briefly in Chapter 9, which I feel deserves additional discussion. Knowing a company's positioning in its market is critical to understanding the proper management and potential synergy aspects of the company after purchased.

Is the company a low price (commodity)/high volume provider? If so, its business model should support this strategy. Here are a few important characteristics of a company that fits into this category:

➤ Its operation should be driven by efficiency. The only way to be a price leader is to squeeze every penny out of a product's profit margins.

➤ Rapid changeover of equipment and technology is also common. The low cost leaders generally implement any changes in technology that provide an efficiency edge.

➤ Inventory levels should be maintained at their lowest possible levels, since unused inventory means increased costs; a low cost leader cannot tolerate this for long.

➤ Automation should be used extensively throughout the company. It might even have its own information technology staff that manages the highly efficient automation operation.

➤ Determine the aspects of the automation that are company developed, custom, or proprietary technology. It might turn out that this technology alone is enough reason to purchase the company, and it never once appeared in a product brochure.

➤ The management reporting systems for a low cost company should be comprehensive and directly pointed at tracking small changes in profit margins and sales volumes.

If you see any of these previously mentioned points not being handled effectively by the target company, one of two possibilities exists:

1. They are not really the profitable low cost leader they purport to be; or

2. Management efficiencies can be applied to the company's operation that should make it even more profitable.

Possibility number two is always good news for a buyer since smaller changes by you can create large investment returns, and possibility number one might be either good or bad, which can only be determined with additional research.

Straight Talk

There has been litigation lately between low-cost suppliers of products and various Internet-based retail companies. The litigation point is that personnel from the low-cost retailers are going to work for the Internet-based retailers. There are fears that proprietary methods and technologies that were developed by the low-cost retail leaders are being transferred to the Internet-based retailers without the standard retailers being properly compensated. The courts will have to work these cases out, but it shows the importance of technology in today's business environment.

What if the company is a premium priced specialty products or services provider? You should find a very different business model than that of the low-cost producer. Here are some points that you should confirm when looking at a specialty product provider:

➤ The products and/or services offered should be different in a very positive way from those offered by other vendors, as with the American Express example cited earlier.

➤ The products and services offered will generally be of a higher quality but of a more limited scope. Think of a high-end audio store that might not even carry the lower-end products that are found at a low-cost retailer.

➤ Some aspect of the customer interaction should be of a premium nature, whether it be the sale process itself, post sale support, return policies, extended warranties, service, or any number of other possibilities.

➤ Margins are important, and so are efficiencies, but you should rarely see service sacrifices in the interest of squeezing the profit margins.

➤ These companies clearly understand their customers, and they should have a high level of repeat business.

➤ You may also find a higher level of "partnership" between the company and its vendors. There might also be a more limited number of possible vendors, since the products might be unique enough to only be sourced from a few vendors.

Purchasing a high-end, premium customer-oriented company with the intent of cutting costs will definitely cause unwelcome disruption with existing clientele, employees, and vendors. In general, a company cannot be both a high volume and a high price provider. The economics law of supply and demand dictates that the higher the price the lower the demand.

And how long do you think it would take other companies to enter the market if there was a chance to sell high quality, high margin products in large quantities? Not very long, since the profit motive for entering this type of marketplace is very strong.

Only in rare instances where the company has some type of legal protection in the form of a patent or a copyright can this basic law be broken. In addition, once that legal protection is broken the original provider will be forced to drop its prices. The protection might end either through an expiration of the patent or through somebody developing a "look alike" product that does the same thing at a fraction of the cost.

Coming back to the original intent of this section, you must know where the target company fits in its particular marketplace. It is a well-known rule of business that the fewer of something that you produce, the higher the manufacturing cost of each one made. Higher costs either decrease profit margins or drive up prices. If the company thinks that it will be a low volume, low-cost producer, run. It just won't work and probably hasn't worked, which could very well be why they are selling in the first place.

Hot Tip

Success breeds, and also attracts, success. When a company starts to make money in a particular industry, others will be attracted to it with the intention of gaining larger than average profits. Always understand that the more successful you and your company become, the more likely you are to have someone enter the market to specifically compete on your turf.

If the buying company is a low-cost producer and the target company is a high-price, high-quality producer, you should take a close look at the corporate philosophies. Using a high-volume business model while managing a premium provider will undoubtedly cause conflicts. The low-cost oriented buyer might even see a flight of target company customers after the purchase, simply because these customer might well expect the buyer's low-cost mentality to be applied to their previously high-quality vendor.

Understanding the targeted company's business model, understanding its customers, and clearly understanding what has made it successful to date is mandatory. This approach is the best way to ensure that major strategic mistakes that would sour the purchase aren't made early after the acquisition is finalized.

Valuing What They Know

What would it cost to replace the specific knowledge contained within the target company? This doesn't just mean hiring a person to fill a slot. It means replicating, in every mission-critical respect, the needed knowledge that sustains the company's current level of operation.

In large part, this is what you are purchasing when you buy a company. This knowledge might be in the form of books, instruction tapes, and procedure manuals that are used by existing personnel. But it might, and often is, contained inside the heads of a few people.

A natural question that comes up during the purchase process is whether you could, on your own, do what this company already does. This appears to be an attractive option since it saves you the money, hassle, and risk associated with buying another company. In fact, it comes with its own price tag.

Here are a few things to consider as you work your way through this question:

Hot Tip

It is possible to purchase manuals, but it is often difficult to purchase people, their expertise, and their cooperation.

➤ Is the operational-specific knowledge generally distributed throughout the company or localized with a few key people?

➤ How was this expertise acquired? How long did it take?

➤ Is the expertise legally protected so that you would need to work around legal restrictions in the process of developing your own, in-house version?

➤ Can the market sustain two companies performing the same services or producing the same products? If the market can't sustain another entrant, which is exactly what you would be if you created your own, you have immediately eliminated this non-purchase option. You will need to purchase the expertise to play in this particular game.

➤ Has there been a successful personnel turnover since the first level of expertise was achieved? If so, this means that the expertise was transferred from one person to another, which also means that it can probably be transferred to your company. This bodes well for your company having a successful acquisition.

➤ What would it cost your company in personnel, equipment, legal, research, opportunity, and production costs to develop the expertise internally? Whatever the amount of time you assume, you should probably add 50 to 100 percent to the initial estimate. These things always take longer than expected. This is one time you don't want to be caught short on time.

➤ Could other companies enter the market with this expertise while you are trying to create it yourself? A good idea attracts others who want to take their share of the market pie. Purchasing the expertise for the right price gets you quickly into the market with a proven name and expertise level. That is worth something.

➤ What other opportunities would your company not pursue if it developed the targeted expertise internally? What would be the revenue and, more importantly, the net income lost from not being able to pursue these opportunities?

➤ Does your intended product or service depend on rare supplies that are scarce, such as enriched plutonium, or other people experienced with the mixing of clay slurry at high altitudes and low temperatures? (I'll bet most of you thought that a slurry was only a drink. Get my point?) These rare resources and people are in limited supply, and they must be confirmed available before you can even look at entering the market through internal development.

It is often seductive, and usually inaccurate, to assume that you can develop and produce a comparable product or service within a reasonable time frame. Sure, it was harder for them to develop it the first time, but it is still generally no cakewalk to duplicate their success. It costs time, effort, and money.

Straight Talk

Don't expect the rest of the world to stand still while you either purchase a new company or develop internal expertise. The word often gets out about your intentions. Competitors already positioned in your intended market will take defensive steps to protect themselves, their customer base, and their market share. In addition, your entry might drive up raw material prices for rare commodities, cause a price reduction on the part of your competitors, or drain the marketplace of rare personnel talents, which drive market entry prices higher. Your company makes a difference and can shift market status quo, which should be accounted for when performing your analysis. If you think that your company won't make much of a market difference, perhaps you should forget the idea altogether.

So how much would it cost? The specifics will vary with each set of circumstances, but here are several steps that you can take to determine ballpark figures. The answer is in the details, but a rough first cut can save lots of later shuffling.

1. Estimate the personnel costs, on a monthly basis if possible, required for the internal development effort. This includes design, marketing, research, procurement, testing, shipping, legal, and other costs.

2. Estimate the equipment costs. You might already have equipment idle time in-house, which helps on this count. If not, then it must be purchased, financed, and somehow accounted for.

3. Estimate the production costs associated with the trial runs, initial production, and full production levels.

4. Determine the initial marketing and sales effort costs. Creating product or service awareness costs money and time, usually in an inverse relationship: The shorter the time the higher the costs involved.

5. Calculate the gross margin associated with the product sales, noticing that this number will change, and hopefully increase, over time due to learned manufacturing efficiencies.

6. Calculate the total development and the initial market introduction costs by adding together the numbers determined from steps 1 to 4.

7. Divide the total startup costs obtained from step 6 by the gross margin figure determined from step 5. You now have a rough estimate of the break-even point in unit sales that must be reached before you start making any money at all. Is this unit sales number realistic?

8. Calculate your best "guesstimate" of the sales, cost of sales, and fixed expenses as projected out for a three to five year period. From these guesstimates, calculate your expected total net income before tax for the period in question.

9. Subtract the development and introduction costs obtained in step 6 from the projected income total found in step 8. This is the amount of money that you most realistically project you will make over the three to five year period of analysis.

Terms of Acquisition

Intangibles Those aspects of a company, product, service, or situation that cannot be easily quantified. These are often subjective items such as level of quality or specific design preferences.

These nine steps look like a lot of work, and they really are. Nevertheless, without taking these steps there is no way for you to have a benchmark comparison between developing the expertise yourself or simply purchasing it.

You can now compare the value from step 9 to the estimated purchase price. It is now time to start evaluating the intangible aspects of the decision, such as the cost associated with being out of the market for the three to five years needed to develop and market your own developed product? What if market financial conditions change, causing an increase in financing costs? Purchase today and lock in the financing. Develop yourself and subject yourself to future positive or negative changes.

Detailed company valuation procedures are presented in Chapters 15, "Making an Offer They Can't Refuse," and 22, "How Much to Ask for and Other Negotiations." Once you have the projected company purchase price and the cost of developing similar expertise internally, which you can estimate from the procedure that is presented here, you can credibly compare the costs of internal development to purchasing.

Special Agreements That Are of Value

Make a point of getting to know the target company's key customers and vendors. I have typically found the 80/20 rule to apply to these situations: 80 percent of the business is done with 20 percent of the customers or vendors. This doesn't mean that you shouldn't get to know the others that are of critical strategic importance but of lower dollar volumes. It just means that you must get to know this critical 20 percent before you can say that you truly understand the targeted company's production and sales operation.

Pay particular interest to any special, longer term, agreements that might have recently been signed. These agreements might represent a solid business arrangement on behalf of the target company's management. General Motors recently signed a series of multiyear steel purchasing agreements, which locks in a fixed price and a guaranteed supply. Only time will tell if this was a shrewd move on GM's part or not. It is certainly an area worthy of discussion if you were looking to purchase GM.

It is also a good idea to research any long-term agreements the target company might have with any of its customers. You would inherit the implementation of these agreements, and you want to make sure that they include terms and conditions you can live with.

Patents, Copyrights, and Trademarks

Placing a value on intellectual property, such as patents, trademarks, and copyrights, is a lot like purchasing artwork. If you simply must have it and you have the money for it, you will set the market value by the amount you are willing to pay. Why? Simply stated, there is only one of these items out there. The patent means that the patent holder owns the rights to that particular product. If you want to produce it, you must pay for that privilege or you must develop a comparable product that does not infringe on the patent.

The analysis approach presented in the "Valuing What They Know" section of this chapter provides an initial basis of comparison between the asking price for the intellectual property asset in question and your costs for developing your own. You have to start somewhere, and might as well start with the numbers.

Product patents are more defined in their analysis than copyrights and trademarks. For example, how do you place a value on the Coca Cola trademark, and is it even feasible to assume that you could create that type of market awareness and brand loyalty? Pepsi, RC Cola, 7 Up, and Dr Pepper all try.

Creating a viable competitor for a copyrighted work is also a completely subjective area. Buyers might have welcomed the first copyrighted work in an area where the second one might just look like a duplicate of the first and be shunned.

In valuing intellectual properties, I suggest that you first start with the numbers to get your best estimated objective cost comparison. You can even then perform a parametric analysis where you vary parameters like future costs of sales, decreasing prices due to competition, increasing or decreasing interest rates or other parameters so that reasonable high and low numeric ranges can be determined.

In the end, you will probably have to rely on old-fashioned instinct to tell you if the costs being discussed are reasonable for your situation. Ultimately, this is what business managers are paid to do.

The Least You Need to Know

➤ A company cannot survive trying to bridge the gap between high volume sales and high prices. Choosing one approach or the other is usually best.

➤ Special agreements may add value or add cost depending on their terms and timeframe of effectiveness.

➤ Instead of purchasing expertise, you could develop it inside your own organization. A detailed financial analysis provides insight regarding the least expensive approach.

➤ Entering a market, either through acquisition or internal development, changes the marketplace. Competitors will respond in some way, and you should anticipate their most likely reactions.

➤ Patents, trademarks, and copyrights set their own values, within reason, since they are one-of-a-kind items. What you are willing to pay sets the market value.

Leverage Their Expertise with a Franchise

There really was no secret about it. Micky just loved teaching reading skills to children. It made her feel like she really made a difference in these kids' lives and she liked that.

Micky was a good teacher, but she was tired of having to constantly work around the whims and dictates of administrative people who signed her paycheck but knew nothing about literacy education.

Her brother had suggested that she start her own school, but Micky was really uncomfortable with the business side of things. She was a teacher, but she was also willing to learn business practices if it meant that she could finally do things the way she wanted them done.

She had heard good things about a new franchiser named Words for Kids, but she knew very little about their business operation. Micky had a little money saved up; she also knew a few other teachers who felt the same way she did and who might be interested in joining her in a new school venture. These thoughts had brought her to the franchising expo. Only by learning more about what was offered could she determine if she could teach and still make a decent living. For Micky, that would be a dream come true.

Terms of Acquisition

Franchiser   A company that offers to replicate its proprietary business model to others in exchange for an initial fee and a recurring franchise royalty (fee).

Franchisee   The person or company that purchases the proprietary business model.

Franchising is a way of business life in the United States. Business people either sell to or buy from a franchise-related business on a regular basis, often without knowing it. You might want to purchase a franchise for any number of reasons. You might want to get started with a new business in which you are interested, but have inadequate experience. Or you might own a company that would benefit from the inclusion of a franchise as part of the its overall company mix.

In each case, you will need to understand the basis of the franchise relationship, and you will need to know what to look for in assessing the opportunity. This chapter presents an overview of franchising, and then spells out some of the opportunities and trouble spots associated with purchasing a franchised business.

Franchising in a Nutshell

Franchising, lead by the immensely successful franchises, such as McDonalds, Dunkin Donuts, and Burger King among countless others, took the country by storm in the 1980s. Franchising is a great idea under the right set of circumstances, which explains the popularity. The U.S. Department of Commerce reported that 1996 showed around $800 billion in franchise sales (45 percent of all U.S. retail sales) and that around 8 million people are employed by franchise operations. This is big money.

Hot Tip

The Federal Trade Commission regulates franchise operations in all 50 states, and it requires the disclosure of specific minimum information from any franchiser. In addition, many states require their own level of franchiser disclosure. A disclosure document must be filed with the appropriate state regulatory body before the sale of franchises in that state can commence.

To get a deeper understanding of the franchise relationship, let's cover a few basic concepts:

➤ A company develops a successful method for performing a specific function such as changing automobile oil, food preparation, or personal fitness training.

➤ The company then standardizes its methodology under a legally protected brand name.

➤ The company prepares a set of franchise agreements and performs the required legal filings with every state in which it intends to sell franchise locations. It is officially recognized as a franchiser at this point.

➤ Interested parties purchase a franchise to offer these specific services or products in a given geographic or market area. Once the purchase is completed, the buyer is then known as a franchisee.

➤ The franchiser then provides various benefits to the franchisee, such as financing assistance, volume purchase pricing, national advertising, training, and business location research, among others.

➤ Franchisees pay a franchise fee to the franchiser, which is usually based on a percentage of its sales revenues. This fee relationship usually continues for as long as the franchise is in operation.

You can see from this quick overview that there are substantial benefits associated with purchasing a franchise, but that you also pay for access to these benefits. A major benefit is that you need not be an expert in a particular field, since the franchiser has that expertise and can train you adequately enough to apply their model to your particular business situation. In theory, you provide the money and the personal motivation and they provide the expertise and training. Oh, if it were that simple.

Some businesses become franchisers because they want to expand their market exposure in a rapid fashion and cannot afford to do it on their own. Franchising allows motivated franchisees to get started in their own businesses, based on a proven franchiser business model, giving them a higher likelihood of success. But don't assume that buying a franchise is a success guarantee.

The problem often lies with the franchiser not having adequately prepared the training and support aspects of the franchise network. After all, the franchiser's primary function is to ensure the success of the franchisees. All of them. However, if the franchise network grows quickly due to excellent franchise sales efforts, the franchiser might find itself stretched to the point that it cannot provide the agreed upon products and/or services to the franchisees. This leaves the franchisees in a precarious position because they might not have the years of experience needed to succeed without franchiser assistance, or the franchiser might not be adequately prepared to deal with the myriad questions that inevitably come up from new franchisees.

Terms of Acquisition

Disclosure document   A required filing with the Federal Trade Commission and many state regulatory agencies.

Uniform Franchise Offering Circular (UFOC)   A detailed set of franchise information disclosure guidelines that have been adopted by many states.

Other problems start to appear as the franchisees become more experienced, successful and confident in their own business management abilities. Many franchisees start to believe that they could perform financially as well on their own and do not need the support of the franchiser, and they continue with the relationship simply because they have a signed agreement. Paying the franchise fees might become a point of resentment causing friction between the franchiser and the franchisee. More than one franchiser-franchisee relationship has ended on a litigation note.

It is also possible that the franchiser is not maintaining its part of the agreement, causing the franchisees to complain that they are not receiving adequate services from the franchiser in exchange for paid fees.

The franchisee needs the franchiser to succeed so that the promised purchasing economies of scale, national advertising, research, and new products or services are obtained. Otherwise, the financial model, upon which the franchisee made its purchase, does not apply. The franchiser needs the franchisees to succeed, or the franchiser won't be able to sell any more franchisees on its business and operational concept.

This relationship is definitely a complicated two-way street. Treating a franchise relationship as you would any type of partnership or other business marriage is the right approach.

Hot Tip

Check with the Secretary of State's office as a starting point for specific franchiser information. If they don't have any information, they will generally be able to point you in the direction of someone who does.

Getting to Know the Franchiser

The more you now about the franchiser the more you understand the reality of daily life after purchasing a franchise. The franchiser is like the parent in the relationship in that it defines many of the daily working rules, and single moves by the franchiser can have dramatic impact on the franchisees.

Straight Talk

A few years ago a large franchiser that offered its particular brand (flavor) of fried chicken purchased one of its competing franchisers. It may have sounded good on paper, but the details of consolidating the two businesses created a lot of heartburn. Often these two competitors were just across the street from each other. In a post-purchase environment, the consolidated franchiser had two of its own locations competing for the same customers. Many existing franchisees saw this as a violation of their franchise agreements and took the franchiser to court. The importance of knowing your franchiser and its future business plans cannot be overstated.

If possible, talk with other member franchise organizations to get their perspective on the franchiser. After all, these other locations are already part of the franchise family, and they can tell where the skeletons are hidden, if there are any.

Check out the franchise prospectus provided by the franchiser to new prospective franchisees. What is it offering in the new agreements that may not be included in the one you inherit with the purchase of an existing location?

You might find that the earlier agreement has more favorable terms than those contained in the later agreements. Why? Risk and reward. The earlier adopters took a higher risk and rightfully should have expected a higher reward for taking that risk. The later franchisees are purchasing a proven business model along with a lower risk, and their terms and conditions might well be less attractive.

Here are a few references that may get you started in your franchise research:

➤ Franchise Buyer, a journal for prospective franchisees, [phone] 312-649-5200.

➤ Franchising World, a trade magazine the covers topics of interest to franchise company executives and the business world, [phone] 212-628-8000.

➤ American Association of Franchisees and Dealers (AAFD), [phone] 1-800-733-9858 (over 6,000 members).

➤ Franchise Consultants International Association (FCIA), [phone] 901-682-2951, for professionals dealing specifically with the franchise side of business (over 2,800 members).

➤ International Franchise Association (IFA), [phone] 202-628-8000, for information pertaining to international franchising (850 members).

➤ Women in Franchising (WIF), [phone] 312-431-1467, specifically oriented to franchising opportunities for women.

➤ Small Business Administration (SBA), www.sbaonline.sba.gov, 1-800-827-5722, for general small business information and franchising information in particular. SCORE might also be able to round out your business purchase/sale decisions with a little seasoned wisdom.

Terms of Acquisition

SCORE A part of the Small Business Administration (SBA), which provides experienced, often retired, executives who will consult with small business owners on a wide variety of business matters. Contact the SBA for a local SCORE office.

How Long Has the Franchiser Been in Business?

This is a pretty basic question, but one with tremendous repercussions. If the franchiser is new to franchising and you are new to both franchising and your industry of choice, then you can expect to be in double jeopardy: from your own limited experience and from the franchiser not knowing what to expect from a new franchisee. Factoring an unknown risk factor, which means assuming longer times and more business development expense than initially estimated, is the right thing to do under these circumstances.

131

Determine how many franchise locations have been sold. If there are only a few and they have been selling for a number of years, that indicates a limited acceptance of the idea, except under rare circumstances. If this is the case, you will want to take a close look at the franchiser's financial condition. The last thing you want to be is the last franchisee on a sinking franchiser's ship. It could be a very long, sobering, and disheartening experience.

Just because a franchiser has been in business for a long time does not immediately spell success, but it surely helps in the credibility department. This is another time when talking with the existing franchisees is invaluable. It is a good idea to talk with some that are happy with the relationship and with some that are disgruntled. After all, they all have valid opinions that might affect your opinion.

Buyer Beware

Listen with a careful ear when talking to new franchisees. They are still on their honeymoon period, and they might apply zeal and motivation to covering a franchiser's existing flaws. On the other hand, if the new franchisee is treated the way you would want to be treated, this is good news.

Here are a few questions to ask the franchiser as a starting point. If you are not happy with the answers to these questions, then you will likely find other flaws as well:

➤ How many franchise locations have you added in the last 24 months?

➤ How many franchise locations have you lost in the last 24 months? Why?

➤ Is there any pending franchisee litigation? For what reasons, and for how long? What are the requested damages?

➤ What does the franchiser view as its primary obligation in the relationship? What does it expect from the franchisee?

➤ Have the fees changed in the last five years? If so, how much, and for what reasons?

➤ Has the franchiser changed management or ownership in the last three to five years? Why?

➤ Is the franchiser publicly or privately owned and financed? Are there any pending, major financial deadlines or other covenants? How would these affect the franchisees?

➤ How many new products/services has the franchiser added to its franchisees in the last three to five years? How many of these are actually making money for the franchisees, and why or why not?

➤ What types of national advertising were performed in the last 12 months, and what is planned for the next 24 months?

➤ What percentage of the existing franchisees are actually showing a profit, and how long did it take them?

Asking these questions will be like fighting a hydra. For every one question you ask, two more will come up. Don't be afraid to ask. After all, most of us date for a while and try to meet the family before we get married. Purchasing a franchise is similar to a marriage in many ways, and it deserves close, methodical scrutiny. Should things not work out and you decide to sever the relationship, like any divorce, it will be a messy, expensive process that is best avoided by more comprehensive advance research.

Key Personnel, Methodology, or Arrangements

You have heard this from me before, and you will hear it again as you read through this book. When purchasing a company, you want to know where the specialized information that made the company successful resides. If it resides inside someone's head and it is not well documented, what protection is in place to protect the franchiser and franchisees from the loss of this person? If it resides in methodology and procedures that are well documented and proven, the risks are less but still worth investigating.

As a franchisee, you rely on the franchiser to keep the franchisee network current and on the leading business edge. Knowing where that edge has historically come from is a worthy research project.

It is also a worthwhile effort to verify the status of any national purchasing/sales agreements that the franchiser might have in effect. Understanding the stability of these relationships is critical to your performing a financial analysis that accurately reflects the financial risks and rewards of becoming a franchisee.

Should the agreements terminate or require a cost increase, your operating costs will increase driving down your gross margins and income. All of this, through no control or fault of your own, because the franchiser had to make a change.

An objective assessment of the truly unique nature of the franchiser's offering is another good idea. It might be that the offering was unique when first started, such as offering hamburgers at a low price that are easily purchased from the car. Any good idea will be copied if not legally protected, eventually turning what was once a unique idea into just another similar offering.

> **Hot Tip**
>
> You might find that the franchiser has purchased ideas from the franchisees and offered them throughout its franchisee network. This approach provides an instant national presence for the franchisee's idea, and it could generate substantial revenues. The franchiser and the franchisees both win in this situation.

Does the franchiser have legal protection on its products and/or methodology? If so, how much longer will that legal protection be in force? What protection is really provided, and have competitors already figured out ways to work around it?

How much of the franchiser's value is associated with its name, and has it diligently protected its legal trademark rights?

133

Has the company had recent successes or failures with introducing new products or services?

All of these things contribute to either enhancing or diminishing the franchise value. Many are not under the direct control of the franchisee, and they must be maintained by the franchiser. If it has historically performed its responsibilities in an effective manner, there is every reason to expect that it will continue doing the same in the future unless something has recently changed. The same assessment applies if it has not performed its functions properly.

Only you can make the determination as to whether the franchisee purchase is the right decision for you. And, you can only make this determination when you have adequate, accurate information with which to make this decision.

What About the Competition?

Nothing attracts success like success. The more successful a market and the approach to that market the more likely it is that other companies will want their piece of the business pie.

The good news about being the first into a market is that you get to define the standards against which other entrants are compared. The bad news is that the new entrants build on the success of the trailblazers in creating their ideas and companies. If the early leaders are not careful, they might find themselves trailing instead of leading.

Franchise business is highly competitive, and it is transacted at a rapid pace. If you are not sure about this, take a look at the various printing and copying services that are currently available. As technology moved forward, some of the early franchisers chose to stay with their traditional printing methods. At some point, the technological advances associated with the Internet and the rapidly decreasing cost of computers will make traditional printing for smaller printers less desirable from a customer's perspective.

Straight Talk

Nothing will humble a business faster than resting on its past successes and not setting new goals and challenges for itself. At some point, someone will make an attempt to take some of the previously earned success away, and customers will leave if the new company provides a better value. This is particularly true with franchise operations because they can develop a national presence very quickly.

Keeping ahead of the competition is critical, even if you are among the early leaders. Always check out the competition on both a local and a national level. If the franchiser is in the lead and had a head start to begin with, you are in great shape. If the franchiser is ahead, but the local franchisee is lagging, you might have an excellent opportunity for a turn around at the local location. If both are lagging and competitors that are more contemporary are entering the market on a regular basis, you should seriously consider looking elsewhere for your investment.

The exception to this last point would be if the total franchise network provided a sound marketing base that needed a sound, yet well directed, kick to turn amazing returns. In this way, a few well-placed investments and decisions could turn an older franchiser that is suffering from stagnation into a well-run, hungry competitor. Not only could this situation be fun to manage, but also the investment returns could be enormous.

The Least You Need to Know

➤ A franchisee/franchiser agreement is like a marriage. It is better entered into slowly and with an eye for the long term.

➤ Franchisees are heavily dependent on the franchiser for new products, services, and technologies.

➤ It is usually less risky to start a franchised business than an independent one. This is especially true if you are not an expert in the chosen field.

➤ A franchisee can be seriously hurt if the franchiser does not manage its financial responsibly.

➤ The FTC and state agencies require specific disclosure filings from any franchiser before franchise sales can begin.

➤ Never ignore, or underestimate, the competition.

Chapter 13

Reducing Competition by Buying 'Em Up

In This Chapter

➤ Selectively revealing customer information

➤ Relating buyer and seller customer information

➤ Selling only the customers and keeping the rest

➤ Special competitive company considerations

➤ The importance of secrecy and discretion

"I'm just not comfortable with this," said Judy to her sales manager. "They are asking us for information about our customer list, and they are also currently our biggest competitor. I would love to see their customer list. I know that they want to see ours. I just don't like it."

Jim shook his head in agreement. After all, these were his customers. Many of them he had personally discovered, closed, and serviced for several years.

"On the other hand, you can't blame them for wanting to know more about our customers. After all, they are buying the company and have a right to know something about the future customers that they are inheriting," sighed Jim. "Do you trust them to honor the non-disclosure document? They did sign one, after all."

"I trust them as much as anyone, but I am still uncomfortable with revealing this much information to them, this early in the sales process. There has to be a way to provide them with the basic information they want while still protecting the detailed information we want to protect. There just has to be a way."

More than once, you might have wished that your competition would go out of business. They have probably forced you to drop your prices, undercut you on a bid, taken one of your best customers, or even hired away some of your employees. That is competition, and these things come with the territory. You probably understand this, and still wish that they would just go away.

You might be in a position to make that happen. Why not simply buy them? You get your employees back, you decrease the competition, and likely expand your customer base. You probably know a lot about your competition simply because you compete against them all the time. You might also know if one of your competitors is thinking of selling or might be open to the prospect. Work your way through this chapter to learn the various benefits and pitfalls associated with purchasing a competitor.

Competitors Are a Special Case

Purchasing a competitor presents some very special and interesting competitive situations. It is a little like having dinner with someone you admire, respect, and distrust at the same time. If this company can survive as your competitor, it must be doing something right. Right? If it has taken business away from you in a competitive bid situation, it must have something going for it that a customer felt was more attractive than what you had to offer. Right? Otherwise, you would have gotten the business instead of your competitor. Face it. There are probably things that you could learn from them; just as, there are things that they can learn from you.

Terms of Acquisition

Good faith That intangible quality that is difficult to describe and yet very real. Without it, distrust shows up and most negotiations will be seriously disrupted or simply fail. With it, many obstacles can be overcome, but it usually requires flexibility on the part of both parties in the negotiations.

That is what makes purchasing a competitor an interesting process. The negotiations are little like the peace talks that occur while fighting is still happening in the trenches. You don't want to reveal too much information, yet you need to reveal enough to show good faith.

Once you get serious about purchasing a competitor, and they get serious about selling to you, you will both definitely reveal information about each other during the remaining process. This is information that you would probably not reveal under normal circumstances, yet it is information that must be revealed for both sides to determine the viability of the proposed transaction.

Purchasing any company is a complicated process. Purchasing a competitor, or being purchased by a competitor, presents its own unique set of circumstances, which makes the process more interesting but also more risky.

Are They Really Serious About Buying or Selling?

This is the first, and probably most important, question you will ask when investigating a competitive purchase or sale. How serious are they? Is this simply a ploy to obtain additional competitive information, or do they really want to buy your company? Do they really want to sell, or are they simply interested in learning more about your financial structure and management processes?

This is a tough question to answer in a quantitative way, because it deals with human motivations, which I continually find myself struggling to figure out. Do ya' know what I mean?

Here are a few starting questions that, when answered, might help you to determine the buyer's sincerity:

➤ Has it made a public announcement about its intention to buy another company that fits your company's profile? Or, has the seller publicly announced its intention to sell?

➤ Has the seller experienced recent changes that would precipitate a sale? (See Chapter 17, "Why Sell Anyway," for a partial listing of instances that might prompt a sale.)

➤ Is there an obvious synergy between the two companies? Does the seller have something that the buyer could obviously use, or vice versa?

➤ Does the buyer's management have a history of purchasing its technological or market expansion as opposed to developing it internally?

➤ Does the buyer's management have a history of managing companies to a certain size or condition and then selling?

➤ Does the buyer have the money to make the purchase? If it is a public company, get a copy of the latest financial report to verify its financial condition. Decide on a ballpark selling price for your company, and then ask a financial expert if this company could reasonably fund the purchase. If not, put this issue on the table before pursuing too deeply into sale discussions.

Don't feel restricted by this list. It is only a starting point. Spend the time up front coming up with others that apply to your particular situation. My point is simply that you are best served by asking these qualifying questions early in the process. In this way, you do not reveal privileged information to someone who is not seriously interested in the first place.

If these questions offend the other party, that tells you something right off about their level of commitment and openness to the process.

Hot Tip

Remember that "Need to Know" policy used within the nuclear weapons industry. If a person doesn't need to know it, they are not told. A similar approach applies when dealing with buyers and sellers in general, and with competitors in particular.

Are Your Customers the Same?

One thing that you and your competition typically share is customers. It is highly likely that many of your customers also buy from your competitor. This could be for any number of reasons, but it often stems from salesperson relationships; specific product or service differences; situational issues, such as availability of products or services; or other customer-specific issues.

Because of this customer sharing, you can expect that the purchase of a competitor will bring with it many of the same customers that you already have in your existing customer pool.

Terms of Acquisition

Diversification procedure   The business practice of spreading important business purchases or sale activities over multiple companies. In this way, should one company have trouble, the others can be relied upon until an alternate new source is found. Without diversification, a single company on which you are heavily dependent could go under, taking your company with it.

Don't be fooled into dismissing this customer sharing as inconsequential. You might be tempted to dismiss the revenue from these common customers, but realize that a large common customer will likely have different divisions with separate budgets. Is this "common" customer actually the same division or a different one?

Your company might be working with one division, while your competitor might be working with another. This is new sales revenue from a new customer as far as the buyer is concerned, and it should not be treated as simply more sales revenue from the same customer.

On the other hand, your customer might split its purchases between you and your competitor as a vendor diversification technique. If you purchase your competitor, the money that was previously going to the purchased company will likely not transfer to your company, because this defeats your customer's diversification procedure. Sales revenue to a competitor under these circumstances should be subtracted from the expected post-purchase sales totals.

You might also find that some customers would appreciate being able to combine purchases between the two companies into a single business relationship. There are administrative costs associated with splitting purchases, and many customers appreciate the reduction in work and administration that comes from consolidating business relationships.

The fundamental understanding to retain from this section is that you will most likely share customers with the competitor with whom you are negotiating. You don't want to give away this customer information too early in the process, but you should fully expect that the general information would need revealing at some point in the negotiation.

Which Customers Come with the Purchase?

The competitor that buys your company will want to know which customers come with its purchase of your company, because the marketing and sales aspect of a company are an integral part of its value.

The seller, on the other hand, has a vested interest in not revealing this information. If the sale does not go through for any number of reasons, the seller that reveals its detailed customer base information will always wonder if its competitor is now using the proprietary information obtained during the sale discussion process.

At some point, the buyer and seller must come to some accord that protects the seller while providing the buyer with adequate sales information.

A staged disclosure process has worked for me in the past, and you might consider it for your situation.

1. Both buyer and seller should sign a non-disclosure document that limits either party from using the revealed customer information. Understand that neither party can really be excluded from continued relationships with their present customers that happen to be common to both buyer and seller. Different divisions within the same company, in my opinion, should be treated as separate customers.

> **Terms of Acquisition**
>
> **Specifically Vague** Providing information that is general in nature but specific enough to answer the other party's initial questions. Stating of general facts without much detail attached.

2. The seller prepares a generic listing of total sales by numerically listed customer. In this way, the buyer learns the general breakdown of sales by the customer base. This, in itself, is an important part of the buyer's understanding.

3. The same disclosure process can be performed for the products and/or services involved. Present a breakdown of sales by numerically listed products. Once again, the buyer gets a general feel regarding whether the product sales are concentrated in a few products or spread relatively evenly across the product line. The more *specifically vague* you can make this listing, the better.

4. Notice that no customer-specific information has been revealed at this point. The seller is still fairly well protected, and the buyer has learned some important business information that allows it to assess the value of continuing with the process.

5. Depending upon the specific business types involved, this specifically vague level of disclosure might need refinement with respect to geography, fiscal period, distribution channel, market segment, or other pertinent criteria. Keeping

proprietary information proprietary while still addressing the buyer's questions is an art form and, in my opinion, it's just good business.

6. Once you are far enough along in the process, the buyer should be able to commit based on some general assumptions. For example, a letter of intent can be signed, which states that, based on pre-defined criteria, the buyer fully intends to pursue the purchase. In this way, the seller has some level of protection regarding the disclosure of detailed customer information. If it meets the agreed upon criteria, the buyer will buy. That is as much as you can realistically expect at this stage.

7. Once the detailed customer information is disclosed, you can expect a detailed discussion about the value of the customer list, which represents the backbone of your company's sales activities.

This staged approach adds more steps and complexity to the customer-information disclosure process, but it provides both the buyer and seller with the needed protection. The seller certainly doesn't want to reveal its customer list to a buyer that does not later actually finalize the purchase. The seller has spent large dollars and invested a great deal of time in creating that customer list. The list should be guarded like a company secret, because it is.

Straight Talk

We had another saying in nuclear weapons that dealt with secret information. "It is only a fact when someone who should know confirms it as being true. Up to that point it is simply conjecture." Even if the other party says something like "We all know that this customer is <*a specific customer*>," don't take the bait. Simply nod your head and say something specifically vague like "Interesting." Why reveal more than you have to? Let them wonder. It makes it more interesting, extends the game a little, and, most importantly, it protects your secret company information until the final moments when it must be revealed.

Strange as it may sound, the buyer might not want to know the detailed information unless it is really needed. After all, the buyer also exposes itself to legal problems should the seller construe that the information, provided under non-disclosure, was used against the seller. More than one lawsuit has developed from this type of situation.

Getting the Real Scoop

Life starts to get interesting when the buyer obtains detailed information about your customer list. The buyer might want to contact the seller's primary customers to determine their overall level of satisfaction. As the seller, you might not want this to happen, especially if your customers do not yet know that you are selling your company.

Legal agreements, signed between you and the buyer, must be in effect to protect you against this possibility. If your selling the company is already public knowledge and you really want this buyer to purchase your company, it might be a good idea to go along with the buyer when the buyer visits your major customers.

You are served on two counts with this level of attention: first, you ensure that your customer gets the right information about your company and the status of the sales process and second, you make sure that your customer reveals the needed information that moves the buyer closer to actually making the purchase. If you cannot go yourself, make sure that the person representing your company is well-informed about the Dos and Don'ts that pertain to this customer in particular and to the overall sale process in general.

If you have several interested buyers, you might consider getting a letter from your major customers that answers some of the most commonly asked buyer questions. Your customers want you to sell to a company that will maintain a healthy business relationship after the sale, but they also need to perform their daily jobs while you are selling. If your business activities become disruptive to your customers, you might alienate them, this is never good news for either you or the prospective buyer.

If possible, keep the buyers from visiting your major customers. They shouldn't really need to talk with them personally as long as they believe your accounting and sales numbers, understand your industry, and really want to purchase more than just your customer list. (See the later section on selling only your customer list.)

Hot Tip

Making a major business decision is a lot like jumping off a bridge into a river. Once you have jumped, it is silly to regret jumping. Control the jumping process and work toward a smooth, painless landing. Having second thoughts while in flight can do little more than cause confusion and increase the likelihood of a crash landing.

How Much Will You Really Make?

If you are the buyer, I suggest that you get an idea of the seller's revenues obtained from these customers over the last three years. Has the customer list stayed relatively the same? Have sales increased or decreased with the major 20 percent of customers over that period? What future sales prospects can the seller tell you about relative to these major customers? Are there any special agreements in effect that protect future sales revenues with these major customers? From this information, you can get an estimate of future sales revenue.

After all, you are not much interested in historical sales data. You want to determine a reasonable estimate of future sales revenues. Trend analysis is an excellent starting point for projecting the future.

Try this process for estimating overall future sales numbers:

1. Determine the sales revenue numbers from the last three to five years. The more historical years of data you can obtain, the better.

2. On a piece of graph paper, mark the years along the horizontal (X) axis and mark the sales increments along the vertical (Y) axis.

3. Plot the historical data on your chart. You should now have a series of three to five data points on your chart.

4. Take a ruler and place it on the graph paper in such as way that the ruler edge lays along a line that approximates an average of the sales figures.

5. Draw a line along the edge of the ruler so that it extends three to five years into the future.

6. Place marks along the drawn line at the points where the line intersects the location of the future year, as shown on the X-axis. The Y-axis value represents the projected future sales figure.

This procedure is a rough estimate, but I assure you that more than one marketing research report has used this procedure to project future market trends. It may not be fancy, but that doesn't mean that it is without value.

Here is where you can apply all of that detailed information you learned about the seller's customers. You might know that certain of the customers would be lost with the sale. You might also know that others would increase orders once the two companies are combined. You might also want to apply a "fudge factor," which enables you to create a conservative projection of future sales. Decreasing future sales by a percentage, say 20 percent, under that which was projected from the regression analysis gives you what might be considered a more realistic estimate of future sale revenues.

These sale revenue estimates will be used when determining a detailed company valuation as presented in

Terms of Acquisition

Regression analysis   The process of mathematically determining a future value based on existing data. The procedure, usually performed on a computer, determines an equation that matches the existing data. It then inserts future values into the equation to mathematically estimate future values.

Linear regression   Assumes that past and future values will fall along a straight line. Works well for numbers that change at a fixed rate.

Non-linear regression   Assumes that past and future values fall along a curve (or arc) instead of a straight line. This analysis technique is used when predicting future values that change rapidly in either a positive or negative direction.

Chapters 15, "Making an Offer They Can't Refuse," and 22, "How Much to Ask For and Other Negotiations."

Buying Their Customers and Not Their Debts

Here is a little trick you might not have considered, and it is a trick that is best used when selling to a competitor.

What if you could simply buy the customer list and leave the company, its owner's stock and associated assets in the hands of the previous owners? In some cases, the most valuable thing a company owns is its customer list. Many assets will have liens attached to them, often causing them to have a minimal net value. And don't forget that purchasing the company's shares simply exposes the buyer company to the potential of future, unexpected litigation.

Straight Talk

The seller might be interested in changing business emphasis so that the new venture does not compete with the buyer's activities. In this case, the seller might be willing to sell the customer list to a buyer, agree to not compete with the buyer in its core area of business, yet still retain the right to contact existing customers for non-competitive business opportunities. In this way, the seller wins by receiving money for the list, which can be used to finance the new business venture. Customers are not angry because they are well taken care of, and they might even use the seller's new services. Small businesses might find this approach useful.

Selling the customer list, along with a non-competition agreement, may serve both the seller's and the buyer's objectives. The seller is served in that its most valuable asset is sold at its highest possible price, its customers are taken care of, and future customer responsibility has been transferred to the buyer.

This type of arrangement is commonly used between companies in the services industry. If the seller is ready to quit business, has fully depreciated its assets, and doesn't want to leave its customers in an unserviced state, selling the customer list presents an excellent option.

All of the cautions presented earlier, with respect to protecting the customer list, must be applied to this situation as well. After all, in this case, the customer list is the only thing being sold. The seller must work to optimize its value to the highest degree possible.

The Least You Need to Know

➤ Competitors almost always share some customers.

➤ Disclosing customer information in stages, and with signed non-disclosure agreements, serves both buyer and seller.

➤ Regression analysis allows you to estimate future sales levels based on historical information.

➤ Selling only the customer list might be attractive to certain small business sellers.

➤ Once you have revealed a detailed customer list, you can never take it back.

Part 4
Actually Buying the Business

Once you have the target company in your sights, you must then determine its strong and weak points, only after which can you determine its worth. It doesn't stop there; you must then determine how you will pay for it. Part Four is important information for any business buyer.

Chapter 14

To Buy, or Not to Buy ...

> ### In This Chapter
>
> ➤ Objectifying the assessment process
>
> ➤ Understanding what you do and do not believe
>
> ➤ Evaluating management trust level
>
> ➤ Confirming initial motivations
>
> ➤ Trusting your intuition

They had been arguing for over two hours, and they seemed to be going nowhere except at each other. They had been looking at this particular company for nearly four weeks now, and had obtained a ton of information—literally. Now it was decision time, and it was Kevin's job to get the group to some type of consensus.

In front of him were the results of his first, private polling of the group members. He had specifically asked two questions: 1)How closely does this targeted company meet our acquisition objectives, and 2)What are the five most valuable assets obtained from the company if purchased?

As he looked through the answers, he started to understand the confusion and frustration. First, there seemed to be a wide difference of opinion about how well the targeted company met the acquisition goals. Secondly, the most valuable aspects were consistent between most members, but they varied among the three having the loudest argument.

This was valuable information, but now Kevin needed somehow to get them talking instead of yelling. Clearly these three viewed things from a different perspective, and Kevin wanted to know why.

Much of your hard work and attention is coming to a head in the next few chapters. It is now time for you to decide if you are actually going to make an offer to buy this company.

This is a checklist and confirmation sort of stage. You will now need to understand if your overall intentions with the purchase will be fulfilled if you can get the company for the right price, which will be discussed in Chapter 15, "Making an Offer They Can't Refuse."

In this chapter, you will take the time to assess the general status of the company and the information upon which you base that status assessment. After all, if your information is suspect, so is your resulting assessment.

Assessing What You Really Know

Think back for a few moments to the beginning of the acquisition process. In Chapter 2, "Start at the Very Beginning ...," I challenged you to take a close look at your motivations, as either a buyer or a seller. I presented the need to create a core team that would work on the acquisition, or sale, project, and the need for their secrecy.

Make a listing of the top reasons that you wanted to purchase a company in the first place. Here are just a few reasons to get you started, although your list is undoubtedly longer at this point:

➤ Was the motivation strictly financial in nature?

➤ Did strategy play a part in your motivation?

➤ Was there an unexpected event, such as a death of a partner or legislative change, that prompted your interest in the purchase?

➤ What were your financial boundaries?

➤ How much were you willing to spend and over how many years?

➤ What restrictions did your board of directors place on your acquisition intentions from both a managerial and financial perspective?

➤ When did you want to have the purchase accomplished?

➤ Did you want, and expect, that members of the acquired company would become employees of your company?

Buyer Beware

The closer you get to a project, the better it might appear simply as a result of the increased familiarity. After gaining a lot of details it is often valuable to take a few steps back to evaluate the target from a more objective perspective. It might very well continue looking positive but this time it is based on objective analysis, not emotional involvement.

Taking the time to write down your objectives is critical. As you learn about the target companies, you will likely become more diffused in your objectives and become more sympathetic to their view of things. This is not bad news in that you start to adopt the thinking processes of the target company and to acquire a more solid understanding. However, it can cause you to stray from your initial objectives. Having them in writing, from the beginning, enables you and your acquisition team to compare what you know today against what you wanted to accomplish when you first set out on your acquisition journey.

Each team member, on his or her own, should answer the posed questions based on their assessment. The individual assessments should then be compared. If there is a lot of similarity with the assessments, you probably have at least obtained consistent information as part of the process. If not, it is possible that one person knows something that has not been shared with the rest of the group. It is also possible that the various members simply see things differently, which is the basis of an excellent discussion regarding the various perspectives.

At some point, you must make a decision to buy or not. That part is simply a fact. But understanding the various perspectives on the information obtained allows you to verify the obtained information or uncover holes that could affect the price and even the final outcome of the acquisition.

Do You Trust What You Know?

Carrying the prior topic a little further, you might consider preparing a form for each team member, including the executive members, to complete. Here are a few components of the form:

➤ List each of the key initial objectives as a separate line item in the form of a question about how closely the targeted company matches this objective.

➤ Set a rating system of 1 to 10, with 1 being a low match and 10 being a perfect match.

➤ Ask that each member of the team insert their own assessment, from 1 to 10, of how closely the various criteria are matched by the targeted company.

➤ Total the individual line item assessments for each team member.

➤ Multiply the total number of line items by 10 to get the total for a perfect match (10s on each line item).

➤ Divide the individual assessment total by the perfect total to get a percentage match assessment.

This may seem like a lot of work, but it is pretty simple if the line items are put into an electronic spreadsheet. Then each member can complete the spreadsheet on his or her own system, and return

Hot Tip

Just because you all agree doesn't mean that the information is accurate. You might all be working from the same incorrect information. Consistency simply means that you all agree based on what has been presented and/or obtained.

it to the coordinating team member. The spreadsheet can be set up to tally the totals and percentages automatically.

Comparing the various percentages allows you to determine the level of consistency across the team. If it is consistent, you at least have consensus among team members. If there is a wide spread of 10 percent to 15 percent or more, the members see things differently. Looking at the individual line item breakdowns might provide areas of discussion. Some people might rate particular areas a high match with others being lower. At least you now have a starting place for communication. From this communication, you might find out information that would not have come out otherwise.

Do You Trust the Targeted Management Team?

OK. I might sound like a cynic using this topic title, but it is certainly a point worth considering. As my brother says, "Just because you're paranoid doesn't mean that they are not out to get you."

Straight Talk

"*Caveat emptor*" is Latin for "Buyer Beware." Heck. Even the Romans worried about the honesty and/or the intentions of sellers, and from what little I know about the Romans, the concern was probably warranted.

Anyway, the intent is not to present a philosophy lesson, but to show that questioning the seller's motivations and integrity is a good idea. With all of that said, the question still stands: "Do you trust the targeted management team?" This doesn't question whether they would steal from you, but rather whether or not you have heard the whole truth about the company.

Here are a few flags to watch for that might indicate something is going on under the surface of your negotiations:

➤ Is there language in written communications that appeared to be specifically vague?

➤ Are there direct statements that seem to contradict what you actually saw while researching the company?

➤ Did the company not want you to visit on short notice, and did things look different from one visit to the next in either a positive or a negative way?

➤ Did certain people get called away or not appear in what you considered important meetings in which their attendance would have added important perspective?

➤ What if you are a publicly held company, and your stock price drops upon announcing your intention to purchase the company? Does this mean that the investor community knows something your don't, or is it just overreacting to any news of change?

➤ What is the historical level of integrity that the company's management is known to maintain? If high, has there been any reason for you to doubt its maintenance through your negotiations? If not, have you factored into your assessment a lower than desired truth factor?

Understand that there is a world of difference between somebody NOT telling you something that you did not ask about, and flat out misrepresenting or misstating the truth. I would call the first "selective disclosure" and the other "lying."

Few people offer negative information unless specifically asked for it. In an IRS audit, few people tell the examiner that he or she missed these points "over here" that would mean that you owe more tax. You expect the IRS auditor to find the areas in question. The same is true for the seller. Unless specifically asked about a potentially negative issue, it might not be revealed.

Straight Talk

Anyone who watched the President Clinton impeachment proceedings has reached some opinion about the use of the English language and hairsplitting. If you have ever trained for a legal deposition, your attorney always will coach you to 1) make sure that you completely understand the specific question being asked, and 2) answer only the specific, confirmed question asked. It makes for a very long trial and deposition process, but it makes sure that a person under oath is not construed as having said one thing while meaning something else. I will let history and the scholars debate President Clinton's actions. I only state here that you should be aware of these practices, and if you feel your questions are being addressed with legal hairsplitting answers, you might want to look at rephrasing the question.

I suggest you take this type of selective disclosure as part of the sales process. If you find that someone specifically and deliberately misrepresented or misstated the truth, you have a sound reason for questioning their accuracy on other statements.

153

Also know that people will generally answer the SPECIFIC question you ask and not the one that you "kinda meant to ask." Sellers will generally look for the best possible light in which to present their company. Unless your questions are specific and to the point while remaining non-threatening, you might find yourself looking at a bunch of generalities that might mean one thing on the surface, but really mean another at the detail level.

You should also remember that the targeted company's management team would likely become your company's employees. Will they fit in or will they simply bring problems with them? Will the prior owners honor their commitments to assist with a smooth transition, or will their attention waver after they receive their first payment? The advance structuring of the deal is an important part of making sure that the post-purchase phase proceeds as it was expected when the agreements were signed.

What Is Your Confidence Level?

Here I come back to "gut instinct" again, but I really trust human intuition backed up by research and information. If all of the data indicates one thing but your instincts are telling you another, I assert that something critical is missing. At some point, most research projects hit a point where all of the various puzzle pieces almost spontaneously mesh into a total picture.

Rushing the deal is almost never a good idea since you undoubtedly find the puzzle contains holes. If you can live with the uncertainty posed by those holes, then move forward. However, if the holes concern you, dig deeper to determine specifically the additional information you need to obtain. You will really kick yourself if you go against your instincts and later find out that you were right. Nevertheless, living in fear of making a wrong decision has caused more than one executive to retire early. Only you can determine the proper balance.

If you have the time, stamina, and confidence in what you know, the management team and the achievement of your initial objectives will be where they need to be. At this time you will either feel comfortable enough to move on to making an offer or decide the deal is just not right for you and your company.

Hot Tip

I suggest not pressing the financial dollar value issue too much with your team, since that assessment might not have been performed yet. This procedure simply allows those with valid input to express their contentions.

Determining What You Are Really Buying

As a final, high level exercise, I suggest that you and the other members of the team perform another simple task.

Have each member of the team list five answers to the following question, in order of most to least valuable:

"What are the five most valuable aspects of the targeted company? If possible, place a proposed purchase price on each individual aspect listed." This second point is optional.

This really brings the entire analysis process down to a simple listing of the primary reasons to purchase this company and the value of that purchase to your company.

We will get more specific about determining a purchase price in the next chapter, but this exercise narrows the focus, ensuring that the most valuable assets are obtained for a fair price. Again, if all team members agree on the top five, you are either all confused or the acquisition picture is clear. If there is a wide spread, then something is, once again off balance. Communication within the team is the most effective way to resolve any disputes.

The team coordinator might have to expand the list to seven or eight aspects to accommodate what are valid yet different perspectives. However, you now know what you are buying, and should have a rough benchmark of what it should cost.

The Least You Need to Know

➤ Reviewing initial objectives ensures that you have not lost track of the main goals while looking at all of those details.

➤ Your acquisition team's members have a lot of aggregate knowledge at this point. Tapping it while looking for a consensus ensures that all the most important information is revealed.

➤ The targeted company's management team might have selectively revealed information instead of showing both the good and bad with equal candor.

➤ There is a difference between blatantly misrepresenting the truth and only answering questions asked. The legal aspects should be confirmed with an attorney.

➤ Ask specific, direct and non-threatening questions and make sure that they are answered.

➤ Don't underestimate the value of gut instincts. If your business intuition is telling you something is either very right or very wrong, you should listen and look for objective confirmation.

Chapter 15

Making an Offer They Can't Refuse

In This Chapter

➤ Knowing where to start the bidding

➤ Determining today's value for future events

➤ Working around a secretive seller

➤ Working with business appraisers

➤ Understanding the limitations of analysis

There would probably never be a good time to bring this up, so it might as well be now, thought Jill as she looked at the expectant seller on the other side of the table.

"We have a little problem here," Jill started out. "We don't know a lot about your company at this point, but according to our analysis of companies comparable to yours, you are asking what appears to be around 30 percent more for your company than other comparably sized companies. How do you justify the price differential?"

Ron, the owner of the company being sold, smiled at the comment. His accountant had told him to be ready for this question, and he was.

"We know those other 'comparable' companies, and even looked into buying them ourselves," said Ron. "When we looked at their operations, we realized that we could do better on our own. So we did."

"That's fine, as far as it goes," said Jill. "But your asking price must be backed up by some type of objective assessment that would help me to understand why you are worth that extra

30 percent, or I'm afraid we are done. I like your company, but it just appears too expensive for what we would be getting."

Ron reached into his briefcase and pulled out a few sheets of paper. He now knew that Jill was serious, and he was willing to share his more detailed analysis. Placing the papers in front of her, he looked her right in the eye.

"I'm glad you asked," he responded with a gleam of pride in his eye. "This is a discounted cash flow analysis that we carried out looking ahead for a 5-year period. Take a look at these numbers and tell me that we are not a bargain at this price."

Eventually, the buy/sell process comes down to pricing. Either they are going to specify a desired selling price or you will specify a buying price. In either case, you must determine the purchase price that is right for you. The more foundation you have for that price the more likely you are to get it, since your pricing assumptions can be used as negotiating points against what might be more emotional arguments posed by the seller.

There are a few different techniques available for determining the price of an asset, which is really all that a company is when you come right down to it. It is an asset that provides a certain amount of income or return. The price you pay today is usually based on the future expected income.

The various pricing models fall into one of several categories:

➤ Calculating the equivalent current value of all projected future incomes and expenses.

➤ Comparative pricing when the targeted company's price is based on the selling price of other companies sold within the industry.

➤ Rule-of-thumb formulas where a given parameter is multiplied by a factor, which then determines the right price.

Other pricing models will be presented either in detail or for general information purposes. As you can see, there are numerous ways to determine a company's value and resulting purchase price.

Picking the right technique for your situation is based on the underlying financial assumptions associated with each analysis type and industry-specific experience. Reading this chapter will provide you with a solid foundation for determining the right technique for your situation. You will likely use an accountant to perform the specific calculations.

Hot Tip

Some investors won't even look at a company with a valuation of less than $5 million. It is just not worth the time and attention needed to evaluate such a small purchase.

Predicting the Future

No matter what technique you use for valuing a company, you must always remember that you are buying the future. Past performance is interesting, and certainly an important indicator, but the past has already happened. Relying on past glories is always dangerous, even when they are your own glories. These past glories belonged to someone else (the seller), and they are really of no intrinsic value to you at all, so use them as an indicator only.

Look to the future. Even the techniques that use a current financial number in conjunction with a multiplier are looking toward the future, in that they assume that the future will at least be as good as today.

Unless you can confidently assess the future financial performance capabilities of the company, you really can't place a justifiable current value, or purchase price, on the company today.

Projecting Future Sales

I talk in great length about future sales and customer values in Chapter 19, "Preparing Your Financials," so check that chapter for the details. Notice that this chapter looks at the topic from the seller's perspective, which is simply the optimistic side of your, the buyer's, perspective. The seller will want to estimate future sales to be as high as possible, since that makes the company look more attractive, and more valuable. You want to believe that the sales will be higher, but negotiate from a more conservative, yet realistic, position, since the lower the future sales estimated, the lower the purchase price.

Again, notice that spending time estimating the future is required to assess today.

Projecting Future Expenses

Expense prediction is also covered in Chapter 19, and I will only spend a few moments here on this topic. Once again, you and the seller are on opposite sides of this topic. The seller wants the future expenses to look lower, while you will want them to be estimated on the higher end. Why? Because the lower the assumed revenues and the higher your assumed expenses the more conservative, and possibly realistic, your projections. This combination usually translates into a lower current purchase price.

Understanding the expenses, and the assumptions, associated with the numbers reported on the financial statements, is a little mundane, but very important in predicting the company's future expense needs.

After you have predicted future financial estimates, you must now assess their worth as paid for with today's money, which is exactly what you are doing when you purchase a company. You are paying for the future with today's commitment. Read the next section to learn the basics associated with performing a present-value analysis. It is a little abstract, but you will find it very real when your accountant uses this technique to place a value on an asset or the company you plan to purchase.

Straight Talk

Once you have an estimate of future revenues and expenses, you can predict future net incomes, which is really what you wanted to know when you started. The pro-forma income statements shown in Chapter 19 demonstrate how future revenues and expenses are used to predict future net incomes before and after tax. You can perform this analysis on either an accrual or a cash basis of accounting, with cash typically being the most accurate but also possibly the most difficult to prepare, since the historical reporting was probably done using accrual accounting methods.

Weighing the Future—Today

You have probably heard that "time is money." It can also be said that time either makes money or costs money. In this section, I will present a very important, but often abstract concept, referred to as "the time value of money."

Think about this: What if someone could ask you for 10 thousand dollars today and offer to give you back the same 10 thousand dollars five years from today, with no interest income at all? You probably wouldn't do it since you would be losing money on the deal. After all, you could put that 10 thousand dollars into a bank account and at least make a few hundred dollars a year in interest. That interest would be lost if you had given this person the 10 thousand dollars with no interest return at all.

Now, factor in the possibility that you might not get the money back. Now, the interest rate that you need to charge, for the loan, goes up. Why? Well, why would you give this person a loan, if you have only the chance of making the same interest income but additionally expose yourself to the chance of losing the money completely?

This trade-off of risk and reward is done by business people every day, although perhaps not in a formalized, numeric fashion.

We all know that a dollar promised tomorrow is not as sure as a dollar in our hand today. As a result, lenders require that you pay a "risk premium" for any money loaned today that will be repaid with future dollars.

Straight Talk

Any time that you provide/loan money today, you make certain assumptions about the likelihood of repayment. You also compare the expected income from that loan to the amount of money you would receive from a risk-free investment, such as a bank savings account. You may not realize it, but you do this.

Think about this scenario for a moment. Assume that you loan $1,000 to someone with a stable income, and charge them an interest rate equal to what you would receive from a bank savings account. Also, assume that you expect them to pay it back over a five-year period. You are essentially giving up the interest from the bank for the interest you expect to get from the person receiving the loan.

Notice that the "present value" of the loan is $1,000 (since that is what you are lending them today) combined with the future interest income to be obtained from that $1,000. Now assume that the borrower falls on difficult financial times, and tells you that he or she cannot make payments for a while. How much is that $1,000 loan worth to you now? Less, since the likelihood of you receiving the future payments, as originally expected, just dropped.

A discounted cash flow analysis is a formal way of attaching firm numbers to a subjective scenario, such as I just described.

The entire goal of the analysis is to determine the amount of money, if in your hand today, that would equal all of the future money amounts you expect to receive.

The analysis requires three basic components:

➤ The expected future cash flows, whether treated as negative flows (expenses) or positive flows (income).

➤ The amount of time between today and when the future cash amounts under analysis are obtained, or spent.

➤ The discount factor applied to the future cash flows that bring it back to the current day, providing an equivalent value today.

I am not going to get into the details of the calculations, since they are relatively complicated

Hot Tip

Any finance book will contain a pre-printed table of discount factors that can be applied to future cash amounts to bring them back to a current, or present, value. Calculators and spreadsheet programs also perform these calculations.

and beyond the scope of this short chapter. However, I do want you to understand the meaning of the different factors and how they combine to create a present value number. Your accountant can perform the analysis for you, once the two of you come to an agreement about the various factors involved.

The important concept to understand is that the more risk associated with the actual receipt of future payments the greater the discount that must be applied to this future money when bringing it to a present value. In addition, the further out this amount is in the future the less impact it will have on the present value of that future money. If you think about it, this makes a lot of sense. A lot can happen between today and 5 or 10 years into the future. So its impact on today should be taken with a large grain of salt, which really means "highly discounted" when talking about a discounted cash flow analysis.

For purposes of simplifying this discussion, I use only future net-income-before-tax numbers, and I do not include various adjustments to this number, such as the impact of depreciation, tax brackets, or other items that your accountant might feel materially affect the anal-ysis.

Refer to the following figure for a simplified discounted cash flow analysis for a company with annual revenues of around $20 million and growing. Notice that Year Three shows a large loss due to expenses you expect to incur based on knowledge obtained from the due diligence portion of the acquisition process.

Remember that my goal with this discussion is to present the concepts. You can work out the factual details with your accountant. I strongly encourage you not to plan to perform this analysis on your own, since it is fraught with pitfalls for the uninitiated.

Terms of Acquisition

Materiality   An accounting term that designates a number or ac-counting assumption as having a relative size or importance in relation to net income or financial position. The larger the impact the more "material" it is assumed to the analysis.

Discount factor   The amount used to decrease the current effect of a future financial event. The larger the discount the less the current effect.

Investigation of the following figure shows the important results of this analysis:

➤ That the $1.5 million loss in Year Three is really only worth a $1.068 million loss when looked at in present day dollars.

➤ That the 60-year income life of this company, from the end of Year Five forward, is worth $19.586 million if the same assumed NIBT performance is maintained. This figure is then discounted back to the present time by applying the Year Five discount factor of .5674 to the $19.586 million to contribute $11.113 million to the $26.767 million figure shown.

➤ Subtracting the current value of liabilities from the current value of future projected incomes provides an estimate of the current shareholder equity. This number represents the current value of all outstanding stock.

XYZ Present Value Calculation - Discounted Cash Flow Analysis (000)

Discount Factor Precentage: 12%

	Year 1	Year 2	Year 3	Year 4	Year 5	Terminal Value
Revenues:	$20,000	$22,400	$25,088	$28,099	$31,470	
Net Income Before Tax:	$2,000	$2,400	$(1,500)	$3,456	$4,147	$4,147
Present Value Factor:	0.8929	0.7972	0.7118	0.6355	0.5674	8.324
Present Value of future Annual Net Income:	$1,786	$1,913	$(1,068)	$2,196	$2,353	$19,586

Total Assumed Present Value: $26,767

Less: Present Market Value of Debt: (16,906)

Shareholder Net Present Value: $9,862

Notes for Analysis:

Terminal Value assumed for 60-year period.

Simplified Discounted Cash Flow Analysis

Notice that this analysis incorporates the third year's negative income expectation, the long-term future value of the recurring income stream (assumed constant for this analysis) and the current market value of what the company owes. In short, the shareholder net present value figure ($9,862,000) represents a fair purchase price for the company in question based on the information included in this analysis. Additional information may sway this price in either direction, but at least you have a starting point.

Strategic factors might drive this figure up or down, but it truly reflects a valid starting point for negotiations. Notice that it is completely objective and incorporates the various future expectations.

Hot Tip

Any present value analysis is only as accurate as the future projections and the assumed discount factor. Don't ignore the assumed discount rate because you can turn a bad investment into a good one, on paper anyway, just by changing the discount rate.

Is it accurate? Only the future will tell. Is it valid based on the information contained and the current investment climate? Yes, if the right discount factor is chosen.

Choosing the Discount Rate

Bear with me for a few more moments, because this is important. Choosing the right discount rate is an art form that can be pretty complicated, but it should not be ignored.

The Capital Asset Pricing Model (CAPM) method of determining the discount rate is probably the most commonly accepted in the valuation of larger companies, although it is not without its critics. It does, however, incorporate the expected return from a risk free alternate investment and a premium for any asset that deviates substantially from other stocks, such as those tracked on the S&P 500.

Here is the formula used for calculating the CAPM factor, which is then assumed as the discount rate used in the present value calculation shown in the prior section:

Expected Return (ER) = Risk Free (RF) Return + [Beta * (Expected Market Return (ERM) – RF)]

Where:

Expected Return (ER) represents the expected future return that the stock should provide, which also becomes the discount rate (ask your accountant for further explanation).

Risk Free (RF) Return represents the return you would expect if you put the money into a risk free investment, such as a bank savings account.

Beta is a factor calculated by industry analysts that tracks the deviation of a stock or other investment vehicle as compared to the overall market as a whole, such as the S&P 500. It measures the volatility of a stock, which also represents its risk with respect to the rest of the market.

Expected Market Return (ERM) is the overall market performance as determined by a market indicator, such as the S&P 500.

As an example, assume that the Risk Free (RF) rate is 3%, that the Beta for our target company is assumed as 1.2 (20% larger pricing swings than the general market), and that the Expected Market Return (ERM) has historically been 10%. Putting these values into the equation yields the following result, and assumed discount rate:

Expected Return = .03 + 1.2 * (.10 – .03) = 11.4%

Using the 11.4% discount rate for present value calculations not only takes into account alternate risk free investments but also accounts for the expected higher risk associated with this company's stock as compared with the rest of the market.

Straight Talk

Using CAPM in conjunction with a solid present value analysis provides a way of calculating the present value of a company that currently shows a negative net income. This explains some of the feeding frenzy surrounding the incredible performance of Internet stocks in 1999. These companies show negative net incomes yet command hundreds of millions of dollars in market capitalization. This is simply because investors, in performing their present value calculation, assume large enough positive future cash flows to create a positive present value, even when discounted using the CAPM model. Fascinating, don't you think?

Finding the proper beta is not always a simple task, and different beta sources may provide a different beta for the same stock. I suggest that you eliminate any beta that makes no sense for the company, such as one with a negative number for most companies. Then perform the analysis with the high and low values. This should provide you with the reasonable high and low price for the company.

Check with your brokerage house for the beta value of a specific publicly traded company. You might need to find the specific company, but once you have the company name your broker can almost certainly provide you with the beta. They will probably be impressed that you even asked.

Is CAPM a perfect answer? No. But then, nothing really is, except perhaps 20/20 hindsight. CAPM does provide an excellent valuation starting point, however, which can be used to calculate the present value of a complicated future income and expense stream.

Basing the Price on Comparable Companies

You sometimes are lucky enough to have the information from another comparable company sale upon which to base your purchase price. This is called the "comparable transaction" valuation method, since you are basing your price from another, comparable transaction.

This technique is used in real estate all the time. You ask your agent to perform a market analysis, or even pay an appraiser, to determine a fair price for a particular house. They look around in the area at other sold houses similar enough to yours to be used as a comparable basis of price comparison.

By compensating for the positive and negative aspects of the house as compared to those already sold, a fair price is determined.

Hot Tip

You might find that performing a discounted cash flow analysis would provide some insight about the accuracy of the comparable company price comparisons.

The same can be done for a business, although the analysis is more complicated due to additional factors, many of which have been outlined in this book.

Notice that the terms and conditions of the sale must be public knowledge, which might be a problem if you are selling a smaller company. These companies often transfer from one private company to another, with the terms and conditions remaining confidential, usually as part of the agreement.

An alternate approach is to find a publicly traded company that, according to its quarterly or annual report, operates in a similar method to the target company. The market valuation of this publicly traded company provides a benchmark against which the target company's value can be compared. If the company's stock sells for $10 per share and there are 1 million shares outstanding, then the market valuation of the company is $10 million. This value sets a general range against which the target company can be compared.

Straight Talk

If the target company is larger or smaller than the valuation of a comparable company which is being used as a basis for comparison, you might even try pro-rating the valuation to match. Assume that the target company has sales of $8 million whereas the comparable public company has sales of $16 million and a market valuation of $10 million. Everything else assumed equal, which they almost never are, you could assume that the target company is worth 50 percent of the public company which gives it a valuation of 0.50 * $10 million, or $5 million. This isn't a perfect technique, but it is a place to start.

Rule of Thumb Pricing

When dealing with smaller companies that have revenues under $5 million, or so, you will likely run into rule of thumb valuation techniques. These techniques take an easily obtained and substantiated number, such as annual sales or number of clients, and multiply it by a specific factor. The result of this calculation provides a starting point for negotiations.

This approach is attractive in that it avoids many of the accounting pitfalls associated with privately held companies. After all, understanding what was historically done in a company only provides insight if you understand the assumptions associated with the history. Moreover, you have to be given the historical information in the first place. Right?

What if a small business owner, especially one who views you as a competitor, decides not to show you his or her financial numbers but is willing to share some overall information, such as annual sales and number of clients? From this information, you should be able to determine some general parameters about the company simply by extrapolating the performance of your own company under similar conditions. From this analysis, you can determine a fair price for the business without delving too deeply into the confidential information of the target company.

The multipliers do the same thing. Assume that a travel agency that you are interested in purchasing has annual sales of $750,000. A common multiplier for travel agencies is .05 to 0.1 times annual gross sales, which places a valid price range for this agency between $37,500 and $75,000 (0.05 * $750,000 and 0.1 * $750,000 respectively).

Notice that confidentiality does not have to stop a transaction if you find a multiplier you are comfortable with. Remember also that a company that performs better than the industry average might have a higher multiplier, whereas one that is suffering problems might command a lower multiplier. As always, the fairest answer is in the details.

Hot Tip

You can find multipliers for industries by checking with industry associations or simply by checking with the reference desk of your local library. As always, simply use these multipliers as a starting point and not as a fixed financial point.

What About Using an Appraiser?

Just as an appraiser is called in to place a market value on a house, a business appraiser can be called in to place a value on a business. This is not an instantaneous process, and it requires cooperation on the part of the seller, but it does provide an objective view of the company.

The American Society of Appraisers has been around for a while and its members charge a higher fee for a business appraisal, but this valuation is considered by some to be the most accurate. The Institute of Business Appraisers is a newer organization whose members also provide appraisals, often for a lower fee.

You are probably looking at a $5,000 to $10,000 fee for a credible appraisal for a conventional

Buyer/Seller Beware

Avoid appraisers who base their fee on the final valuation of the company or on the sale price at which it finally sells. This appraiser now has a vested interest in the final valuation price, which can easily affect the appraisal results. A flat fee is usually a safer bet.

business. The fees will vary based on the level of complexity involved. The appraisal will take several weeks, at a minimum.

The Least You Need to Know

➤ No average valuation can precisely value any company, but it can be used as a starting point for adding or subtracting value based on the specific company's situation.

➤ Working with an accountant when performing a detailed valuation analysis will keep your numbers consistent and can provide independent verification.

➤ A discounted cash flow analysis is helpful in determining the present value of future financial events, with CAPM providing a solid discount rate.

➤ Rule of thumb valuations are often used for small, secretive companies where detailed information is not available.

➤ Appraisers charge a fee for performing the valuation analysis, which might not be a bad idea if you have concerns about performing the analysis yourself.

Chapter 16

Financing the Deal

In This Chapter

➤ Understanding purchase finance options

➤ Using convertible securities

➤ Seller cautions when accepting stock

➤ Using the company to finance its own purchase

➤ Employment agreements and contingency payments

"Well, our fears have found us," said Judy as she smiled at the other owners who were seated around the conference room table. "We have a firm offer in our hands. It is for the full $12,000,000 asking price, but there are some interesting requests included by the buyers."

At that point, she turned the floor over to Mike, her CFO. He had really done most of the negotiating, and he knew the details far better than she did. But that would change in the next 48 hours, she vowed to herself.

Mike stepped up to the white board and started to write as he explained the offer.

"They are offering the full $12 million to be paid for as follows: they plan to pay $2 million in cash out of an XYZ account; they plan to get $2.8 million in bank financing secured by receivables and other assets; and they also have a company loan lined up for another $2 million. That is a total of $6.8 million in cash." Everyone around the table was smiling. Cash was good, and they all knew it.

"They also want us to have some skin in this deal, which is why they want us to also offer them a $2 million loan as convertible securities, paid out over 5 years and to accept $3.2

million in XYZ stock." Mike totaled the column to show that all of the numbers added up to $12 million, looked back at the group, and smiled. *"Any questions?"*

Setting a purchase price and having someone offer to buy your company for that price is one thing. Actually being paid that amount is another. Company acquisitions often involve large sums of money and complicated financing to make them work. Reading through this chapter will provide you with a better understanding of the various financing techniques, their benefits, and their pitfalls.

Why Financing Is Important

The need for financing might seem obvious, but it provides a back-to-basics starting point for this chapter.

Most of us have taken out loans when we purchased our homes. We struggle through the paperwork, complain about the loan officers, and grouse about the amount of time that it takes to approve the loan. And we still do it. Why? Simple. We don't have the cash on hand to pay for the house, or we don't want to substantially deplete our cash reserves.

Hot Tip

A dollar today is always worth more than a dollar in the future. Financing is a great way to shift the payment of today's dollar into the future, on someone else's credit.

We are using the bank's financial power to help us purchase the house. In financial jargon, we don't have the liquidity on hand, or we do but choose not to use it, to purchase the desired asset.

Even if you have the money, you still might not want to put it all into an asset purchase. Cash is the lifeblood of any household's finances and certainly of any business's. Running out of cash is like running out of food or air. You just don't last very long without it. Conserving cash is a sound business strategy, within reasons, and many companies fund purchases just to keep more cash on hand to cover them should the future take an unexpected downturn. (Remember the Quick Ratio analysis presented in Chapter 7, "Let the Ratios Be Your Guide"?)

And if one company purchases another for $20 million, it has to come up with $20 million. That is a lot of money for almost any company. Certainly, the larger companies have an easier time obtaining the money, but a $20 million purchase will be analyzed to determine the transaction's optimal financial structure.

The example I plan to use throughout this chapter assumes that XYZ Company purchased ABC Company for $12,000,000. Everyone is in agreement about the purchase price. Now XYZ must find a way to pay for it.

XYZ has several items of value that it can use to fund the purchase:

➤ ABC has its own assets, such as cash, Accounts Receivable, Inventory, and unnecessary assets that can be sold or used as collateral to obtain money.

➤ XYZ has its own assets that can be used as part of the purchase, sold, or used as collateral to obtain funding for the purchase.

➤ XYZ has stock that can be sold to obtain cash to pay the ABC purchase price tag.

➤ XYZ can provide the ABC owners with XYZ stock in exchange for a portion of the purchase price.

➤ Both ABC and XYZ are expected to continue in operation, and this should provide a future income stream. This income stream in combination with various assets might qualify either or both for a loan that can be then used to pay off ABC's owners.

As you can see, there are a number of financing options available to XYZ as it goes about financing the purchase.

The financing can be obtained from any number of sources, depending upon the amount needed and the security provided as collateral for the money. In addition, the specific security instruments used will be determined by the lenders, collateral available, and willingness of XYZ and the lenders to strike a financing deal.

Typical Financial Components

XYZ will most likely want to use as much of ABC's value as is possible to fund the purchase. Think about this concept for a moment. The seller is selling the company for any number of reasons, and the buyer agrees to pay the seller a specified amount of money. The buyer is then going to use the sold company as collateral to pay the buyer for the purchase. It really is elegant, if you think about it.

There is good news and bad news in this situation, depending on whether you are the buyer or seller. And the good news/bad news ratio changes with the deal structure, as you will see later in the example.

Hot Tip

Example Assumption: Assume that XYZ is willing to put $2,000,000 in cash into the purchase. It must still come up with $12,000,000 – $2,000,000 = $10,000,000 more to complete the purchase.

A first place to look for financing is a commercial lending bank. After all, ABC probably already has an established relationship with a commercial bank, so obtaining credit from this bank might be easier than working with an unknown.

As any businessperson knows, banks are rarely overly free in their lending practices. The line that "A bank will only give you money if you don't need it" is truer than most of us would like to admit, but it is not absolutely true.

In fact, in the initial stages of the acquisition funding you might find the commercial banker to be a friendly advocate within the bank and an ally in obtaining alternate financing.

Banks lend money expecting to be paid back. They never lend money expecting the loan to go into default, which, in turn, forces them to collect the collateral and then resell it to get their money back. However, banks lend as if that the worst case scenario is the one applicable to this transaction, whether it is true or not.

Banks will typically lend money on physical property like land or a building, accounts receivable, inventory, and equipment. Very small loan amounts might be provided to established customers on an unsecured basis, but almost always banks require a personal repayment guarantee on the part of the business owners anyway. They always plan to get their money.

Terms of Acquisition

Loan to value ratio   The total percentage of an asset's value against which a loan will be provided. An asset worth $1,000 against which the bank will loan up to a 60 percent loan to value ratio, means that you can borrow up to $600 using this asset as collateral.

Banks will lend based on a loan to value ratio. Loans secured by real estate might get you 50 to 60 percent of the real estate's appraised market value. If it is already financed to that amount, then it does you no good at all. However, if the property has built up substantial equity, it might be a source of purchase funding.

Inventory will also typically yield a 60 percent, or so, loan to value. Accounts receivable, depending on their quality, which is based on customer payment history, may get you as much as 80 percent loan to value. Equipment might get you as high as 50 percent, but don't count on that high of a loan value if it is computer equipment, since is well known to have very short market value life with rapid depreciation.

Using the $3 million in AR and inventory should get a loan from the bank of 60 percent of $3 million = $1.8 million. Using the real estate equity, the bank should be willing to refinance the underlying existing notes and also to fund a portion of the real estate market value up to 60 percent of the $2.0 million market value, but this nets only $1.0 million since there is an underlying $200,000 note already secured by the property ($2.0 million × 60% = $1.2 million. $1.2 million minus $200,000 = $1 million).

Hot Tip

Example Assumption: Assume that ABC has accounts receivable and inventory valued at $3 million. Also, assume that its real estate holdings have a market value of $2.0 million. Equipment liens equal approximately the equipment value.

Notice, though, that the bank is willing to provide the ABC/XYZ combination with $1.8 million (inventory/AR) and $1 million (real estate) = $2.8 million.

Of the $12 million purchase price, XYZ has now has $4.8 million, meaning that it still must come up with $7.2 million more to pay for the company.

Now here is another interesting point about the financing we have seen so far. Notice that we still have not really used up any of ABC's borrowing power, although it might look that way. Here is why.

The cash from XYZ is without repayment, so does not draw down ABC's borrowing power at all. The loans secured by AR and inventory will be repaid as soon as the AR is collected (60 days or so, at maximum) and the inventory is converted to cash (usually less than 6 months). Therefore, ABC is still in its initial debt condition for all intents and purposes.

ABC most likely still has a positive cash flow that can be used to pay off a loan. This is the next likely source of funding.

Debt Funding of the Purchase

It may turn out that the company has adequate positive cash flow to be able to repay a loan to help finance a portion of the purchase price. This type of funding has a potential down side in that it uses up the company's financial resources to help fund the purchase. If the loan is too large and the company falls onto hard time, it could loan-payment itself right out of business.

A standard commercial bank will typically not fund this type of financing, so debt financing must usually be obtained through alternate sources, such as venture capitalists, insurance companies, or merchant banks. It is basically secured by the agreement of the company to pay the interest and principal payments on the note.

Let's assume that ABC has sufficient cash flow to handle a $2 million loan, paid off over a 5 to 10 year period at some specified interest rate.

An important aspect of this type of financing is that the note is typically subordinate to the primary lender, which in most cases is the standard commercial lender.

This is an important consideration in the mind of the person providing this loan. If the company has financial troubles, the lender in the first position (the bank) is paid off before the subordinate lenders. Hopefully, there is enough value in the company to allow everyone to be paid, but the lender in the subordinate position will want some

Terms of Acquisition

Debt financing Occurs when a company takes out a loan to pay for things, such as special research projects, expansion, or the company purchase.

Highly leveraged When a company has committed so much of its value (and cash flow) to loan agreements that it has little left over to pay for anything else.

Subordinate lender A lender who is paid only after some other lender is paid in full.

level of compensation for the increased risk. There it is again. Risk and reward! See? You thought I was exaggerating earlier, didn't you?

To compensate for this increased risk, the subordinate lender will want a higher interest rate than the lender in first position. This is particularly true when you consider that the bank, in our example, is not only in first position but also has provided a loan secured by assets, which the subordinate lender does not have.

Expect to pay 1-3 percent, or more, incremental interest over that charged by a bank for the first position, secured loan. This may not seem like a lot of money, but it all adds up as every bit of financing cost removes little more of ABC's future financial flexibility.

At this point, the sellers have received over 50 percent of the sale price in cash ($6.8 million of the $12 million), which is pretty good. XYZ might now want to look to the sellers to help finance the rest of the price through a combination of loans, stock, and/or other financial methods.

> **Hot Tip**
>
> Notice that XYZ must still come up with another $5.2 million (the prior $7.2 million less the $2 million in subordinate loan).

The Strategic Aspects of the Deal

At this point, it is appropriate to talk about the strategic aspects of the transaction. The simple fact is that the buyer may only want the sellers to retain an active interest in the future operation of the company. This is very common when a small, privately held company is purchased, since the founder/owner is typically an integral part of the company's success. Losing that founder/owner might seriously decrease the future value of the company.

There are a number of ways to keep the prior owners interested:

1. Have the sellers retain a portion of the selling company's (ABC) stock. In this way, they have a direct vested interest in ABC's future performance.

2. The sellers could provide a loan to the buyer, which keeps the sellers interested because future performance will pay off the loan and poor performance will put the loan in jeopardy.

3. Employment agreements are set up between the seller and buyer, where the seller receives a set income for a period of three to five years, which is often higher than the seller's previous salary.

4. Contingent payments can be set up so that the seller gets paid a higher amount at a future date if the sold company meets, or exceeds, expected performance goals.

5. The seller can be asked to provide a loan in exchange for convertible securities, which provide a fixed return over a specified period of time and can later be converted into common stock, at the seller's discretion.

6. The seller is asked to take the buying company's stock (XYZ) in exchange for an equal value of seller stock (ABC). This is a less direct interest, but this keeps them both interested at some level.

Having the Sellers Retain Some Stock

This option keeps the sellers personally, and financially, interested in the selling company's future performance. Notice that this option only works if the selling company is kept as a separate financial entity and is not merged into the buyer's financial structure.

If you are a seller and agree to this as a financing option, I suggest that you negotiate some type of guaranteed "out clause" that allows you to recover the value left in your stock either by forcing the buying company to purchase the shares at some agreed upon price or by allowing you to sell the shares on the open market if the company is taken public.

Having the Sellers Lend the Buyer Money

The sellers have the ability to lend money to the buyer. There is nothing to stop a seller from offering the buyer a loan to be paid off over a specified number of years and at a premium interest rate. This note would almost definitely be subordinate to the commercial and merchant lenders, which means the interest rate on this note will likely be higher. Again, the buyer does not need to come up with the cash and the seller still has a vested interest in company operation.

Notice that this option really does not require that the seller maintain a management place in the company operations or on the board, which might pose a good solution for both companies. On the other hand, it does force the seller to put substance behind his or her commitments regarding expected future performance.

For this reason alone, many buyers will want the seller(s) to finance a portion of the sale. It minimizes the buyer's cash outlay, and risk, while also keeping the seller honest. After all, his or her future loan payments will have to come from

> **Hot Tip**
>
> The sellers will likely want to retain some level of management control, which might immediately cause problems for both the buyer and the seller. It is also possible that the sellers might want out completely, or the buyers may not want the former owner's interference. If either of these possibilities is true, this financing through stock transfer option is probably not viable.

future incomes generated along the lines of the pro-forma financial statements he or she presented as part of the prospectus.

Set Up an Employment Agreement with the Seller

Smaller sellers are often asked to stick around for a few years after the sale is finalized. In some cases, the buyer wants the seller to run the company for a period of time as a learning period for the buyer and as a transition period for prior customers, vendors, and employees.

Change is often viewed as scary, and minimizing the potentially negative perception associated with the change can help create a smoother transition. Keeping the prior management in place provides continuity while also providing a training ground for the buyers.

The seller usually demands a higher salary than previously received and should also negotiate protection should the new management not turn out to be to his or her liking. After all, why would a seller lock himself or herself into a five-year contractual obligation to perform a job he or she would never have taken in the first place? Sellers should always add protective language to this agreement that covers such items as changes in buyer management, resale of the purchased company, and other major business changes. If the employment agreement is considered a substantial part of the purchase price, an automatic escalation clause that pays all expected money up front should the employment agreement terminate for any action other than those of the seller should be seriously considered.

Contingent Future Payments

This is a hook that many entrepreneurs just cannot resist. "I will give you $1 today as we have already agreed. But if you can help me do what you already said can be done, I will instead give you $1.50 in two years." This is a contingent future payment arrangement in that a future payment is arranged that pays a premium to the seller if specific performance objectives are met.

Straight Talk

Employment agreements and contingent future payments are likely grounds for misunderstanding and hard feelings on the part of both buyer and seller. The seller must financially cover himself or herself should things happen as a direct result of the buyer's actions, which causes the seller to not achieve his or her goals. A minimum level should be negotiated as part of the initial agreement. The buyer puts any payments off into the future, while the seller doesn't put all of the contingent money at risk.

Contingent future payments are often used in conjunction with employment agreements. Are they fraught with risk for the seller? Yes, since he or she no longer has a controlling interest in the company. But is the potential of a lot more income in exchange for meeting certain, reasonably achievable, goals too enticing to pass up? Often, yes again.

This type of arrangement, along with the employment agreement, requires that the buyer and seller work together after the sale. If you are not comfortable with working together after the sale, you should seriously reconsider accepting or offering either of these longer term relationship arrangements.

The Seller Takes Convertible Securities as Payment

Convertible securities present an interesting financial option to both the buyer and the seller. A convertible security is a note or a loan that the seller offers to the buyer, which is paid off just like any other loan, with a few exceptions.

The convertible aspect comes into play, typically, toward the end of the loan's life. At that time, the seller, who is the holder of the note, can opt to accept company stock instead of cash payment as note payoff. This is a good option for the seller in that the note provides guaranteed income during the life of the note, making it less risky than accepting company stock.

As an added benefit to the seller, the convertible option allows the seller to take advantage of any stock appreciation that might have occurred over the life of the security. This could provide the best of both worlds for the seller: payments are received over the life of the security with the possibility of highly valued stock (or cash) provided at the end of the term.

The buyer benefits in that the company stock is not diluted at the time of purchase by having to issue the seller's shares at that time. That possibility has been pushed off into the future. Also beneficial is that only interest payments are made on the loan over its life, and all interest payments are deductible and the seller's payment has been successfully put off into the future. Future dollars are always worth less than today dollars. Remember?

> **Terms of Acquisition**
>
> **Stock dilution**   The offering of more company stock for sale when the net income of the company does not increase. The extra shares have the effect of dividing the same net income by more shares, which in turn decreases the earnings per share. This decrease will typically decrease the stock price via the price/earnings ratio.

The Seller Accepts the Buying Company's Stock

The seller is often asked to take the buying company's stock in exchange for a portion of the sale price. This can be an attractive option for both buyer and seller, but it holds some serious downside risk for the seller.

First, the number of shares that change hands is based on the relative valuation of both the selling and buying company stocks. Assume that ABC's shares are valued at $10 each, and XYZ's are valued at $20 each. This means that two shares of ABC stock equal the same value as one share of XYZ. So, 10,000 shares of ABC stock would turn into 5,000 shares of XYZ stock. And the exchange should be tax-free since we are assumed to be exchanging common shares of stock in ABC for shares of common stock in XYZ. See your tax professional for more complicated stock exchanges.

From the seller's perspective, he or she has given up shares in ABC for shares in XYZ. So far, so good. The question now is how valuable are XYZ's shares, really? Can they be traded freely? If not fully registered with the SEC, there might be restrictions on how many shares can be sold, by whom and by when. If the seller accepts a director position within the buyer's company, additional stock sale restrictions are imposed. In short, don't think that a stock exchange is a painless, risk free venture. It isn't.

Hot Tip

Sellers should review the information provided in Chapter 5, "The Various Business Arrangements," for the details regarding the benefits and pitfalls of stock transfers as payment for your company's purchase.

And what about the value of the buyer's stock? If it increases, then the seller is happy. If it drops, then the seller has sold that percentage of his or her company at a real discounted price. Notice that the seller is assuming future risks with respect to the performance of XYZ as a total entity, and not just the ABC portion. In this light, XYZ should be evaluated as an investment, not as a buyer, since the seller is buying a large chunk of XYZ's stock. As you well know by this point, a stock's value is based on its future earning potential. How does XYZ stack up?

From the buyer's perspective, a stock transfer is pretty attractive. It requires no cash outlay today and may only nominally dilute the buying company's stock. If the number of XYZ shares issued to purchase ABC are substantial compared to those already issued, XYZ's stock value might be substantially diluted, which will certainly attract the attention of XYZ's current shareholders. In either case, XYZ's management had better have a good financial story to tell its shareholders.

Overall ABC Purchase Financing Summary

Here is one way in which the purchase of ABC by XYZ could be financed as outlined as this chapter's example:

Financing the purchase of ABC by XYZ		
Original Sale Price	$12,000,000	
Cash Payment to ABC	$2,000,000	Cash from XYZ to ABC
Commercial Bank Loan	$2,800,000	Secured by real estate, AR, and inventory

Merchant Bank Loan	$2,000,000	For 5 years at loan rates + 3%
Loan from Seller	$2,000,000	Convertible securities for 5 years at loan rates + 2%
Stock from Buyer	$3,200,000	Transferred at $20 XYZ market share price.

Whether this deal is good or bad for either the buyer or the seller is dependent on the particular situation of both the buyer and seller. As you notice in the table, the buyer gets $6,800,000 in cash along with income obtained from the loan. In addition, the seller can benefit from XYZ stock increases, directly or indirectly resulting from the ABC purchase, through both the convertible security and the stock. The bad news is that a decrease in XYZ stock can seriously impact the overall selling price that the seller receives.

The buyer likes this deal because $4.8 million of it is provided by assets, which are only secured at 60 percent of value. The buyer only comes up with $2 million in cash to purchase a $12 million company! The balance is through stock, which may, or may not, materially affect XYZ's overall stock performance.

This is certainly not the only way to finance XYZ's purchase of ABC, but it illustrates many of the commonly used financing options so that you can evaluate them for your particular circumstances.

The Least You Need to Know

➤ Buyers must work with their lenders from early in the due diligence stages.

➤ The buyer's offer to the seller cannot be made until financing is in place, which makes working with lenders critical.

➤ Sellers can finance part of the purchase price through loans, convertible securities, or stock.

➤ Sellers should be cautious of transactions that include a large amount of stock, especially if that stock is not freely publicly traded.

➤ An asset-rich company is easier to finance, and sell, than one heavily leveraged, which sellers should consider when preparing to sell.

Part 5
Preparing to Sell Your Business

If you think that you can decide to sell your business today, put it on the market tomorrow, and then get top dollar for it, well, you are just mistaken. Sorry. Getting top dollar for your business means extensive advance planning. Part Five tells you how to get started.

Why Sell, Anyway?

In This Chapter

➤ Investigate your motivations for selling

➤ Timing the sale

➤ Family and close company special circumstances

➤ The dangers of a bored entrepreneur

➤ Selling to expand your dreams

Grace had always feared that this moment would come, and here it was. Across the table from her sat Michael, the husband of Grace's former partner who had recently passed away. He was clearly distraught over the loss of his wife, and he was looking for a way to get his life back on track.

"I know nothing about the daily operation of this business," said Michael. "Judy was the designer in the family, and you would definitely lose money if I started designing houses for you. Plus, I'm really tired right now, and don't feel that I can pick up where Judy left off."

Grace knew he was right. First off, Michael had no interior design expertise at all. Secondly, Judy had been the special design talent that had made them a household name in Austin. The name would carry over without Judy because other employees had picked up her style. Finally, Grace had wanted to expand, and Judy had always resisted.

Perhaps it was time to sell the company to a larger one. Michael could get the money he wanted, and Grace could get the expansion she wanted along with other management colleagues. She really didn't want to run this ship on her own.

The impetus to sell your company can come from any number of directions and at any time. The market could change, someone could pass away, an unsolicited company might offer to buy you, or the founders might simply get bored and want to do something different. Whatever the reason, selling is a big step that should not be taken lightly. Nevertheless, when it is time to sell, you want to be clear on your motivations, which better ensures that you get what you want out of the sale.

This chapter presents a number of reasons for selling your business; your situation might fit into one or several of the categories mentioned.

It's Valuable to Be on Top

Selling a hot company in a hot market is always better than the other way around. Let's face it. People want to associate with winners, and if your company is on a winning streak, people will be more likely to pay more for it.

Should financial markets alone determine whether you sell or not? Probably not. However, if you are going to sell, you and your shareholders are better served by selling while both the market and your company are in their best shape.

Straight Talk

The best part of being on top is that you are not generally under any pressure to sell. If the timing and the offered deal are right, then sell. If not, then wait. The down side of being on top is that everyone knows who you are, and if your company is publicly traded you might have unwelcome suitors trying to purchase in an unfriendly, or hostile, way. As with most things in life, you have to take the bad with the good.

Determining when your company performance is at its peak is often a job for a fortuneteller, but you can do some simple trend analysis to see where your company stands.

Here are a few simple exercises you can perform to see where you stand with respect to the rest of your market, in particular, and the overall market, in general:

➤ Has your company shown a profit for the last five fiscal quarters? If so, you are immediately a viable financial investment.

➤ Are your historical net-income-before-tax results increasing over the prior five quarters, or are they erratic in nature? Financial markets like consistency, and the more consistent the income figures the better your company looks.

➤ Has your company been gaining market share with respect to other companies in your industry? If so, you look even better. If not but your income continues to grow, it means the management is doing something right with respect to operations.

➤ Has your company recently obtained the rights to a patent, trademark, or other intellectual property item that has a long life and hot market potential? If so, selling now while the iron is hot may not be a bad idea. This is especially true if the technology is relatively unproven, such as might be the case with a new pharmaceutical drug where time may reveal unknown side effects related to taking the drug.

➤ Did your company just receive a major contract that extends over a number of years? This provides income consistency that is always attractive to a prospective buyer.

➤ Is your company in a hot market segment that is showing above-market-average stock price returns? If so, then you might want to sell even if some other financial parameters are not in optimal condition. Remember that you are always competing with other investments, and if the other investments are not performing as well as your company's stock, it is still a solid investment.

Any one of these reasons, along with numerous others, might be reason to assume that your company is on a solid upswing. A combination of several simply makes the case even stronger.

The point is that you must do some research for yourself to determine the performance of your company with respect to the others in the industry.

When the Market Drops Off

Playing the stock market is a lot like playing craps in Las Vegas. If you know the rules, you can even make money when the shooter (person with the dice) is losing. You can make money when they win and when they lose. It may sound a little unethical or unrealistic, but it is true none the less.

The same is true with the stock market, but the opportunities for making money in a down (bear) market are fewer than those in an increasing (bull) market.

The good news for you business owners is that a well-run company is good news in either a bear or a bull market. In a bull market, there is more money to go around, and there's a lot of optimism

Hot Tip

Waiting until you start to see a down-swing in your company's performance before you sell is generally not a good idea. Nobody knows for sure when an upswing will end, but everyone gets cold feet and more risk averse when things start to take a negative turn.

about the future, which generally allows you to command a higher price for your company. A bear market generally brings a less optimistic view of the future and its earnings potential, and companies will generally sell for a lower price, unless the company is well-run and/or has some particular strategic advantage. Somebody makes money in a bear market; it might as well be you and your shareholders.

Hot Tip

Throwing good money after bad is never a sound financial policy, although it is one that many of us unwittingly practice. If your company really is precariously positioned when assessed against an extended market downturn, you must look at either selling the company or acquiring the resources needed to get through the slow times. Waiting, and doing nothing, will only push a questionable situation into a negative one that could cost you and your shareholders dearly.

What if you are not one of those prepared companies? Should you sell in a bear market? This good question can only be answered by knowing the specifics of your company. Here are a few things to consider when making this decision:

➤ How is your particular market segment affected by the bear market? If it is expected to suffer and customers expect to cut back on purchases, this does not bode well for your company's future sales.

➤ If your company has the cash or credit reserves to weather an extended downturn, and your competition does not, you might be the last company standing when the bull market returns. This could be great news.

➤ Suppose, on the other hand, that your company has a large cash reserve on hand that is used up weathering the bear market. If the market downturn lasts longer than anticipated, you could put your company in a precarious position should you have to sell later.

➤ Selling a company with cash, receivables, and a good debt-equity ratio is much easier than the other way around.

➤ By the way, having too much of your company's assets in cash and receivables makes you a takeover target; the purchasing company simply wants to get its hands on your current assets.

If you believe that an active market downturn might take your company with it, I suggest that you move quickly and professionally toward selling your company. The earlier you sell, the more you will probably receive for your company. If things really get bad during the downturn, you are better off holding cash in your hand instead of stock in a company heading toward financial disaster.

When Technology Changes

How would you have liked to be the owner of a horse and buggy manufacturing company on the day that the first Ford automobile drove down the street? Or, how would you feel if you were the people at Western Electric who turned down Alexander Graham Bell when he offered to sell the patent rights to the telephone for $100,000?

Technology changes markets. And this has never been truer than today with the incredible impact of the Internet being felt in a more pronounced way every day.

Technological innovation rarely turns a market on its ear overnight, but it can do it over the span of a few years. If you are a company whose livelihood is jeopardized by the introduction of new technology from one of your competitors, you might look seriously at selling your company. Here are your basic choices when faced with this situation:

➤ You can develop your own technology that competes with that of this technologically advanced competitor. Advanced Micro Devices has done an excellent job in this area while competing with the Intel processors.

➤ You can band together with other affected companies to pool your resources in a defensive/offensive move against the new major threat. This might mean a merger or two, but the resulting consolidated company should be stronger and better able to weather the change.

➤ You could talk to the technologically advanced competitor and offer to sell strategic assets that will assist them in getting to market more quickly.

➤ Heck, you might even offer to buy the company that developed the new technology in the first place, and run the new product through your own distribution channels.

➤ Sometimes a lawsuit is filed against the new technology company with the underlying, and completely denied, intent of draining company resources. Distracting the newer company delays market penetration, and might even put the company out of business before it has a chance to do any substantial damage. This is called "legal blackmail," and it is commonly practiced when companies find themselves in a threatened circumstance.

One thing is sure. If you do not take some type of steps to protect yourself against major technological changes within your industry, you could end up like the guy watching the Ford roll down the street who figured it for a passing fancy. He probably wound up getting a job on the production line at Ford after bankrupting his buggy business.

I'm Bored—Let's Sell

Boredom has caused the downfall and sale of more small businesses than most people want to admit. Entrepreneurs like new ground and challenges. When the challenges turn into routine business operation, most entrepreneurs will look for ways to spice things up. If they do not get themselves under control, they can spice up a good business into a crisis situation, which is what entrepreneurs deal with best. Do you see a pattern forming here?

If you are an entrepreneur whose business is doing well, you should first congratulate yourself for a job well done. You should then look at the job you ended up with in your successful business. Some entrepreneurs have admitted to me that they would never have hired on to take the job they currently had, and the only reason they do it is that it is for their own company. They just don't like the daily administrative management of an established company, and they would like to get out to do something else.

Hot Tip

Entrepreneurs who treat the sale of their company as another challenge might find the process rewarding and stimulating. Those who treat it like losing their little baby will probably get less for the sale, and they will probably suffer more emotional upset in the process.

If you are in this position and have convinced yourself that you need new challenges, you might be better served by selling your company before you do something that compromises its financial condition.

If you sell to a larger company, they may want you to take on a larger responsibility within the acquiring company, which could provide all of the excitement your little entrepreneurial heart desires.

If you merge with another company, you might be needed to manage the new merged entity, which, once again, could be fun and different.

Selling should provide you with enough financial resources to start another company, knowing that you will probably have to sign non-compete agreements as part of the sale of your first company.

Selling also should provide you with the freedom and money needed to do some of the personal things that you ignored when making your first company a success. Hang gliding in the Andes mountains, anyone?

One entrepreneur friend sold his smaller company to a larger one that already had a national presence. He instantly moved the products produced by his smaller company to national level simply by selling to a larger one that fit his strategic desires.

Management or Family Squabbles

This next topic is an unfortunate fact of life, but it happens frequently in closely held companies. People don't always get along, and the higher the personal stakes the riper the opportunity for personality conflict.

More than one happy relationship has broken up over money, and a successful, or even unsuccessful, business can cause personal friction between shareholders or owners.

If that friction starts to creep into the daily operation of the company, it can undo years worth of work in a short period of time.

You might have expected that your children would run the business after you retired only to find out that they have no interest in the business, or that they are simply incompetent and would run it into the ground.

As mentioned elsewhere, the death of an owner, a majority shareholder, or even your death (sorry) will prompt the sale of a company. It might be to pay off the other partners in a partnership, or to divide up the deceased person's estate.

One member of a family run business might want a newer house, or a new child might be on the way. Consequently, this family member might want to hold his or her portion of the family

Buyer Beware

If you are looking to purchase a family owned/run business, you should spend some casual time with the family members themselves. These interactions can be complicated, and they will work substantially either for the benefit or for the detriment of the company. Either way, you inherit the family members and their relationships, after the purchase is finalized.

business as a liquid asset. This usually requires the sale of the corporation unless the other members decide to buy his or her share and have the financial resources to execute the purchase.

Family members have a power over other shareholders that is typically not possible in a conventional business environment. If I don't like a specific shareholder or officer in a publicly held corporation, so what? I don't have to spend Christmas with this person. I do with family members.

The Financial Stakes Are Too High

One area that most entrepreneurs rarely know about, or fully appreciate, is the impact a growing business will have on their personal financial picture. They want the business to grow, and they do everything in their power to make that happen. Then the creditors start to come into the picture and the entrepreneurs financial picture changes forever.

Any time a company obtains a loan for equipment, land, buildings, inventory purchases, expansion, or any of a number of other typical business needs, the lender almost always wants a personal guarantee from the primary stockholders that the loan will be repaid. Notice what just happened. The protection of your personal assets that was supposed to happen when you incorporated was just shot to pieces. The bank can now come after your personal assets if your corporation defaults on a loan.

When these loans are for a few thousand dollars, you rarely worry. When they grow to being hundreds of thousands, or millions of dollars, things change. Any of us can come up with a few thousand dollars, but I know of very few people who could come up with several million.

Hot Tip

Most major creditors will want a personal loan guarantee from any corporation shareholders with more than a 20 to 40 percent ownership stake. Few people understand this *de facto* requirement when starting their own business, but they definitely understand it the first time that they obtain a major loan and never, never forget it after that.

For this reason alone, some entrepreneur/owners decide to sell their company. What was once fun now holds their personal assets, and the financial well-being of their family, at risk. Some owners simply decide to get out. Selling is a viable way to accomplish this goal, but make sure that you understand the reality of your situation when you decide to sell.

Don't let your personal fears drive your decision, or you could end up with a purchase agreement that you later might regret. If your company is doing well, and from an objective viewpoint, is performing financially in an attractive manner, you should seriously consider holding out until you get what the company is really worth. Just because you suddenly get nervous doesn't mean that your company is now a bad risk. You are just nervous. Take a deep breath, go on a few customer calls, evaluate your most recent financial statements using the ratio analysis presented in Chapter 7, "Let the Ratios Be Your Guide," and then determine for yourself how things look.

You might still decide to sell, but the desperation should not be there. If you still feel a sense of foreboding, then sell. Your intuition might just be telling you something that doesn't appear in financial statements.

The Least You Need to Know

➤ It is usually better to sell when both your company performance and the overall market are at their best.

➤ A down market can spell opportunity for a well-run company that shows solid investment returns.

➤ Selling before reaching bottom allows you to keep more of what you worked for.

➤ Beware family and management squabbles both as a buyer and as a seller.

➤ If you are bored, find a hobby; sell the company if you find yourself disrupting the operations to add spice to your entrepreneurial life.

Chapter 18

Getting Ready to Sell

In This Chapter

➤ The importance of advance planning

➤ Systems make your company more attractive

➤ The importance of confidentiality

➤ Properly using your financial contacts

➤ Keeping key employees when selling

Mike and Jill, owners of a small manufacturing company that they have been trying to sell, looked at each other with frustration on their faces. They had a really interested buyer who, based on Mike and Jill's reputation alone, had at first seemed very open to moving to the next stages of the purchasing process. That was before he asked about personnel and manufacturing procedures. Mike and Jill explained to him that everyone on the production line knew how things were done and that when problems came up they could always go to Jim, the production supervisor, who had been in production since the company began.

This information wasn't good enough for the buyer. "I have no assurances that your people will stay on board if we purchase your company, and if anything happened to Jim it appears that most of your production knowledge would be lost with him," remarked the buyer.

Mike and Jill really wanted to tell him that he was wrong, but they both knew that he was right. They had even taken out an insurance policy on Jim just to cover themselves financially should something happen to him. They had always wanted to document what Jim knew, but they had always been too busy to take the time.

Jill turned to Mike and said, "I guess it's time to learn what Jim knows. I think he will work with us, since the more that the others know the less he has to be involved with the little stuff. He might actually get home at a reasonable hour and we might be able to sell to the next person who is really interested."

Mike shook his head as he pulled a quarter out of his pocket. If it came up heads, he would be the first to interview Jim; tails, it would be Jill's turn.

No better time to get started than today.

Preparing to Sell

This chapter runs through several highly recommended changes you can make to your business that will help it to sell at its maximum potential. Shift your thinking to a clear understanding that selling your business won't happen overnight. And to sell your business for its maximum potential requires advance work on your part. The good news is that all of the advance work you do improves your daily operation, which is good news whether you sell or not. It often turns out that the prospect of selling motivates us to make the improvements we wanted to do anyway.

Selling a business, like most things in life, is almost always more complicated than anyone expects. The single most important piece of advice I can give you on selling your business is to start preparing for the sale long before you actually decide to put it on the market.

Why? Simple. It takes time to get things set up in such a way that someone not familiar with your operation can see its intrinsic value.

Have you ever sold your house? If so, just before putting it on the market, you probably did all the things to the house that you had planned to do to while you were actually living in it. These might be putting on new siding, upgrading the windows, giving your bathrooms a facelift, adding that new roof, landscaping, and other things that make your house more attractive.

Straight Talk

Financial people get concerned when they see business people make radical decisions on fundamental business areas such as selling a business or changing top management personnel. If you plan to sell your business, and not raise a lot of eyebrows, you must be adequately prepared to present your personal reasons for selling along with the financial aspects of the sale. This is particularly true for small business owners who have likely had their business become their personal identity to the local business community.

I swore that I would make the changes (like the ones mentioned above) while I lived in the house, so that I could enjoy them, but almost always wound up making the most expensive repairs at the end. Why? Because it improved the resale value of the home, allowing me to get the highest possible selling price for my home. And I could never justify the time and expense required to make the changes while I was simply living in the house.

The same logic often applies to your business, which makes little sense. Start early getting it ready for sale. Early can mean as much as two or three years before actually putting it up for sale. The earlier you start the more natural the changes will appear to a prospective buyer and the better your business will run—which is a good thing, whether the business sells or not.

Make Sure the Money Adds Up

The reason you and everyone else start a business is to make money. It doesn't mean that you don't like what you do; it just means that making money is a business fact of life.

As soon as you possibly can, you need to prepare valid financial statements that can stand up to close scrutiny by a trained accounting professional. It is never too early to get these statements accurate and financially consistent. Those of you familiar with my business philosophy know that I strongly believe in automating your accounting procedures from the start. You will have to automate eventually, so you might as well do it right from the beginning. At some point you will need financial statements for either your own management purposes or to work with financial colleagues, such as a bank or investor.

If you do not have financial statements that can be credibly reviewed by a prospective buyer's accountant, you have started out the sale process on shaky ground. After all, you are trying to convince someone else who is most likely not familiar with your business that owning your business is a solid financial decision. How can that person make this determination without comprehensive, consistent, and current financial statements?

To gain the confidence of prospective buyers, you must create a detailed review of your financial and accounting procedures and determine how your financial statements will look to someone who is not familiar with, or emotionally involved with, your business. If the statements make sense, you are probably in good shape. If the financial statements only raise more questions about the financial aspects of the company, you probably

Hot Tip

For more information on financial statements, refer to Chapters 6, "The Financials Speak for Themselves," and 7, "Let the Ratios Be Your Guide," of this book or to my other book, *The Complete Idiot's Guide® to Starting Your Own Business, Second Edition.*

need changes to your financial reporting processes or the data itself needs careful evaluation.

If, after a close look, you find that your company is in great financial shape, congratulate yourself. If you find problems or just suspect that something is wrong (gut instinct), you need to engage an accountant to review your financials with an eye for finding any inconsistencies that might give rise to discrepancies (accounting errors) that might negatively impact your statements. If inconsistencies are not found, a further look at operations is required.

Straight Talk

I used QuickBooks for my accounting needs with my last business. Being busy, I was not rigorous about verifying the entered accounting data and rarely took the time to evaluate the financial management aspects of my company. I showed the financial statements to my banker while applying for a line of credit, and he mentioned that some of the numbers did not make sense to him. He also noted that my salary expenses were too high for a company my size. He suggested that I reduce my employees by one person. I initially negated his suggestion but then went back and looked at the numbers with an objective eye only to find out that he was right. Letting a person go opened up enough financial breathing room, which allowed me to save up a financial cushion.

Systemize Your Processes

Have you ever talked to someone about something that you cared about dearly and found that they just didn't care? Or perhaps they didn't understand? Or perhaps you were so close to the situation that you assumed that they knew what you knew, which is almost never the case? In conversations with my spouse, it could be a combination of any or all of the above. But she is stuck with me and we eventually find out where communication broke down, getting the conversation back on track. It often costs me an expensive dinner, but problems always get worked out.

You might not get more than one chance to convince a prospective buyer that purchasing your company is a solid investment. You need to "tell your story" to a prospective buyer. You want to remove as much uncertainty from the communication as you can.

Understanding what you have to sell is important or you cannot truly appreciate its value to an objective party. In addition, the buyer wants to understand what he or she is buying and your word about how things work just isn't enough. No offense meant.

As soon as you think that you might want to sell your business, you should start looking at it as a system—that is, a process of everyday employee activities that have been created into a routine that anyone on the outside can learn and follow.

Systems have inputs and outputs. Between the input and output is a process of some kind. If you are a manufacturing company, your inputs are typically raw materials and product specification information. Your output is typically a final product that meets that specification, which is then shipped to the customer. The process involves all of the work done to get the project from the input to the output.

If you are a services company, your input is some type of work request from the customer. It may require some supplies and the labor of your skilled people. The output is the desired end result of work done by your company, which might be a clean building for a cleaning service or a report for a consulting company.

If your people "just know" how to do things and much of that "just knowing" is not documented, you are now selling a concept. There is nothing tangible that you can show prospective buyers, convincing them that you have been anything more than lucky. Consistently lucky, maybe, but lucky just the same. How does that buyer understand that there is really a process in place—one that can be repeated? It is your job to help him or her get to that level of understanding.

So, start looking at every aspect of your business for any possibility of its being systemized.

Procedure Manuals Are Sellable

Systemizing also applies to the administrative aspects of your company. Assume that you have a two week vacation policy that isn't written down but everyone knows exists. This has worked well in the past and you fully intend to maintain this policy. How do you prove to a prospective buyer that this is your policy? You can tell them that this is your policy, but they must now verify the statement with employee interviews and reviews of past payroll records.

Terms of Acquisition

System   Is a process of turning daily routines that you or your employees "just know" how to do into specific procedures that someone else can learn and follow.

Input   Refers to the various items and/or skills required to make a process work properly.

Output   Is the final result of the process.

Terms of Acquisition

Policies   The internal laws around which employees operate, typically including guidelines for vacation, sick leave, and other rules.

Procedures   Deal with operational topics, such as the creation of a final report, performing an audit, or testing a particular product. They often include detailed, step-by-step instructions for performing specific tasks.

However, a better way to go is to simply include the specific details of your vacation policy in your corporate policy manual. Why? Because it is in print, it is published internally, and it is theoretically in the hands of your employees. This is no longer a thing that exists only in your head or in their minds. It's a policy that exists in the collective thinking of the organization. It simply makes it more real when written down.

Straight Talk

People respond well to physical evidence that something exists. Showing a person one of my books always reinforces my credibility more than simply telling someone that I am an author. When I tell people that I am the author of over a dozen books, they perhaps politely ask a few questions and then change the subject. End of discussion. If I tell them I am a writer and then place one of my books on the table, they look at the book, see my name, and invariably say with surprise, "You wrote this?" The same is true for procedures. Telling someone that you follow specific procedures is one thing. Giving him or her a procedures manual shows that person that it's for real.

Policies are those internal guidelines around which employees operate, almost like the "laws" of the company. They usually include guidelines for such things as vacation, sick leave, hours of operation, dress codes, anti-theft, and other rules. A policies manual is a collection of all company policies that are used by employees for determining proper conduct under specific circumstances.

Procedures usually deal with operational topics, such as the creation of a final report, performing an audit, or testing a particular product. They often include detailed, step-by-step instructions for performing specific tasks. A procedures manual is a central location where procedures are stored so that employees can refer to them as required in the performance of their operational duties.

A word of caution is due at this point. Make sure that your procedures manual is current or it can do more harm than good. You need to talk-the-talk and walk-the-walk, meaning that you actually need to follow the procedures outlined in the manual. If the prospective buyers compare your actual procedures with those outlined in the book and find a discrepancy, you might wind up with a perceived integrity problem on your hands—which is probably the worst thing that could happen to you when selling your business. Once they start to question the truth of what you say, the transaction almost always stalls, falls apart, or costs you something else as part of the negotiations. After all, would you completely trust someone who had already misrepresented the truth to you?

Automation provides an excellent foundation for establishing and following procedures. Accounting procedures can be built right into the software. Commercially available or custom developed applications can be used for maintaining marketing communications and sales contact histories. Materials reporting (MRP) systems can be used to track raw inventory, work in progress, and finished goods that are ready to sell.

My point is that working with automation requires that you formalize your thinking and standardize your procedures. Only standardized procedures can be implemented by a computer, since it really cannot make any unpredicted, unanticipated decisions on its own. The good news is that it decreases the dependence on the human being. The bad news is that automation requires substantial amounts of time and/or money in the beginning, along with a sustaining, periodic investment to keep things current into the future.

Formalize Customer Agreements

Handshake agreements work with many established customers. I have closed deals for tens-of-thousands of dollars with large, established customers simply on the word of my key contact. My philosophy is one should always try to get it in writing as a precaution should something happen to that person or should the project not work out to everyone's satisfaction. But I have also had long-term arrangements with customers that never involved a written contract simply because getting it in writing was not feasible, and I felt the customer was a solid credit risk. This often happened when dealing with municipalities where the paperwork involved with a contract is complicated, and I know that a governmental agency will pay its bills. I also had an unwritten, long-term arrangement with IBM, who always paid on time and presented minimal credit risk.

Terms of Acquisition

Raw inventory This consists of asset items that were purchased so that they can be combined to create a finished product. It includes items like screws, nuts, paper, ink, wire, and other basic materials.

Work in progress Designates asset items that are in the process of being converted from raw materials into finished goods that can then be resold. This is sometimes called WIP by manufacturing folks.

Finished goods These are items ready for sale to a customer. Notice that raw inventory, combined with some type of a process, creates finished goods.

When you sell your business, your customer relationships become one of your most prized assets. If those assets are not documented, the verification of those relationships becomes more difficult. For this reason, I suggest that you take a close look at creating a standardized agreement that you sign with your customers. This takes the guesswork out of your existing relationships, and it provides another level of confidence to prospective buyers.

You will benefit today from standardizing your agreements. It's easier for you to deal with customer agreement problems when everyone signs substantially the same

Seller Beware

While I do recommend customer agreements in general, keep in mind that customers can react in strange ways when you try to formalize what has traditionally been an informal relationship. If it comes down to a choice between keeping the customer and formalizing the agreement, always keep the customer. An agreement without a customer is useless, where a customer without an agreement can still be a customer for years to come.

Hot Tip

Your banker can be a potential ally. You are the president of your company, and you deal with your banker. This means that your banker also deals with other business presidents. He or she has also seen business plans from various companies just as he or she has seen yours. Do you see a pattern forming here?

agreement. When every agreement is an exercise in creativity, it makes it more difficult to keep them all straight. And it also makes it more difficult for your sales people to sell, since your customers know that everything is negotiable if they can get to you.

I have found that standardized terms and conditions, backed up by a written agreement, is the least disruptive, most productive process. And, it will make it easier to sell your business later on.

Let Your Bank Know—in Confidence

Contrary to what you may think, your banker is not a penny-pinching adversary, but actually a potential ally. It is important that you let your banker know about major financial changes, especially if you have loans or other agreements that define what you can and cannot do with respect to business ownership.

The bank just wants to make sure that any outstanding loans it has made to you and your company will be repaid. New ownership adds a new risk into the banker's mind, and you should be prepared to minimize their perception of the risks. And the new owners might have to take over your financial obligations, including those to your bank, so it makes sense to involve them in your plans.

You do also want to ensure that your banker knows from the start that you and the business are not in financial trouble—unless you really are in trouble and think that the bank can help you out. The last thing you want is for the bank to call a loan when you are trying to make the company look as financially solvent as possible. Another thing to avoid is having your banker find out from a source other than you that your company is up for sale. They will wonder why you didn't tell them yourself, and you are once again on the defensive for what would otherwise be considered a sound business move on your part.

How much should you tell your banker? Only what they "need-to-know" (see below for more on this). Your banker has a fiduciary responsibility first to the bank and secondly to you, which means that he or she will act first in the bank's best interest and secondly in your best interest. Your banker cannot ethically discuss your financial situation with anyone outside of the bank without your permission, so don't expect your banker to talk about your sale without you specifically authorizing him or her to do so, either verbally or in writing.

Letting your banker know that your company is for sale, and allowing him or her to discuss it with specific other companies who might be prospective buyers, may get your business presented to the executive levels of that company. And having it referred from your banker adds credibility to your selling efforts. Working with your banker is always an interesting balancing act, and the act continues when you decide to sell your company. As with most things in life, honesty is the best policy, and that certainly applies here.

Keep It to Yourself

Honesty may be the best policy, but providing information on a need-to-know basis is in a solid second place.

You and the other members of your staff who are directly involved with the sale of the company are the only ones who need to know about it. At some point, if your company is for sale for a long period of time, word will get out and you will have to address your employees. But that time is usually somewhere down the road, and not in the early stages of the sale process.

Terms of Acquisition

Need to know basis This expression refers to when a person reveals information only to those people who absolutely must know that particular piece of information.

Letting even little items slip can cost you dearly while you are trying to sell the company. If employees think that the company is for sale because of financial problems, they may decide to start job hunting. If they succeed and leave your company, you have decreased the value of your company to a prospective buyer. If they succeed and your company does not sell, your daily operations have been hampered by their loss and for no real reason.

Finally, people might start assuming that you, a principle member of the company, are planning to leave the company. If they are there to work specifically for you, they might leave for any number of personal reasons that have nothing to do with business or money. And if the company, once again, does not sell, you have lost key employees and some credibility for no reason at all. Needless to say, all of these problems could be avoided if the sale is kept secret until finally completed.

Breaking the News

In reality, no matter how secretive you are, the word eventually gets out. Secretaries type and copy documents that will be related to the sale. People will see changes around the company and speculate on your motivations. If you leave their minds to work in a vacuum, they could very well come up with disaster scenarios that are far

Seller Beware

If employees speculate that the potential buyer is someone for whom they would not work, they might start job hunting. Remember that you straddle the distance between the new buyer and your employees until the sale is completed.

worse than, or have nothing to do with, what is really going on. At some point, you are going to tell your employees something, and you should plan that strategy from the beginning.

When you do break the news, make sure that you present it in a way that is beneficial to the employees, customers, and other owners. If they think that you are being greedy, you might have a lot of resentful people on your hands. If they think that their jobs are in jeopardy, they might jump ship. You must be sensitive to their side of the conversation and prepare your presentation so that it presents things in the most positive light for everyone involved.

Here are a few things to consider when finally relaying the information to employees, customers, and other owners:

➤ Remember to present the information in a way that is positive for those listening.

➤ If you have a gripe about the new owners, keep it to yourself. That is your problem, and it should not become your employees.

➤ Let them know that their jobs are not in jeopardy, or that those who are caught in reorganization will be given proper financial and personal consideration.

➤ Perhaps you are far enough along in the sale process that you can present the new owners. A favorable handoff from you to them is like gold to the new owners.

➤ Make sure that the new owners understand the impact of their statements on your employees. You know them better than the new owners do, and you might help them avoid mistakes during the transition period.

➤ Keep the details of your arrangement to yourself, and simply let them know that you are satisfied with the deal and that you are in no personal jeopardy. Your old employees might be more dedicated to you than you think, and you want to put their minds at ease with respect to your side of the sale.

Make Tomorrow Look Just Like Today

The most important thing that you must do in selling your company is also perhaps the most difficult. You must make tomorrow look just like today. By this I mean that employees, customers, vendors, creditors, and other owners must not see a major disruption of standard business operations. If you are going nuts inside, don't display it at work. Get it out of your system with a friend, a family member, or by taking up kickboxing. Whatever it takes to keep the ship on course.

Straight Talk

I usually favor more communication over less, but I believe that the stages of negotiations involved with selling your business should be kept to yourself and/or those on your core staff. Your emotional ups and downs, which will almost always happen as you progress through the sale stages, can ripple through the rest of the company. This is rarely a good thing, and it should be avoided. You might very well leave the company after the sale is completed, but the employees will likely stay on. Keep it to yourself until it is time to let everyone else in on the details.

Remember that change is frightening to most people. The more perceived risk that they associate with your decisions the more worried they will be that something will go wrong. As a result, they will be watching for any signs of change. Nobody ever complains about a positive change, such as a salary increase. Negative change, be it ever so slight, even something as seemingly minor as changing from a name-brand coffee to generic can raise flags in people's minds, causing them anxiety and costing you the time and energy required to keep their fears under control.

Note that if your intention is keep "business as usual" once a sale becomes public knowledge, there is no real reason for people to get anxious. There is no guarantee that people won't still get anxious, but without real justification for their fears, most emotionally healthy people will also treat you in a "business as usual" way.

If your business is in turmoil, it will be less attractive to a prospective buyer. This makes your business more difficult to sell and will probably cost you money due to an uncertainty-induced sale price reduction. Risk/reward. The higher the perceived risk on the buyer's side the more reward they will want—which means a drop in sale price or the negotiation of less favorable terms for you.

Help the Buyer with Financing

Once again, let's talk about your banker. Whoever buys your business will have to finance the purchase. If it is Bill Gates, congratulations—I think. At least he should have the money to fund the purchase himself. However, the last time I looked there was only one Bill Gates, which means that your potential buyers will probably need to find ways to come up with some money.

Anyone providing credit to the buyer will primarily be interested in two things when evaluating the extension of credit: How solid is the business and how credible is the buyer?

Your current creditors already know your business. The fact that they have already lent you money means that they believed in you and your business at least once. I suggest that you involve them in the sale process and ask them if they might consider providing credit to the new buyer. You might be doing your creditors, the buyer, and yourself a favor.

Be careful, however, when approaching your creditors to help your potential buyer; there may be a conflict of interest. They have an interest in seeing the company sold so that they can recover their existing loans, and they also want to ensure that that the new buyer will properly repay existing debts that carry over with the sale. But, if they are providing credit to the new buyer, they want to see that the company does not wind up with so much debt that it becomes a financial risk. Make sure that you select creditors who won't try to squeeze you, but will work with you to find the best deal for all involved parties.

You probably already have creditor relationships that you have not used in part of your current operation. Determine which of these creditors would be open to funding a new, credible buyer. Then sell them on the future potential of your business. This lets them know your business reasons for wanting to sell and lays the groundwork for the new, credit-worthy buyer.

The more attractive your business looks and the easier you make it to finance the sale, the more likely you are to sell in a reasonable timeframe while also getting the price you want.

The Least You Need to Know

➤ Companies that have systems in place are less risky to buy and consequently easier to sell.

➤ Accounting processes and statements must be under control so that they present a consistent and accurate picture of your company's financial health.

➤ A procedure manual allows the buyer to have something more than your word on how things are done at your company.

➤ A seller should only reveal information to those people who have a "need-to-know"—until the word hits the street.

➤ When employees, creditors, vendors, and customers are about to find out about your intention to sell, you are best served by telling them the facts yourself.

➤ Helping your buyer find financiers can be very helpful to all parties involved—but be cautious about whom you approach.

Preparing Your Financials

"These numbers don't look very good," thought Philip. "I know that we are making money, but it sure doesn't look like it from these financial statements."

And that had pretty much been the reaction of the prospective buyers, a publicly owned company, who had just today looked at his financial statements. Philip told them about some of his aggressive expense/depreciation/deduction policies, but they seemed to lose interest after spending a few minutes with the statements.

There was value in his company. He knew that. He just had to figure out how to display that value financially in a way that the bean counters would understand.

We can talk all we want about strategy and planning, but ultimately, any business venture comes down to an assessment of the financial situation. If your financial reports are not right, your credibility will be undermined along with the price you will receive for your company.

In this chapter, we look at the financial aspects of selling your company. Advance preparation will make your financial statements and you look better. That translates into a quicker sale and higher sales dollars when the offers finally come.

The Financials Must Sell Themselves

The ultimate goal of everything you create or do with respect to the sale of your company should be clearly targeted toward improving the likelihood of that sale happening. This is also true of any financial decisions you make during the period of the sale.

Hot Tip

You cannot take back any historical expenses, but you can control what you spend from this point forward.

Most larger companies have dedicated finance and accounting departments, which typically have trained professionals who pride themselves on the precise accuracy of their accounting numbers. As an employee, I always thought these people got in the way of doing business, and I still often think that I was right. (Of course!)

However, as I have matured as a businessperson and run several of my own businesses, I have come to not only appreciate but rely on valid accounting information. You really can't make effective financial decisions if you don't know the current state of your finances. These departments, although they often drive me nuts and should not dictate what happens in the company, are an integral part of effectively, and profitably, running a company.

Sorry for the digression, but I feel better. Hope you do too. Thanks for listening. Back to the topic of this section.

Whoever purchases your company is going to go over your financials with a magnifying glass, so they have to be correct. I cannot emphasize this enough. It is not just that your company will not sell if your financials are questionable, but I assure you that the process will be longer, harder, and almost definitely cost you money with respect to the sale price.

Here are a few important points to understand when evaluating the current status of your financial reports:

➤ You have developed accounting procedures over the years that might be either documented or tacit. Those procedures are reflected in the financial statements.

➤ A listing of your current accounting and financial reporting procedures and policies is a good place to start. This list tells the reader how the numbers were prepared, which gives a basis of comparison against what would normally be expected.

➤ If you are a publicly traded company, your historical financial reports are pretty well locked in by the information that you publicly disclosed. Changing these numbers at a later date is possibly illegal and certainly expensive.

➤ Privately held, small companies, usually take more liberties with their financial procedures and accounting, since they are the only ones, other than the IRS, to whom reporting must be done. This reporting is almost always prepared to minimize net income, which also minimizes taxes. (See recasting in the next section.)

➤ Obvious unusual items, like a negative liability account balance or a negative expense, will raise flags. If they are REALLY supposed to be there, then you should be ready to explain them. More likely, there is an accounting error somewhere that needs correction before you let others review the reports.

It may appear, once again, as though I am pushing you in the direction of advance preparation to avoid future problems, instead of waiting until the problem finds you. Well, I am.

Straight Talk

I recently sold a house with only the inspection pending as a contingency. My real estate agent suggested that I change the filter on the furnace, so that it looks like it was changed on a regular basis. A clean filter implies a clean house. A dirty filter implies less attention to maintenance, which might make the inspector look harder for defects. Overly cautious? Maybe. But I changed the filter, and things appear to be moving to close as planned. Replace a 79¢ filter to make an overall inspection go more smoothly. That is a solid return on investment in my book.

An ounce of prevention may very well save you hours of dancing and unnecessary expenses finding a financial cure.

Historical Income and Net Worth Reports

Buyers purchase a company expecting some future performance levels. Determining the most likely future performance levels is often based on past performance. Therefore, although buyers purchase their version of the future, they often base their future expectations on past performance.

You and I do the same thing every day of our lives, but we may not be so blatant about it. Assume that you have a friend who is consistently 30 minutes late. He or she asks to meet with you at 3:00p.m.. Will you push to arrive on time? We all will do our best, but if your past experience tells you that the other person will most likely NOT be there at 3:00, you might not worry as much about arriving on time.

The same overall impression is left with a trained financial person who reads a set of historical financial reports. They make assumptions about your past performance against which your future projections are compared. If the future doesn't track with the past, you had better have a story to tell regarding the discrepancy. Just don't count on being lucky, and don't just hope that they won't find it. More than likely, they will.

Therefore, the trick is to create the historical reports with as much positively oriented accuracy as possible and to then make a pro-forma projection of a reasonable future based on that past.

Should you have recent large changes to the financial condition of the company that cause the future projections to deviate substantially from the past, explain those changes in the financial report footnotes. Don't leave them unanswered because the questions will come up, putting you on the defensive.

Track your company's historical information for the past three to five years. Only go for three years if years four and five add little to the picture or can seriously undermine your current state. Most business people will discount those years anyway if the recent years show markedly better performance.

Recasting for Small Businesses

You small business owners have a special situation that must be addressed, especially if you are potentially selling to a publicly held company.

You manage your company to minimize net income, while obviously making a solid personal income. A publicly held company manages to maximize net income, which increases earnings, which increases the stock value when multiplied by the PE ratio. Remember all of this from Chapters 6, "The Financials Speak for Themselves," 7, "Let the Ratios Be Your Guide," and 8, "Making It All Less Taxing?"

Terms of Acquisition

Recasting This is the process of removing unnecessary expenses from historical financial statements so that they more accurately reflect a realistic financial assessment of performance. It is often done by small companies to remove "special" expenses incurred to decrease net income and taxes.

Assume, for example, that the prospective buyer is a publicly held company that shows a 15 percent net income before tax (NIBT) on sales of $10 million. Also, assume that this company has a stock price of $15. This means that every dollar of annually reported earnings, when divided by the total number of shares, increases the share price by $15. After all, isn't this what the PE ratio means?

This is the level of future performance that the investing public thinks is reasonable for this company, or they wouldn't purchase a stock with this particular set of earnings, price, and PE ratio.

Now assume that this company purchases your company, which you have specifically managed to show a loss of $100,000 for each of the last two years. Assume also that your company has annual sales of $2 million, or 20 percent of the parent (buying) company's total annual revenues. Your accounting approach minimizes your taxes, which was good as far as you were concerned. However, it is likely not good news for the buyers.

Notice that the income performance of the purchased company will decrease after the purchase. Here is why. A dollar in sales revenue for the purchased company returns a loss of 10 cents. Take a look at the numbers shown in the following situation. (Assume that no dividends are paid by either company and that the effect of taxes can be neglected, only to simplify the analysis.)

➤ The company's total projected revenues were previously $10 million, and are now $12 million after the purchase.

➤ The NIBT for the parent company used to be $1.5 million, or 15 percent of $10 million. It is now $1.4 million ($1.5 million – $100,000) or 14 percent.

➤ Notice that the earnings will drop, which now means that the amount of pro-rated earnings that can be multiplied by the PE ratio also drops, although the number of outstanding shares remains the same. The net effect is a drop in the stock price.

➤ If the buying company's management is compensated based on stock performance, they just lost personal income because the stock price just dropped as a result of the acquisition.

➤ Slick accounting and financial maneuvering on your part just put a huge boulder in the path of selling your company to a publicly held buyer.

This is an extreme example because you cannot consistently operate your company at a loss or the IRS will want to chat with you. But the point should come across that diminishing your earnings, which is great for a small business, is not great for a publicly held company and therefore must be addressed.

Assume that you have paid yourself, or other family members, a higher salary than they would have normally received on the open market. These higher expense levels will disappear when the company is sold since the newer management will not have the emotional reason for helping them, or you, out in this same way. Assume that you have a car allowance for each of your managers, who also happen to be relatives. These expenses will likely also go away with the purchase. Perhaps you belong to a country club, where you transact business four days a week. (Uh-huh! How's your tee shot?) These expenses will likely also not be paid by the buying company.

Hot Tip

Never forget that you cannot change the past, but you can shape the buyer's perception of the future. That is the point of recasting your financial statements.

Notice that all of these expenses help you or your family out while decreasing net income, which ultimately decreases taxes. The buyer must be made aware of these discretionary expenses, and realize that they will not be incurred after the company is sold. In fact, taking them out of the past financial reporting might actually show that the company made a profit. This is recasting your financial statements.

Re-creating the past financial reports so that they do not include these non-transferred expenses recasts them in a light that the buyer can appreciate. Now, the buyer can validly assess the value of your company based on a realistic set of financial numbers. Notice that if your recasted numbers show the company making a profit, or possibly even a NIBT, of higher than 15 percent, you are now adding to the share price instead of hurting it. Your company instantly became more attractive to the publicly held corporate buyer. Get the picture?

Take a look at the following figure to see how recasting your historical financial reports can turn a company that appears to be losing money into one that shows a positive NIBT. Assume that your salespeople (your brother and sister) get an 8 percent commission instead of the buying company's standard 5 percent; that you have an extra $215,000 in salaries that you pay your wife, mother, children, cousin, and other family members that would not transfer to the new owner; and that $25,000 in various G&A expenses would not be needed, or approved, by the new owner's internal accounting policy.

Removing the impact of these expense numbers by adding them back into the NIBT number shown (–$100,000) proves to the buyers that a more realistic assessment of their expected income is a positive $200,000 or 10 percent of sales. This may not match our sample buyer's goal of 15 percent, but it is a lot better than losing $100,000.

Is recasting starting to make sense to you? It should at this point.

Straight Talk

It is OK to be a small business owner who aggressively, and legally, does everything possible to reduce the impact of taxes by reducing income. You just don't want your past financial manipulations to get in the way of the prospective buyer seeing the true financial value in your company.

Creating Pro-Forma Financial Reports

Historical financial performance reporting is relatively cut and dry. Although it allows for some level of creativity, you are still working with past numbers that have already happened. The issue is not whether the numbers exist; the issue is where they should be reported. So far so good? Good.

Predicting the future is not as simple, and it is certainly open to interpretation. After all, no one can know what will happen in the future until it becomes the past. OK. Enough Zen. My point is that the future is open to interpretation and that buyers purchase the future. Bridging the gap between the past and the future is the role of the pro-forma financial statements.

Pro-Forma Income Statement	Purchase Year				
	FY 1998	FY 1999	FY 2000	FY 2001	FY 2002
Sales and COGS:					
Sales Revenue	2,000,000	2,300,000	2,645,000	3,041,750	3,498,013
Cost of Goods Sold	1,200,000	1,380,000	1,587,000	1,825,050	2,098,808
Gross Profit	800,000	920,000	1,058,000	1,216,700	1,399,205
Operating Expenses:					
Rent	65,000	68,900	73,034	77,416	82,061
Utilities	32,000	33,920	35,955	38,113	40,399
Depreciation	12,000	12,720	13,483	14,292	15,150
Salaries	565,000	598,900	634,834	672,924	713,299
General and Administrative	66,000	69,960	74,158	78,607	83,323
Commissions	160,000	169,600	179,776	190,563	201,996
Total Operating Expenses	900,000	954,000	1,011,240	1,071,914	1,136,229
Net Income Before Taxa (NIBT)	(100,000)	(34,000)	46,760	144,786	262,976
Recasting Adjustments					
Adjust Commissions from 8% to 5%:	60,000	63,600	67,416	71,461	75,749
Adjust Salaries to Post Purchase Levels:	215,000	227,900	241,574	256,068	271,433
Adjust G&A for Misc Expenses:	25,000	26,500	28,090	29,775	31,562
Recasted NIBT Values	200,000	284,000	383,840	502,090	641,719
NIBT as Percentage of Sales Revenue:	10%	12%	15%	17%	18%
Estimated Annual Sales Growth:	15%				
Estimated Operating Expense Increase:	6%				

Recasting Income Statement Numbers

		FY 20XX
Sales and COGS:		
Sales Revenue		2,000,000
Cost of Goods Sold		1,200,000
Gross Profit		800,000
Operating Expenses:		
Rent	65,000	
Utilities	32,000	
Depreciation	12,000	
Salaries	565,000	
General and Administrative	66,000	
Commissions	160,000	
Total Operating Expenses		900,000
Net Income Before Tax		(100,000)
Recasting Adjustments		
Adjust Commissions from 8% to 5%:		60,000
Adjust Salaries to Post Purchase Levels:		215,000
Adjust G&A for Misc Expenses:		25,000
Recasted NIBT Values		200,000

The preceding figure displays three things:

1. Two prior years of income performance
2. Income performance in the year of sale, which is noted as such
3. Two years of estimated future income performance

It also shows the recasted NIBT for both historical and future fiscal years. How you display the information is up to you; you can use this figure as a starting point.

Straight Talk

Lawyers sometimes claim that pro-forma statements are dangerous in that they can be interpreted as a "guarantee" of performance instead of as a best-guess estimate. I just don't see how you can sell the future without some type of pro-forma analysis. Leaving their creation up to the buyer takes it out of your hands and puts it into theirs. This is always a risky move when selling.

CPAs have an entire set of criteria that governs their involvement with prospective financial statements, which they classify as either forecasts or projections. Forecasts are appropriate for outside parties but require greater detail and disclosure. CPAs use standard language to explain that the forecasts may differ from actual results. I highly recommend that you use a CPA to assist you in disseminating this important information. You may also want to talk to your counsel about disclaimers that can be added to protect you legally, but do provide this additional, highly valued buyer analysis.

The assumptions are of particular value in this figure and the way that those assumptions affect the buyer's perspective on the financial prospects for this company. Notice that the recast NIBT number for 1998 shows NIBT as a percentage of sales equal to 10 percent, which is under our buying company's minimum. But, look at what happens to these numbers when recast for FY 2000 and beyond. See how the value starts at 15 percent and moves up to 20 percent by 2003?

These higher values put the financial perspective on this company in a completely new light. Instead of this company being a drain on public stock price values, it now contributes earnings dollars due to the higher NIBT values. Each sales dollar now contributes more to the public stock price, via the PE ratio, than the current buying company's sales dollars.

Hot Tip

Don't expect to create your own pro-forma financial statements unless you have an accounting background. You are better served by having an accountant create them for you. They will be numerically consistent, and maybe even right, which is a lot to say about the future.

It is common, at this point, to perform a discounted cash flow analysis on the pro-forma income statement values shown. This process provides insight into the present value of future cash flows, which helps to assess the value of the company as viewed from today. Take a look at Chapter 22, "How Much to Ask For and Other Negotiations," for additional information on performing this important, yet conceptually advanced, analysis.

It is common to create pro-forma balance sheets and cash flow statements. This is particularly true for companies that are concerned about the availability of cash to fund future growth. Growth is expensive, and high growth requires cash. The pro-forma cash flow statement provides these estimates.

Estimating Your Customer Value

Customers are your most valued assets. Without them, there are no sales, which means no income or profits to you. Pretty obvious, don't you think? Well, think about this.

Many companies start taking their customers for granted. They stop making those unnecessary, but appreciated, thank you courtesy calls. Stop sending Christmas cards, stop soliciting them for new business and thanking them for past business. In short, they start to treat their customers as if they will always be there.

I speak a little from personal experience on this, since I was one of those business managers who started taking his customers for granted. We focused so much internal company attention on creating the new products that our customers wanted that we forgot to tell our customers what we were doing. When we were ready, some had already made plans to go with another vendor for those particular, and some other, needs. Now that hurt, but it wasn't the customer's fault. It was ours.

I now work hard to retain our customers, and find that I still goof up. Customer service is very important, and now I will prove to you that it makes financial sense as well.

Every industry has its own set of marketing processes that must be followed. If you are in retail, your first major challenge is getting the consumer to try your store in the first place. If the experience goes well, they will likely come back. If not, you will be lucky to see them again, unless you offer something unique that is just not easily available elsewhere. It costs you advertising, promotion, and discount dollars to get them to come in. Getting them to come back is the least expensive part of the process, and the one most neglected.

Hot Tip

For every single customer complaint that you hear about, there are many more out there you know nothing about. If you don't find out about them or if you manage them improperly, your buyers might disappear, which could cost you big time money on the purchase price.

If you are in a commercial industry, such as equipment sales, that has a regular equipment upgrade period, you can count on happy existing customers purchasing new equipment within a few years. Why would they go elsewhere if you have what they want, for a reasonable price, when they want it, and with minimal hassle to them? They wouldn't, and neither would you or I.

Having been in business, you should have a number of repeat customers. I suggest that you perform this simple, yet interesting exercise:

1. Estimate the number of new customers you obtained last year. (For example, assume 20 new customers.)

2. Now estimate the number of expense dollars you spent that could be earmarked for "new customer generation" marketing and sales activities. (Assume that you spent $40,000 total on new customer generation activities.)

3. Divide the value obtained from Step 2 by the value obtained from Step 1. This provides you with a cost per new customer expense ratio. ($40,000/200 = $200 per customer.)

Getting a new customer cost you $200. Keeping a new customer might only cost you a smile and a little attention.

When I owned a software training business, it was typical for a customer to take several software classes over the course of a year. They might take both a beginning and an intermediate training class on a spreadsheet, word processing, and presentation graphic software package. This is a total of six classes at $200 each, or $1200 over the course of a year. In addition, every year they would take three more classes at $200 each, or $600 in sales revenue per customer.

Hot Tip

A customer is also worth more than a single sale to your company. This customer represents a certain amount of money that they will likely spend over the course of a year ... year after year.

Looking at a typical customer-related income stream provides the following insight over a three-year period:

Projecting Customer Value

Year One Revenues	$1,200
Year Two Revenues	$ 600
Year Three Revenues	$ 600
Three Year Total Customer Revenues	$2,400

If we assumed that this company has a NIBT of 10 percent, then this particular customer yields $240 of net income over a three-year period, after all sales, operating, production, and fixed expenses are paid.

At this point, you might be wondering if this number has any greater significance. The answer is "yes," for certain industries, such as health care, cable TV, vending machines, and others.

Hot Tip

The higher your customer retention rate, the higher the price you can expect to be placed on that particular customer's account. This is good news from a seller, and a business manager, standpoint.

Many of these companies determine their value based on the number of customers they currently have. A dentist's office, for example, might show that it has 500 active customers. If it can show that its average revenue per customer is above the national average for dentists, then that particular practice is worth more from a sales perspective.

The same is true for other recurring service industries, such as house cleaning or car detailing. If the business has a high repeat clientele, it costs less to keep those customers than it does to find new ones. If, on the other hand, you find high customer turnover when compared to the rest of that particular industry, you should expect your new customer sales expenses to be higher than the national average.

As an ongoing management tool, you want to clearly understand the average revenue you expect from each of your customers, and then keep those customers happy. It is always easier to keep a customer than it is to find him or her in the first place.

Projecting customer sales revenues into the future is a kind of pro-forma exercise, and will also be based on historical trends and specific future customer agreements. A discounted cash flow analysis can also be applied to these revenues.

Explain Book Value Assumptions

Finally, a brief note should be added to your reported financial information explaining the assumptions on which the company's book value is determined. Remember that book value has nothing directly to do with the current market value of an asset. It is the purchase price minus the depreciation of an asset or the current remaining balance of a loan.

Understanding the methods used for calculating book values is of value to the buyer. This company inherits the current, depreciated value of your assets if passed to the buyer as part of a company purchase. Book value is also used to determine the seller's gain in the event of an asset purchase. Therefore, book value determination methods are pertinent in most circumstances and to all parties involved.

Make sure that you explain the various book value assumptions, and you will avoid the questions that will inevitably come up later.

The Least You Need to Know

➤ Your financial statements and analyses must stand on their own, without explanation.

➤ Book values should be stated, even if not directly used as part of the purchase negotiations.

➤ Customers have an intrinsic and a financial value that can be estimated into the future.

➤ Pro-forma financial statements are a best guess of the future, and they are well worth creating and providing, after first checking with legal counsel.

➤ Historical financial trends are often carried into the future as part of the pro-forma statements.

Selling Can Be Taxing— Beware!

"Why are they offering me so much money for my company," thought Jenny as she sipped her coffee. "It is not that I don't want the money, but if it seems too good to be true, it often is." She wrapped her hands around the coffee mug and stared at the offer letter.

The deal offered stock in the purchasing company plus a little cash and asked that Jenny provide the purchasing company with a loan for around 25 percent of the purchase price. The interest rate was around 1 percent above what she could get from a local bank; she should be making money on the loan. So, why was she uneasy? Taking another sip, she continued to stare at the letter.

Then it hit her. What if the purchasing company fell on hard financial times? What if the value of their stock dropped? What if they defaulted on their loan to Jenny? She would have to collect from the very company whose stock would comprise the majority of her investment portfolio. At that moment, she realized that she did not know enough about the financial history of the purchasing company.

She stood up from her desk and walked to the window. "Let's face it," she mumbled to herself, "this company would become my future retirement ticket. This is not an investment to be taken lightly." Shaking her head, she walked back to her desk to look up the number of her stockbroker. It was time to do some financial sleuthing.

Tax strategies, if handled properly, can increase the after tax income seen by the seller while decreasing the purchase price paid by the buyer. Buyers and sellers may disagree about a lot of things, but both generally agree with giving as little money as possible to the IRS.

However, tax avoidance strategies can be fraught with hidden dangers that could put the seller in the position of owning a lot of stock that does him or her no good at all. The seller's company and income source was sold to the purchaser, and he or she could be left with little of tangible value in return.

Nobody wants to be in this position. Work your way through this chapter and understand the various considerations involved with structuring a sale deal. This is not only good business, but also one that avoids unnecessary taxes. (Note: This chapter is a supplement to Chapter 8, "Making It All Less Taxing." If you have not already read Chapter 8, you should do so before reading this chapter.)

Income Always Brings Tax Considerations

There is good news and bad news associated with making money. The good news is that you now have more money than you had before, which helps a great deal in making daily life a little more manageable. The bad news is that making money always means that paying taxes is not far behind.

There are various ways that money can be sheltered from the maximum tax bite, but you are almost always going to incur some type of tax bill when you sell a business and receive cash as part of the purchase. Even if your sale is an all stock deal, you must still account for the increased (decreased) stock value as part of your, or the company's, tax return.

Hot Tip

The tax impact of a transaction should always be in the back of your mind when evaluating any deal, but it should not determine the whole deal.

Structuring a deal that minimizes taxes at the expense of making as much as possible off the sale is winning a battle, but losing the war. Sure you paid less in taxes, but you also did not take home as much as possible from the sale of your company.

Your first concern should be with structuring a transaction that pays you what you want along with what you need, and then incorporates tax strategies. Complicated transactions like those associated with selling a business can be stalled if there is not a stake in the ground somewhere, determining a minimally reasonable offer.

I contend that this is your job as the owner/seller. You must define what constitutes a minimally acceptable deal. You can then put the tax guys to work trying to structure the deal so that both the seller and buyer benefit by meeting these deal criteria.

In general, taxes incurred from the sale will be minimized if a few simple strategies are used:

➤ Try to show as much of the sale in the form of a capital gain to the seller, which should then qualify for a lower capital gains tax rate.

➤ Defer income to future years when the seller's tax rate might be lower, which would decrease the overall tax bite.

➤ Avoid double taxation to the selling company and its shareholders, which is achieved with the sale of an S corporation or with a non-taxable transfer to the purchasing company.

Capital Gain Taxes Minimize the Bite

Treating an asset as a long-term capital gain item allows you to take advantage of the IRS capital gain tax rate. This rate is 10 percent for those in a 15% tax bracket, and 20 percent for everyone else. Notice that this saves 5 percent in taxes for those in the 15% tax bracket and saves as much as 19.6 percent for those in the highest tax bracket. At the least it allows for a 33 percent decrease (5/15=.33 or 33%) or almost a 50 percent decrease (20/39.6 = .495 or 49.5%) for those in the 39.6% federal tax bracket.

For this reason, it is highly attractive to look at accepting payment for your company in such a way that the capital gain tax rate applies.

Here is the problem with this approach. The only ways to receive favorable capital gains tax treatment are to sell the company assets, to sell the company stock, or to merge the company and then subsequently sell the newly obtained stock.

Let's take a closer look at each of these options to determine their personal pros and cons to the seller.

Here are some of the positive and negative aspects of selling company assets:

Hot Tip

The higher the tax bracket of the sellers, the more valuable the capital gain tax benefits become.

Positive Aspects

➤ The seller gets to choose which asset items are sold and which to keep.

➤ Sold asset items that have been owned for longer than the minimum 12-month capital gain holding period are eligible for lower capital gain tax treatment (individuals only—capital gain tax breaks are not available to corporations).

➤ The selling corporation continues its existence, which might be very good news if the intention of the sale is to move the company into another line of business where its established name would be of value.

➤ The selling corporation retains any favorable tax treatments it might have earned such as a carried forward net operating loss, favorable unemployment or disability tax treatments, and others.

➤ The company is still an established company, with an established credit rating and financial relationships, making successful business continuance a more likely possibility.

➤ If the selling company is an S corporation, the capital gain tax benefits pass directly to the shareholders, except for cash, account receivable and inventory sale proceeds, which are treated as income.

➤ The sellers get their money up front, without having to wait for a longer period of time.

Negative Aspects

➤ Paperwork must be managed for each sold asset including license transfers, warranty transfers, lien resolutions, and other miscellaneous areas.

➤ If you plan to sell the company, or shift it into another business area, you must still do something with the assets that are left over after the initial, large asset purchase/sale.

➤ Although the selling company receives capital gain treatment on the asset sale gains, the shareholders themselves do not. Double taxation is experienced when the proceeds from the asset sales are transferred to the shareholders themselves in the form of dividends or full liquidation.

➤ The company still exists, which means that the selling owners must still deal with its operation, no matter how trivial it might become. This is a nuisance factor more than anything else, but it can become a liability should someone decide to go after the stripped corporation for something that happened in the past.

Hot Tip

Since the tax implications of any sale can have a substantial impact on the net cash you receive from the sale, I suggest that you review the transaction with an accountant before setting your expectations. The tax laws are incredibly complicated and so diverse that a professional is needed to assess your tax impact.

➤ If the assets have not been held for the 12-month minimum capital gain holding period, any gain on the sale of the asset will be taxed at an S corporation shareholder's regular income tax rate (regular corporations are not able to benefit from capital gain tax breaks).

The sale of company stock is a lot like selling assets, except that the ownership issue becomes a little more complicated. If all stock is sold, then ownership is a simple matter and has been discussed in Chapters 5, "The Various Business Arrangements," and 8, "Making It All Less Taxing." The entity that bought the stock is the new owner. Period.

If only a percentage of outstanding shares is sold, the situation gets more complicated. I will present only a few major items for consideration in this section. I strongly encourage you to discuss the details of your particular situation with your tax professional.

Positive Aspects

➤ Shareholders who sell capital gain-qualified shares will receive capital gain tax treatment on that gain.

➤ The selling company still retains some ownership control over the daily operation of the company.

➤ The selling company has an investment in seeing the purchased company succeed since it now has an investment in its future financial performance.

➤ The purchasing company might be willing to give its stock to the shareholders of the purchased company, making the transaction tax free to the selling company shareholders, at least until the shareholders sell the newly received stock. This decreases the cash outlay on the part of the purchasing company and decreases the tax impact on the sellers who receive stock.

Negative Aspects

➤ The prior owners now have a new set of owners, and probably board members, who must be dealt with.

➤ No cash infusion was seen by the selling company, but its management hassle-factor increased.

➤ If the purchasing company acquired a majority of the shares, it might have the right to obtain a majority voting right on the board as well. This would transfer operational control to the purchasing company, even though the original founders/owners are still managing the company and may still have personally guaranteed company loans. This is a very precarious position for the previous owners.

Seller Beware

As soon as a publicly traded company becomes interested in buying your company, you should check out its historical stock performance. If it has a very low trading volume, you might have a hard time selling any stock that might be included as part of the purchase agreement.

➤ The actual value of stock received will not be determined until a future date, when the stock is actually sold. If the purchasing company does well, having taken stock will be viewed as a great investment move. If its stock drops, taking stock instead of cash at the time of purchase will have a 20/20 hindsight regret associated with it.

Merging stocks is actually a simpler matter on almost all fronts since all assets transfer at their depreciated book values. All transactions are typically stock-for-stock transfers, which should have no tax consequences to the sellers, require minimal cash by the buyer, and minimize individual asset tracking/sale/negotiations. Remember that buyers may not want to fully acquire the company since they would also acquire all known, and unknown, liabilities along with all assets and goodwill. This reason alone is enough for many companies to never purchase another company outright.

Leaving Too Much in the Company Can Be Risky

There is a natural tendency to take as much as possible in cash when selling your company. After all, what is more secure than cash?

Seller Beware

If the stock prices of the publicly traded company that is interested in buying your company have dropped over recent months, its stock might either be a bargain or still be on its way down. Only careful investigation will ensure that you know what you are getting into.

For various reasons, buyers will often want to include some of their stock as part of the deal. These reasons might include a management motivation to keep the previous owners/managers interested in the performance of the new venture. They might include a financial motivation to minimize the amount of cash included in the purchase, making it less of an asset drain on the purchasing company. They might actually feel that the future value of the company stock is so positive that you are truly benefiting by owning the purchasing company's stock.

No matter the reason, the possibility of having stock presented as part of the deal is very real. The questions you will ask at that time are, should you take the stock and how much?

First, you want to ensure that you have a means for selling the received stock so that you can recoup some of your sale price when you choose.

Stock in a publicly traded company can usually be sold on the open market, but your stock might have restrictions on when and how it can be sold, especially if you become an officer in the purchasing company.

If there are any restrictions at all placed on how you can trade your acquired stock, the price of the stock should be discounted from its current market value. You don't know what the future holds for the market in general or for this stock in particular.

Therefore, you want to protect yourself from future negative stock performance by acquiring the stock today at a discount that might be as much as 50 percent off of market price.

Think about this little financial trick if you feel yourself being wooed by the thought of major stock ownership. Assume for a moment that the acquiring company is trading at a price-to-earning (PE) ratio of 25, and your company has a PE ratio of 8, whether publicly or privately determined.

Notice that your company's earnings will transfer to the purchasing company, which now will multiply the stock value by a factor of 25 instead of 8. If the executives on the purchasing side are compensated on stock price performance, then this is a sound deal, especially if they can purchase your company with their stock which is highly leveraged (as indicated by the 25 times multiplier).

Hot Tip

Check out the purchasing company's stock to determine if it is worth owning on its own merits. If you yourself would not buy the stock outside of your purchase agreement, why would you want to acquire the stock as part of your own company's sale transaction? This would make no sense at all.

They haven't done a thing to functionally integrate the two companies, and have already shown an increase in stock price simply due to the earnings multiplier. Is that cool or what? As the buyer who is compensated based on stock price increases, this is a clever approach. As the seller, you want to make sure that you are compensated for allowing the buyer to take advantage of your lower PE ratio.

Taking a lot of stock as part of the transaction while not retaining any controlling interest in the purchasing company puts your future income and wealth in the hands of the purchasing company management. If they live up to your expectations, life is good. If not, you could find yourself, and your shareholders, holding worthless stock that cannot even be traded.

Finding the right mix of cash, loans, and stock that you should accept is a tough question, and one that is heavily dependent on the personality of the sellers. If you are a privately held company with all stock ownership in the hands of a few people, you can probably obtain a consensus about the right mix to accept. If it is just you, assess your own risk profile and accept the combination that is right for you.

If you have a large number of shareholders, you really have to take a more objective approach and determine the arrangement that optimizes share-holder wealth in today's dollars. This will likely

Terms of Acquisition

Accounting or Paper Profit A profit that appears on the financial statements and that is the result of an administrative or accounting procedure or change, as opposed to one that results from an actual change in operation.

require a discounted cash flow analysis, so that you and the other board members are protected should future buyer performance not turn out as expected. (See Chapter 5 for additional information about board member responsibilities.)

Weighing What You Want Against What You Need

Finally, don't finalize any sale transaction unless you get out of it what you yourself truly need. If you plan to leave the company after the sale, you want to make sure that you have adequate cash and/or income to cover your living expenses. If a large portion of that future cash is associated with loans that you provided the company, you probably want to reevaluate the deal. If the purchasing company ever defaults on the loan, your future income can be jeopardized along with what you thought might have been a comfortable early retirement.

Hot Tip

Write down your bottom line requirements before you get too far into the sale process details. The forest often gets lost in the trees, and you always want to make sure that your initial objectives are met once all details have worked themselves out.

If, on the other hand, you are motivated enough to want to keep working, you might be more willing to arrange the sale as a higher risk/higher potential reward transaction. Your income is not jeopardized since you plan to continue working, and your higher risk sale transaction setup might just pay huge returns in a few years.

There is no "right" way to structure the deal. Knowing your bottom line requirements helps you set a floor under which you are just not willing to go, unless your current company is in such bad shape that you just want to be out from under its weight.

Leaving It for Your Heirs

If you are the owner of a closely held corporation, or sole proprietorship, and intend to leave it to your heirs, you should really talk with them about your plans. You just might find out that none of your heirs wants the company, and that they only want the proceeds that would come from its sale.

Should you pass away before the company is sold, its market value might be substantially reduced for any number of reasons:

➤ You will not be around to assist with the sale itself.

➤ You cannot be passed to the new owners as part of the transaction, making the overall transaction less valuable to the buyers.

➤ Nobody knows your business, or believes in your business, more than you do. That is worth something when selling.

➤ Any squabbling that might occur between heirs might force a quick sale as opposed to handling the sale in a solid, prepared manner as recommended in this book.

➤ Buyers look for good companies that are being sold as part of an estate resolution because this generally means highly motivated sellers and a lower price.

➤ If you died without having a will in place, your estate and business might be resolved in probate court, which most certainly is not what you want for your heirs.

For these reasons alone, you should take the time to plan the passage of your company to your heirs. It is difficult for an heir to deal with the loss of a loved one. It is even more difficult to see someone's wishes not fulfilled simply because they had not expressed them in writing or had not taken the time to plan appropriately while alive.

Straight Talk

Any small business owner has pride in the company he or she has created, and naturally, wants his or her family to share in and benefit from its success. However, the simple fact is that they may not want to share in your dreams, and forcing your family into your vision will only cause personal hardship and will probably decrease the value of the business. An honest assessment might mean that you sell the company while you are still young enough to enjoy the sale proceeds. You can then have a good time while you are still healthy, leaving the balance to your spouse or children as part of your estate.

If you are holding onto the company so that it can be passed on to your family, do them a favor and talk honestly with them about their desires. You want what is best for them, and if what's best for them is not the company but its value in more liquid assets, plan accordingly. Nobody can handle that process more effectively than you can.

The Least You Need to Know

➤ Future stock value is riskier than current cash value.

➤ Set up either a succession plan or a sale plan to ensure that your heirs get the most from your estate.

➤ PE ratios should be considered when exchanging stock as part of the transaction.

➤ The right financial transaction structure will vary from one person to the next, so beware absolute "right" ways of doing things.

➤ Selling assets that you have held over 12 months allows personal capital gain tax benefits, which can reduce taxes by up to 50 percent.

Part 6
Putting Your Baby on the Market

Marketing your business is critical to getting top dollar. Creating the prospectus, determining the right price, and being willing to walk away from a bad deal are important parts of the process. Part Six outlines many of the tricks and the traps of selling your company.

Your Prospectus Looks Good

"I like it," exclaimed Mike as he viewed the bound prospectus just handed to him by Judy, his marketing VP. *"You really did a great job on this."*

Judy beamed. They had spent a lot of hours collecting the information, preparing the charts and tables, and making sure that it said what she and Mike wanted it to say. She had worked for Mike for five years at this point, and had learned to trust his instincts. If he liked it, it was good.

"The amazing part to me," Mike continued, *"is that we did all of this over the last five years. I had forgotten about a lot of things until I read it in the report. We really have worked hard to get here, and you did a great job of presenting our story. Now we just need to find people who will appreciate it the way we do. It's time to sell this company. As a matter of fact, I'd buy it myself if I didn't already own it!"*

Here you are, ready to sell your company. How do you let others see the intrinsic value you see in your company? They don't have years worth of experience marketing, selling, and designing your company's specific products and services. They just won't view it the same way you do.

Nevertheless, you have to try to get that message across to them or you will not get the amount of money you want for your company. In fact, if not presented properly, you might not get any offers at all, which is unfortunate for everyone.

The sales prospectus, often called the marketing brochure or offering memorandum, outlines the important aspects of your company. And outlines them in such a way that the reader, and potential buyer, sees the company as a sound investment that is worth every penny of the asking price.

It is your job to convince them that the price and your company are right for them. Don't blame them if they don't get it. After all, who is the customer here?

Taking the time to prepare a professional, accurate, and convincing prospectus is one of the most important things you will do when selling your company. Don't skimp here because it will almost always cost you money in the end.

The Components of the Prospectus

The prospectus is a sales document. Period. The entire point is to move the buyer closer to accepting your asking price and to actually buying your company. You might not be there when the person reads the prospectus, meaning that it not only has to be accurate but also has to to stand on its own merits. Think of it this way: When the reader, who is unfamiliar with your company, finishes reading the prospectus, will he or she feel motivated to buy your company? If so, you are on the right track. If not, the prospectus needs more work. It is just that simple.

The more credible your prospectus, the better your company will appear, making your assertions more believable. A solidly built prospectus might very well reduce the buyer's due diligence requirements, decreasing the sale cycle, which more quickly sells your company.

Here are the common components of a prospectus. As always, don't feel constrained by this listing; just treat it as a starting point. Add any additional sections that are required to paint a complete, positive picture of your company to the reader.

Terms of Acquisition

Prospectus A document that outlines the opportunity presented by a specific investment. Fundamentally, it is a sales document aimed at potential investors.

Company Confidential Cover Sheet

1. Investment Summary

2. General Company Presentation

3. Overall Market Assessment

4. Sales and Marketing Overview

5. Special Assets, Processes, and Agreements

6. Key Management Personnel

7. Past Financial Performance

8. Projected Future Financial Performance

9. Ownership Structure

10. Asking Price and Financing

11. Conclusion

Appendices (as needed)

Investment Summary

Oddly enough, this section is usually written last. All of the information presented in the prospectus is designed to support this section. It is just what it sounds like … a summary of the investment opportunity outlined throughout the rest of the prospectus.

It should be no longer than two pages, with one page being the preferred length. Its job is to tease the reader into wanting to read the rest of the document. The details are in the various prospectus sections. The wrap-up is in the investment summary.

The first paragraph will typically read something like this:

> "ABC Company is a privately held corporation that manufactures specialty widgets. As the national widget market has decreased in overall sales dollars, ABC's sales have increased, allowing it to currently enjoy a 45 percent market share, up from 30 percent only three years ago."

Hot Tip

Keep the Investment Summary short and to the point. Spend a lot of time here making sure it delivers the message you intend: "Buy Me Now!"

The summary goes on to talk about the reason for selling, items that are for sale, timeframe for the sale, and asking price along with any specific financing requirements.

It should close with something like this:

> "ABC is a well-run company with an excellent product mix and a dedicated professional staff and executive management team. An investment in ABC, as outlined in this prospectus, should provide an XX percent annual investment

return, assuming no synergies exist with the purchasing company. Synergies should only enhance the return, making it even more attractive."

General Company Presentation

This is where you start your presentation about the company itself. Here are some basic points that must be contained in this section:

➤ How old is the company?

➤ How was it formed, by whom, and why has it been successful to date?

➤ The number of business locations, employees, and annual sales.

➤ What does the company sell and through what type of marketing channels? (Very general information only.)

➤ General information about proprietary technologies, intellectual property, processes, and any other unique attributes that make this company different.

➤ What its future looks like with respect to future marketing, product, service, or overall business plans (very general).

➤ Why the company is up for sale, presented in the most positive light possible.

This is simply an overview. The specific marketing, product, and financial sections will reveal the details.

Overall Market Assessment

This section covers the relationship between the company, the market in general, and its specific market in particular. Growth trends within the market, obtained by the company, or within the segment should all be presented over a three to five year historical perspective. Future market trends should also be included in this section.

Sales and Marketing Overview

The details of the company's products and/or services mix, marketing strategies, personnel, distribution channels, unique approaches, historical successes, and future goals should be presented in this area. It is also helpful to include competitive information so that industry comparisons can be drawn by the uninitiated reader. This is particularly helpful if you have been taking business away from your competition in recent years. Special customer arrangements/agreements should be included at this point. The general backgrounds of key marketing and sales personnel should be also included at this point.

A detailed analysis of customers, products, geographies, successes, and even struggles might be appropriate in this section. Every company has problems, and the buyer knows that too. Revealing something significant yet not injurious might help to improve reception and credibility.

Finally, take a few moments to discuss the strategic focus of the company. Remember the "drill bits" vs. "holes" discussion we had in Chapter 11, "What Do They REALLY Have Of Value?" Here might be a place to strut your stuff and to show them that you really know what you are talking about and that your success was not an accident.

Special Assets, Processes, and Agreements

This section contains information about any proprietary arrangements held by the company. These might include patents, trademarks, or copyrighted information. Special agreements with vendors, foreign countries, and key distributors should also be included here. Details regarding intellectual property, the scope of protection provided, length of protection, and other pertinent information should be included.

If special processes, which are personnel or technique dependent, are part of the company value mix, they should be presented here. After all, you want the information to convince the reader that you are offering a fair product for a fair price. If the processes or techniques are part of the value, it should spelled out in such as way that the reader understands the value, as seen through your eyes.

> **Hot Tip**
>
> Charts, graphs, tables, and pictures are great presentation tools. Get to know your computer graphics software packages if you don't know them already.

Key Management Personnel

The professional, educational, and pertinent personal background of key personnel should be presented in this section. The minimal people to include are the CEO, President, Vice Presidents, Directors, key board members, key technology personnel, key operations personnel, influential staff consultants, investors, and other important personnel. Remember that you are often judged by the company you keep. By association, your company will be assessed by the people on its staff and board and by its investors.

Just because you are familiar with these people doesn't mean that their names have no clout in the industry. Make sure that you start to look at these people, and yourself, as seen from an outsider's perspective. If someone has a patent, which might be old hat to you, include it in his or her biography. This is interesting and impressive information to others. Make sure that you don't reveal anything of a highly personal nature, but make sure that you do include the information needed to convince the reader that these people are credible professionals, with excellent reputations, who have chosen to work here instead of elsewhere. That, in itself, says a lot about a company.

Past Financial Performance

This section adds financial meat to the skeleton presented in earlier sections. You have made claims about what made the company so great in the past, and this is where the numbers should confirm those assertions.

You should show financial statements for the last three to five years, with comparative financial statements provided for the last two years, including the current year to date.

Details about accounting procedures, such as cash or accrual accounting, should be revealed. If the company took special steps to orient the financial statements in one direction or another, that should also be stated. For example, a privately held company might perform its accounting functions so that income is minimized. This strategy would make the company's historical financial statements look poor to someone who manages to optimize income, which is typically done in a publicly held company. Explaining that this is part of the accounting strategy, instead of an accidental by-product, will improve the financial reception.

If there were special situations that caused radical drops or improvements in financial performance, you should also mention those at this point. Any credible financial person will find them anyway, so why not be up front about them, and show that you are not trying to hide something?

Projected Future Financial Performance

Predicting the future is always tricky business. I once had someone describe the forecasting process as "driving a car while looking in the rear view mirror." There is a lot of truth in this statement, since you can really only look to past performance as a guide to the future, since the future is always changing.

Seller Beware

Check with your legal department before including future forecasts that might be construed as a commitment instead of a best-guesstimate.

Some legal people assert that future forecasts should not be included in any prospectus since they might be construed as a commitment of future performance instead of a best guess. Checking with your legal counsel is always the right thing on a topic like this, and you should always make sure that the reader knows that these are estimates, and not statements of fact. This seems obvious since you are talking about the future, but it is better to error on the safe side and include the disclaimers. (See the discussion about CPAs' involvement with forecasted financial statements in chapter 19.)

By the way, it is certainly OK to correlate information from different sections. Assume, for example, that the company currently has a 45 percent market share and that the market is growing at 10 percent per year. It is certainly reasonable to assert that the company sales will grow by an estimated 4.5 percent (45% of 10%) over the next year, assuming that no market share was lost. These growth percentages can then be used to estimate future dollar-sales growth. The same might apply for manufacturing cost decreases that can be extrapolated into the future from the past along a specific volume curve. If sales increase, so does manufacturing volume, this should decrease production costs. All of these combined indicate increased sales and potentially increased gross margins as well.

Hopefully, you are getting the picture. This is a very important section of the prospectus. Some would contend, and with good justification, that it is the most important section. After all, the buyer is purchasing future performance projections, not past performance histories. Making the best possible financial case for the future is the best possible way to optimize your actual sale price.

Ownership Structure

This is usually a pretty dry section that presents who owns what, for how long and in what percentages. Deadlines, covenants, and other financially related ownership issues are presented in this section. They are going to want to know who the partners are in a partnership, the shareholders are in a corporation, and any family members in a sole proprietorship.

Asking Price and Financing

Here is where you present your case for your asking price. You can base it on any of the valuation techniques presented in Chapters 15, "Making an Offer They Can't Refuse," 16, "Financing The Deal," and 22, "How Much to Ask For and Other Negotiations." The point is that you should have some justification for the asking price, whether you explicitly state it as part of this section or not. At least tell them the general procedure used to determine the price.

If special financing is being provided, or is required by the seller, it should be spelled out in this section. For example, the sellers might be willing to offer a loan to the buyers. On the other hand, the board of directors might have determined that the company could only be merged, for tax reasons. Why waste time with a buyer who cannot, or will not, comply with your financial requirements.

Straight Talk

You should already have financially qualified the buyer by this time. There is no reason to let the prospective buyer read the entire prospectus if he or she cannot comply with the basic financial arrangements. An unqualified buyer has "no need to know." Remember?

Finally, if you have already arranged financing for a solid buyer, you should also spell that out in this section. Anything that makes the workload lighter and makes you look more prepared, is something that makes the purchase of your company more attractive.

Conclusion

This is the wrap-up section of the report. It often simply restates what was presented in the Investment Summary. It naturally should conclude that this is an excellent investment and that the buyer should move quickly to ensure that nobody else buys the company. This section is also written after all the other supporting sections are completed, although you really know what it will say before you start writing.

Appendices (As Needed)

These sections might include product brochures, competitive information, Internet Web site information, samples, detailed biographies, and/or other pertinent information. Anything required to support the mid-report sections should be included in the appendices and referenced from the particular sections.

What to Reveal?

There is still a natural inclination to keep information secret, even at this stage. I feel that it might be counterproductive at this point to keep information from a credible, qualified, and interested buyer.

Terms of Acquisition

Sniff Test An unwritten, non-numeric, yet very real test that we all undergo and perform when negotiating something important. If the other person, or the situation, just doesn't "feel" right, it failed the test, which is never a good sign for future relations.

After all, you should already have a non-disclosure agreement signed, should have met a few times talking about the various general details of your respective businesses, and should have generally given each other what I call the "sniff test." This is where you meet with each other and assess whether the other is a people with whom you want to, or are willing to, do business. Relationships that fail the sniff test often turn into untrusting, antagonistic relationships that become a resource, energy, and financial drain.

If you are sure that their interest is sincere, you really have to move forward by revealing this information. That is, unless, you are lucky enough to have them simply offer you what you want based on your overall financial statements. This would be great news, but it doesn't happen very often. Don't plan on not having to reveal detailed information and be happy if it is not a buyer requirement.

Selling to a Competitor

We spent a lot of time talking about this topic in Chapter 13, "Reducing Competition by Buying 'Em Up," so I won't bore you with repetition here. Let me just say that you should be more on your guard if the buyer is a competitor rather than someone from another industry. Reread Chapter 13 to refresh yourself on the extra steps needed to protect yourself when working with a competitor.

The "Specifically Vague" section is of paramount importance, and you will probably have this talent down to an art form by the time the competitive purchase is finalized. Always error on the side of caution when dealing with a competitor, but also know that your competition might also turn out to be your best buyer. After all, who would better appreciate your business and its industry-specific structure than a respected, and hopefully respectful, competitor? Just like a fine art collector will pay premium prices for the right artwork, which they alone might recognize, a competitor might recognize things in your organization that others might miss or ignore. By the way, this can work either for you or against you.

Watch the Money, Not Your Ego

It is tempting to try to get as much as possible from the sale of your company. After all, this is your baby. This is particularly true for you entrepreneurs who conceived, started, financed, sweated, and dreamed your idea into the reality that you are now selling.

Others won't have your emotional attachment to the business. To them it is a business deal that either makes sense or doesn't. This is not to say that your passion for the business is without value. Just the opposite. Nobody can sell your business better than you can. You just want to be sure that you don't let your emotions get in the way of the business transactions.

People will find flaws with the business. That is a given. Nothing, no one, and no business is perfect. The buyer is there to get the most possible for the least money. The seller is there to get the most possible money for the sale. What you see as a benefit, the buyer might see as a detriment. So what? After the sale, the company won't be yours anyway. Letting go before the sale process begins is the best way to make sure that you transact the best financial deal for your company, which is not necessarily the best one for your ego.

Straight Talk

An ego-inflated company valuation rarely turns into a dollar inflated purchase price. Leave your ego at the door and sell the company for the maximum shareholder value.

Protecting Shareholder Interests

When all is said and done, the sale will be evaluated by your company shareholders and board of directors, based on whether it increases shareholder wealth. As the manager, you have a duty to maximize the investment return experienced by shareholders. As an owner who just sold his or her company, you want to get as much as you can for the sale, since it might be your retirement, play money, or funding for your next company.

At any rate, you really are best served when you serve the interests of your other owners and/or shareholders. Keep them in mind, and you will probably find yourself speaking not just on your own behalf, but on behalf of the others as well.

The Least You Need to Know

➤ The prospectus must be able to stand on its own.

➤ Only show the prospectus to sincere qualified, non-disclosure covered buyers.

➤ Make sure that the prospectus presents a total, rational case that justifies your purchase price.

➤ Talk to legal counsel about revealing future projections.

➤ Sell the company, not your ego, and you will get a better return on your investment.

Chapter 22

How Much to Ask For and Other Negotiations

In This Chapter

➤ Setting the right asking price

➤ Outlining negotiation parameters

➤ Helping the buyer to buy

➤ Protecting yourself with stock deals

➤ Getting out of the way

This was the second time that the buyers had wanted a meeting since finishing their due diligence stage. The last meeting had seemed to go well, yet they had not moved more solidly toward an offer. "How much longer will this go on before they make a firm offer," Judy wondered.

The buyers brought someone new with them to this meeting. He did no talking, but he seemed interested in every word. In a strange sort of way, everyone on the buyer's side of the table seemed to defer to him, even though he said nothing. Who was this guy?

The two negotiators were discussing some fine technical point regarding the calculations methods used in the discounted cash flow analysis that Judy's company provided all prospective buyers. She was a little bored with it, as was the new member of the buyer's party.

Judy asked for a break and offered to buy the mystery gentleman a cup of coffee, which he quickly accepted.

"We would like to buy you more than a cup of coffee," he said to Judy holding his coffee cup like a mug. "I like what I see here, but we need to let these guys do their jobs. If things get

stuck, call me and I will unstick them. OK? We can both benefit from this purchase if it is structured properly."

He handed Judy a business card, which revealed that he was the Chairman of the Board of the acquiring company. She smiled and thanked him. It was nice to be dealing with a decision-maker.

The prior story is anecdotal, but it's not far from the truth in many circumstances. The purchase of a company usually gets very high levels of attention, even in some of the largest companies.

However, the negotiation needs to progress to the point that specific commitments are made and obligations incurred. There is an art associated with getting the sale to that point, and that is the topic of this chapter.

Determining an Asking Price

This is probably one of the most important and difficult decisions you will make as part of the sale process. Asking too little should cause your company to sell more quickly, but it might leave you with a nagging suspicion that you could have asked for more and gotten it. Asking too much may eliminate possible buyers since they feel the asking price unreasonable.

Therefore, finding the right price is a balancing act that is peppered with equal doses of numerical analysis and pure instinct. I suggest that you do the analysis first since that will aid your instinct when needed.

Of primary importance is that any price you ask must be based on the future worth of the company, not its past performance. You benefited from the past, but your buyers won't benefit in any direct way. They might indirectly benefit since your company has a reputation of performing well, but they have to turn that into hard dollars.

Hot Tip

Make sure to refer to Chapter 15, "Making an Offer They Can't Refuse," for details about pricing a business. Its perspective is from that of the buyer, but the valuation techniques presented apply equally to a seller. In the interest of not driving you crazy with boredom as I repeat the same information, I suggest that you read that chapter as a compliment to the first part of this chapter.

Today's Price Is Based on the Future

The buyers are looking forward, and you will initially find yourself looking back. It is important that both of you shift your understanding so that each can comprehend the position of the other when finally negotiating.

Buyers and sellers have the following points in common:

➤ Verified and believable historical financial performance is useful as a benchmark starting point for future performance.

➤ Pro-forma financial statements should be created to project future sales, expenses, and net incomes for a future period, usually between three to five years.

➤ A discounted cash flow analysis provides a credible present value estimate of future cash flows. This is particularly true if the company shows a negative net income or has erratic estimated future financial performance.

➤ A business appraiser can benefit both buyer and seller, and both may choose to get their own, independent appraisal.

➤ The seller is working to get as much as possible for the business sale.

➤ The buyer is working to pay as little as possible for the business purchase.

➤ The buyer knows the possible synergy that the purchased company will have with his or her already existing operations. This synergism can make the purchase even more financially attractive to the buyer, but it might be completely unknown to the seller.

➤ Only the seller knows his or her true motivations. The seller might be willing to keep the business running or thinking of closing shop completely. Only he or she knows for sure.

➤ Supply and demand is always at work. You might think that you are the only interested buyer, or you might think that what you have to sell is very special. Don't believe your own advertising, but investigate the market to ensure that your perceptions hold up under close scrutiny.

Straight Talk

Financial people always look at the value of something today as it relates to the future. Small business owners tend to focus on today and often simply let the future take care of itself. When setting a price for the company, remember that the past performance is already absorbed into the current company financial reports. The future company performance, when translated into a present day dollar value, is what you are really negotiating.

Know Your Own Pain Threshold

After you have performed the various analyses suggested in Chapter 15, "Making an Offer They Can't Refuse," you should then check out your own selling boundaries:

➤ You should first figure out the rock-bottom bare-minimum price at which you can sell. This means the price required to pay off all loans, make current any payroll taxes, and to take care of any other financial obligations. Selling at a price lower than this will cost you money, which you should agree to only if the situation is so desperate that holding on will cost you more money.

➤ Determine the absolute maximum reasonable price for which the company could be justifiably priced. This price can be determined by any of the techniques recommended in Chapter 15 in conjunction with the most optimistic set of possible assumptions. This is the upper end of the sale price range.

➤ Now assess what you really want to get out of the sale for yourself and the other shareholders. Review Chapter 17, "Why Sell Anyway?" for a starting place for this evaluation.

You now know the upper and lower ranges at which the company can be sold and your primary motivations for selling. You are now on solid ground from which to move into the specifics of the sale process.

Choosing the Right Price

Have you ever had a garage sale? Did you ever notice that the things you didn't want you priced low and the things you possibly might keep if it didn't sell you priced high? Did you also notice that as the end of the sale drew near, you were more willing to discount the unsold items that you did not want? Supply, demand, and time. These three components intermingle in every business life and they apply in grand stature when selling a business.

Straight Talk

If you use a business broker to sell your business, he or she should already have worked with business appraisers who will be able to, based on experience and analysis, tell you a solid price range for which the business will sell. Whether you sell it yourself or use a broker, you should understand the justification for the asking price. Don't simply take the broker's recommendation at face value, but ask the detailed questions that make you comfortable with that analysis. After all, nobody knows your business better than you do. The appraiser might have forgotten something of real value that only you or a competitor would recognize.

If you don't really need to sell the company, you might entertain the thought of setting the sale price so high that it would be ridiculous not to sell if someone offered to buy at that price. (You will also preclude potential offers this way.) On the other hand, pricing the company too low might make buyers think that something is wrong with the business, scaring them off.

Even worse, a low price may draw tire-kickers who may be enamored with the thought of buying but who really can't afford the purchase price. These people take up time and cause you to reveal information to more people than you probably had originally intended.

I suggest that you set your asking price at what you feel is a reasonable price PLUS a margin of between 5 and 20 percent added on for negotiation room. For example, if you want $1 million for your company, you should set the price at between $1,050,000 and $1,200,000. Make sure that these asking prices are based on your financial analysis and valuation exercise and not just "what you think it is worth." This is one time that gut instinct should follow a numeric analysis.

If a buyer is not willing to negotiate a 5 to 10 percent price range, he or she really isn't that interested anyway. If you price the business at a fair price and stand firm at your price, you leave the buyer little negotiating room to accommodate things that the buyer might find wrong as part of the due diligence process.

If possible, I suggest you don't reveal your price until you have a seriously interested buyer. Letting him or her make the first offer, based on your prospectus, might set the negotiations off at a higher level than you would have started, with you knowing that he or she is likely starting out at a lower price than he or she is actually willing to pay. Some buyers might let you get away with not setting a price, but most are going to want a starting point to determine if it is worth their while to continue with the process. But it's worth a try.

Understanding the Buyer

When selling, it is important to understand the buyer's motivations. The better you understand these motivations, the more effectively you can present your company in the best light.

Buyers come in a few different flavors; each has special needs and interests:

➤ The strategic buyer is looking for ways that your company can be integrated with his or her other companies to make the combination more valuable than the sum of the individual parts. Sale price is important, but also important is the prospect of the entire organization making more money as a result of the purchase of your company.

➤ The financial buyer is looking at the business as an investment. Either it returns more money than the alternate available investments, or it doesn't. The conversations might be just that cut and dry. If you plan to stay on after the purchase, I

245

encourage you to evaluate the management style of this type of buyer closely, since he or she will become your new boss. It would be a real drag to sell the company only to find yourself dreading going to work because of the new owners.

➤ The owner/operator who is not only interested in the business as an investment but also in it as an employer. This is more common for smaller businesses, but it might also be the case with yours. This type of buyer might well include a portion of his or her salary as income when performing the return on investment calculations.

Straight Talk

It is common today to have a buyer be both financial and strategic in nature, which is really the optimal combination. Many financial buyers are the owners of an umbrella holding company under which they maintain many subsidiary companies. If purchasing your company benefits one of their other companies, the purchase makes sense on both a financial and strategic basis. If you, as the seller, can find this out you might want to tie a portion of your sale price to the overall strategic return if you feel that the future return on this opportunity is better than simply receiving stock or cash today.

Deal Blockers to Avoid

It would be a real disappointment to find an interested buyer only to discover that there is a reason why your company cannot be sold to that buyer. Here are a few things to look for to ensure that you are not wasting your, or the buyer's, time and money:

➤ Are all assets transferable to the new owners? If any of the liens on equipment, real estate, or other assets are not transferable, they must be paid off or renegotiated before the deal can be finalized. An ounce of prevention is definitely worth avoiding the cost of the cure on this point.

➤ Make sure that you and the other owners/shareholder are in agreement regarding an acceptable price range and the type of buyer. It would be a shame to have internal squabbling get in the way of an otherwise excellent sale/purchase.

➤ If you have a troublesome shareholder, you and the other shareholders might consider buying him or her out so that the sale can proceed more smoothly.

Moreover, if done properly, you might be able to purchase these shares at a discount compared to what you will actually receive when sold to the third party buyer.

➤ Have a long talk with your accountant regarding the things that you can, and should, do to allow a major buyer to use *pooling accounting* when reporting the purchase or your company. Pooling will make your company appear more financially attractive to a publicly held company. It would be a real disappointment to lose a viable, financially solid buyer simply because of a few accounting changes. (See Chapter 5, "The Various Business Arrangements," for additional information on pooling.)

➤ Make sure that the buyer has the money to afford the purchase. Otherwise, the buyer might be looking for you to personally finance a portion of the purchase price in the form of a note that you hold, which is repaid by the company you just sold. If you feel comfortable linking a large portion of the sale proceeds to the performance of a company over which you don't have future management influence, this might be right for you. I am just not comfortable with this arrangement except under very specific, unique circumstances.

Taking Stock as Part of the Transaction

It is highly likely that the buyer will want to include some stock as payment for part of the purchase price. This may be good news, or it might be bad news, depending upon the company and a number of other issues. There are few hard and fast rules regarding the acceptance of stock as payment, but here are a few things I suggest that you consider:

➤ Make sure that the stock is transferable and sellable to someone other than the buying company, without restrictions. Otherwise, you could be holding stock with no ready negotiable value.

➤ If the purchase makes you a large shareholder in the buying company, you should negotiate a position on the board of directors. In this way, you retain some level of voting authority over the company's operation. This ensures that the company is run in a way the benefits you, not only as a shareholder but also as a former business owner.

Seller Beware

The caution against holding a note as part of your sale holds doubly true if the buyers are financial and not strategic buyers. Financial buyers, interested only in the bottom line, are far more likely to cut off your note if it makes financial sense than would a strategic buyer who might need your future cooperation.

➤ Stocks are volatile. They increase and decrease in price. That is just part of the stock market game. You should perform your own present value analysis on the stock offered, and use this to determine your own assessment about its current value. If your analysis shows it with a higher present value than the current market value, taking the stock might be a shrewd financial move. If not, negotiating for more shares to compensate for the lower present value is a viable negotiating ploy.

➤ Don't forget that all stock deals involve no tax payments until you resell the stock obtained as part of the purchase. In this way, you can put off capital gains.

What to Expect During Negotiations

Few people actually buy or sell a business in their life. On the other hand, the people who do this for a living do it all the time. You are on their turf when you negotiate with them; so keep your ego in check and assume that assistance from experienced professional during the negotiation stage can only help your situation.

Hot Tip

Look at Chapter 16, "Financing the Deal," for additional information regarding techniques for calculating the entire cost/value associated with a particular purchase transaction structure.

As stated in Chapter 2, "Start at the Very Beginning …," you should already have an accountant and an attorney, or even better a CPA/M&A attorney, on your side. If this person, or these people, has experience negotiating, you might be better served allowing them to negotiate for you. This keeps you out of the limelight and allows you to focus on the substance of the negotiations, instead of focusing on the social aspects of the process.

You should expect the negotiations to proceed on a general level until you get through the due diligence stage. From that point forward, you can expect and you should expect, concrete, substantial comments and movement by the buyer. If they are still dragging their feet, then something is wrong. Usually a slowdown means one of several things:

1. They are not as interested as they seemed to be in early discussions.

2. They discovered something during the due diligence stage that caused concern, and they are not sure how to bring it up or what to do with it.

3. No future event is driving them to make a decision within a specific timeframe.

4. Something has changed since the beginning of the process. After all, the process might take several months, and a lot can happen during that period.

5. You might not be dealing with a decision-maker. This critical point applies to both buyers and sellers. Always make sure that you are dealing with a decision-maker on either the buyer's or the seller's side.

6. Perhaps the due diligence stage revealed that your company is not as solid a fit for the buying company as initially thought.

Items 1, 3, and 5 are basic qualification criteria and should have been recognized by you early in the process. After all, if the buyer is truly interested in buying a company, has a timeframe within which the purchase should happen, and you are dealing with the person who can make the decision, they should buy if there is a good fit. However, if the buyer is not qualified on any of these three items, you will not close the deal unless you are very lucky.

Items 2, 4, and 6 should be expected. The buyers who perform due diligence will discover things about your company that were not previously obvious to them. Don't take their criticism or distance as a personal slight against you or your company. There will be problems with any sale. The secret is to uncover the reasons why they are not buying, address the reasons with a credible, responsible response, and then move on to the next issue. After all the issues are responsibly handled with a qualified buyer, he or she buys. If not, something else is wrong, and you need to keep searching until you find out what it is.

As you would do with any sales situation, check your ego at the door and keep your eyes open. The buyer will give you clues about how things are progressing and will let you know of problems. Don't create problems, but always make sure that buyer-perceived problems are addressed.

Straight Talk

It is amazing what you can observe when you are not the one doing all of the talking. I once attended a negotiation with a law firm at which two other people were actually discussing the negotiations. A more senior member of the firm sat in the background watching everything and saying nothing. Negotiations stalled, and the two people doing the negotiations were starting to get on each other's nerves. I asked for a break and approached the silent person sitting in the back. He confirmed that he was really the decision-maker. I then asked him about stumbling blocks to closing the deal, and he told me every one of them and the deal eventually was closed.

Easier Financing Makes for an Easier Sale

If you have an interested buyer, you can help him or her move in the direction of a closed deal if you have already done some legwork on the financing front.

You probably have working relationships with a number of investors who know you and your company. These people may present excellent possible financiers for your buyer. Once you know the general sale price range of your company and the most likely deal financing structure, I suggest that you talk to your investor contacts to get your company pre-qualified for the money levels involved. In this way, your buyers need only qualify themselves, not the company.

Making the financing easier makes it easier for you to sell. This alone should give you some incentive. Plus, if you plan to keep any or your company's stock or offer financing to the company as part of the purchase agreement, you want to make sure that the buyers work with the most credible financiers possible. Why not your own acquaintances? This makes good business sense for everyone.

The Least You Need to Know

➤ The asking price is based on future income projections.

➤ Determine the reasonable price range based on the high and the low asking prices, and then use your intuition to pick the right price.

➤ Using an attorney to negotiate for you may be a good idea if the attorney understands your business issues and is a seasoned negotiator.

➤ A buyer's objections are the reasons why he or she has not yet purchased. Treat them like gold and address them as best you can.

➤ Pre-qualifying the company for financing can help move the final negotiation stage forward.

Chapter 23

When It Is Better Not to Sell

In This Chapter

➤ Deciding to take your company off the market

➤ Dealing with the fallout of no sale

➤ Selling to your employees instead

➤ Closing down completely

➤ Liquidating can be taxing

Everyone had gone home and John was sitting by himself in his office. It was starting to become clear to him that the company was just not going to sell for what he wanted. Three buyers had gone through the due diligence stages only to decide, at the end, that the company simply was not a good fit for their organization. None had said anything specifically negative; they just had not bought. Six months after having put the company on the market, John had nothing but six months of mayhem and disruption to show for the effort.

Now what? In truth, he really wanted to get back to work. He was tired of living in this limbo state, and he knew that his employees felt the same way.

John was just plain tired. His employees were the best, and they seemed more excited about the company every day. But, he really wanted to get out from under the obligations of the company and do something different. He had started the company over 10 years earlier, and he was ready to do something else. But how, and what? That was the question.

Well, one thing he knew for sure. Getting the business back on track was his first priority. He may be tired, but he wasn't going to let 10 years of hard work fizzle into worthlessness simply because he was tired. As always, a well-run business always presented its own opportunities, as long as you were still in the game.

This is every seller's worst nightmare. You do the preparation work. You prepare your finances. You work with several prospective buyers, and nobody makes you an offer. Or, even worse, the only offer you get is one that is so low that you cannot justify selling. Now what do you do?

That is the focus of this chapter. This is a difficult topic since it really depends on the specifics of the situation and the emotional makeup of the people involved. However, there are options, and there is likely to be fallout resulting from the business not selling.

I hope that you read this chapter before you put your business on the market. After all, this might happen to you if the company doesn't sell. And I hope you never need this information.

What If They Offer Too Little?

It is sobering to have people tell you that your business is simply not worth what you think it's worth. An item is worth only what a buyer is willing to pay for it. Right? What do you do when the only offers you get are lower than you are willing to accept?

An obvious first answer is to drop the price. This is a particularly viable option if you have been told by the buyers that they would not make an offer since there was such a wide gap that any reasonable offer seemed ridiculous. Contrary to how Mergers and Acquisitions are portrayed on television, not everyone is a cutthroat waiting to gouge you. Some people may not make an offer, thinking that a substantially lower offer would simply be insulting.

➤ Is the price too high?

➤ What did your internal analysis tell you?

➤ Is it possible that the assumptions used on your present value analysis or in your future sales projections were so "rosy" that they bordered on unrealistic?

➤ Have the buyers moved on to other acquisitions, or do you think that they might still be interested?

➤ Would it cost you more than you are willing to give up to finally close the deal?

Whatever the reasons, they didn't buy. I suggest that you take one or two of these prospective buyers to a very PRIVATE lunch and have a long, detailed discussion about why they did not buy. Especially if one or two of them, in your opinion, should have bought not only for financial reasons but for strategic ones as well. Something in your assumptions was clearly inaccurate, and only feedback from buyers will help you pinpoint the problem.

Straight Talk

I recently sold a house in Austin, Texas, which is one of the hottest real estate markets in the country. I listed the house for what I considered a "high yet reasonable" price. The house didn't sell for over a 5-month period, which is forever in a hot market. I didn't even get an offer, although multiple potential buyers came back a second and even third time to look at the house. I figured that if they wanted it, they would make an offer. Not so. I dropped the price around 10 percent, and then sold it for cash and at full price within 48 hours of listing it at the new price. I used to have a boss who constantly contended that "It's the price, stupid!" I didn't always agree with him, but he clearly would have been right on this one.

Is it possible that you are not ready to sell? Perhaps you think that you are ready, but to the eyes of an objective observer, you might still be too possessive, causing them to think that the post-purchase period might be fraught with emotional baggage that is just not worth dealing with, from their perspective.

Although you always want to stress and sell the quality of your company and its various assets, you also have to offer them for a reasonable price.

The Liabilities of Not Selling

Let's assume for a moment that you take the company off the market. Now what? What kind of fallout should you expect? I suggest that you can do this without major damage, but only by performing some kind of damage control with your employees, customers, and other owners.

Everyone who knew about the possibility of sale suffered some type of emotional fallout from the experience. They might have spent weeks obsessing about who their next boss would be, whether they would have a job after the sale, whether the division they work in will be closed down, or any number of other areas of potential concern.

At a minimum, you need to talk with:

➤ Major customers

➤ Major vendors

➤ Key employees

➤ Other investors

In short, you now have to evaluate your motivations and talk to the key people in your business life. They need to understand that you still care about the business and want it to remain successful. Any doubt about your motivations will turn into hesitancy on their part, which inevitably turns into less favorable financial relationships for you. Risk and reward. Remember?

What About Your Customers?

Hopefully, most of your customers were not aware of your intention to sell. This would be good news and will minimize the fallout if the company does not sell. However, any prospective buyer of your business who was serious about the purchase probably talked with some of your key customers.

Customers may now start to wonder about your commitment to the business if it doesn't sell. After all, you had tried to sell and didn't. You gave them some reasons for wanting to sell, back in the early stages of putting the company on the market. Now what are your plans?

Straight Talk

Most business people will understand your wanting to sell, and also that it didn't work out, as long as you are comfortable with the outcome and can present it in a credible way. Just as you would rehearse a speech or formal presentation, you should rehearse your failed-sale presentation to major vendors and customers. It might be the most important presentation you give in the precarious time just after taking the company off of the market. You don't have to reveal everything, but it needs to make business sense.

You should expect some reticence on the part of your customers. You might even lose some of them. Once you decide to take the company off of the market, you must go overboard in the service areas to make sure that your customers accept that you are in business to stay and that your relationship with them will remain as positive as always. They will be looking for signs of negative change on your part, and you should work overtime to ensure them that their fears are unfounded. Even if you are depressed or disappointed that the sale did not go through.

And don't use your customers as your therapist. Simply say something like, "We just didn't find the right buyer, and I took it off the market so that we could get back to running our business." And leave it at that. Customers really don't need to know more than the basics. Besides, your actions will speak much louder than anything you can say at this point.

What About Vendors?

Vendors may change their credit relationship with you if they start to think that you are now in business for the short term instead of the long term as they probably thought you were before you put the company up for sale.

I wouldn't expect this as much if you tried to sell a larger company, but you should expect some fallout if you tried to sell a smaller, privately owned business.

What About Your Employees?

Expect that you will have to do some damage control with your employees as well. They are probably relieved that the company didn't sell, but they will have the same concerns as your customers and vendors will. They might think that your loyalty to them has been placed in jeopardy, causing them to be less "company" oriented and more oriented toward protecting themselves.

If reorganization plans were floated as part of the sale process and your employees found out about it, you definitely will have to do damage control. These people are probably already looking for other jobs if they did not like the plan. Acting promptly and sincerely might keep some of the better ones around. However, if they feel that the trust between the company and themselves has been violated, you might have permanently disgruntled employees. If they are not as happy, but still able to perform their jobs in professional and competent ways, then do the best you can to keep things up-beat and positive.

Getting things back to normal and even throwing a company party to celebrate staying autonomous might not be a bad idea. You somehow need to convince them that the company and you are still in business and that their jobs are not in jeopardy. Otherwise, not selling may end up costing you more than the drop in price you would have needed to sell to a viable buyer would have. Now that would really hurt.

Hot Tip

Just as the presentation to vendors and customers needed rehearsal, so does the presentation to your employees. If they don't believe you, then you might lose them along with the prospects for selling the company.

Selling to Your Employees

Perhaps your best buyers already work for the company: your employees. You might find that the employees would be willing to purchase the company by any number of ways including

➤ Leveraged Buy Out (LBO)

➤ Management Buy Out (MBO)

➤ Employee Stock Option Plan (ESOP)

These three plans really mean the same thing to you as the seller. The employees arrange to purchase your ownership shares in the company using the equity in the company as collateral for a loan or through shared contributions. These plans were discussed briefly in Chapter 5, and they should not be forgotten now that you are in Chapter 23. The approach is still very valid, and you might be inclined to offer your employees a better price than you would a stranger. Especially since you now know that the strangers did not want to purchase the company for the price you wanted anyhow.

Notice that these options help to minimize the negative impact of the non-sale on the employees. Instead of the non-sale looking like bad news, it can now spell opportunity for them. I suggest that you approach this topic carefully. If you start down this road and it does not work out, you will definitely have bad feelings within the company.

There is one huge reason why you might consider selling to your employees, in the form of an ESOP, and offering them a discounted price at the same time. You don't pay federal taxes on money received as part of the ESOP purchase as long as your situation meets a few criteria:

➤ Your company cannot be publicly traded.

➤ You have held the stock for three years or more.

➤ You used the ESOP sale proceeds to buy securities in U.S. corporations.

➤ The corporations in which you purchase securities must use more than 50 percent of their assets in the active conduct of a trade or business while a maximum of 25 percent of the company's gross income can come from passive investment income.

➤ You sold between 30 percent and 100 percent of outstanding shares to the ESOP.

➤ There are a few other criteria that are comparatively rare that I won't list here.

Seller Beware

As the seller to an ESOP who then purchases other U.S. securities, you should be aware that the newly purchased U.S. securities will be subject to capital gain taxes when sold. The basis being the value of the shares at the time they were purchased.

If you think about this option, there are some very real incentives for you to work with your employees to make this happen. It not only benefits your employees, but it also saves you tax money in the process. In fact, if you take a buyout from a third party instead of the ESOP, you will have to pay capital gain taxes on the received money, which will most likely be 20 percent. Dropping your price 10 percent and selling your shares to an ESOP allows your employees to purchase the company for at 10 percent discount and allows you to save 10 percent in taxes, and all is well.

There are other benefits associated with an ESOP purchase that improve ESOP dealings with banks that can offer ESOPs more attractive financing due to tax advantages that are passed on to the bank.

Maintaining an ESOP fund has administrative costs and hassles associated with it, but it might be worth it for both you and the employees.

Remember too that you can sell as little as 30 percent of your stock to an ESOP. This might make it attractive for you to sell 70 percent of your shares to an outside investor and the other 30 percent to the ESOP, that portion would, if reinvested as outlined earlier, be tax free. In this way, you get the majority of your money up front while still presenting the employees with an investment opportunity of their own.

You might find that selling to an ESOP is something to be pursued before selling to a separate company. Should your initial foray into selling the company not work out, don't forget about the ESOP and other employee purchase options.

Doing Damage Control on What Was Revealed

Once you take the company off of the market and get back to business as usual, you might start to regret the amount of information you revealed during the sale process. After all, if you talked with a competitor, you probably revealed processes and other information that they would not have otherwise known. You are now back competing with them, knowing that they know more about your operation than you know about theirs.

Forget it. You cannot undo what was done in the past, and it is easy to get caught up in trying to recapture something instead of simply moving on.

This doesn't mean that you shouldn't make appropriate adjustments to your operation based on this added level of exposure. I simply mean that focusing on what you do, and doing it well, is the best competitive weapon in your arsenal.

Don't forget that you also learned some things about them as part of the process. Perhaps you can use that information to your advantage. For example, you might know more about their financial operating models, which might help you when bidding competitively.

My point is this: get back to business and forgive yourself for anything you might have done during the attempted sale process. It can't be undone, and carrying it with you into the future might be your undoing.

Closing Up Shop Completely

It is very possible that you small business owners might decide that operating the business just isn't worth it any more. That your motivation is no longer in competing and winning. That you would rather get out of what you are doing and do something different.

At this point you may decide that closing up shop completely is the simplest and most attractive answer. Well, this process is never simple. Trust me. It takes months to close even a small business. If your business has been around for any length of time at all and especially if you have employees, you will find this process more time and emotion consuming than anticipated.

Straight Talk

Don't underestimate the complexity and the amount of time involved with completely closing your business. If you have achieved any level of business success at all, you will have vendors, customers, landlords, and employees who will require special attention. In addition, fully expect that you will grieve over the loss. Having closed up two businesses of my own, I can safely say that the feelings associated with closing a business are a lot like those experienced when losing a close friend. It takes time to get over the loss. Don't decide to close up shop as an "easy way out"; you might find it more difficult than expected, and almost always irreversible.

I suggest that you first evaluate your motivations:

➤ Are you simply tired and need a vacation? If so, take it while letting everyone know that business should continue as usual. But do take the time off. Recharge your emotional batteries before you make this major decision.

➤ Make sure that you are not reacting to having your pride hurt from the lack of success you had in selling your business. Contrary to how it might feel sometimes, you are not your business. Your professional and personal credibility is not tied to your business, and if you are closing due to a bruised ego, you should adjust your focus. There are many poor reasons to close, and this is one of the poorest.

➤ Are you embarrassed to face your customers, vendors, and employees who participated in the unsuccessful sale process? If so, figure out a way to get over it and to get back to business. Once before you created a working, thriving business environment and you can do it again. But you have to take the first step. Do it.

➤ Are you simply not having fun? Then look for ways to make it fun. Oddly enough, when you are ready to close the doors, you acquire an immense amount of freedom. After all, what can be worse than closing the doors? Why not take a few chances and have some fun? Perhaps the business needed a shakeup to move it to the next performance level.

This is an excellent time to take advantage of those business contacts you have cultivated over the years. Most likely you know some other business owner who has been through a similar situation. Talking with that person about how they reacted and how they handled the situation might help you determine the right next steps for you.

If you still decide that you want out, I suggest that you take a few preparatory steps:

1. Take an objective look around the company and see if one of the employee buyout agreements (LBO, MBO, or ESOP) will provide a workable solution. Just because you have lost interest doesn't mean that the employees have. Why put the company to sleep if someone else wants to nurture it and make it grow? And you just might make more money in the process!

2. If Step 1 does not present a viable option, review your assets and determine which you might want to keep for either personal or future business reasons. You will have to ask the other owners for similar feedback.

3. Determine which assets have liens attached to them along with the minimum sale price needed to cover the lien. It would really be a shame to sell your company and still owe money when finished.

4. Don't expect to get anywhere near what you paid for furniture, computers, and other operating equipment. That $250 desk might get you $50 in a sale, so adjust your expectations accordingly.

5. You might want to simplify the process by calling one of the liquidaters in your area. These people come into your business, make a listing of everything that is for sale, and offer you one price for the whole lot. This is an easy approach, but I have found that their prices are substantially lower than I have typically been willing to accept.

6. Offer to sell equipment and other items to your employees. They might have had their eye on specific items for a long time, and this is a great way to give something to them at a reasonable price for both of you.

7. Talk to your vendors to see if they are willing to take back any of your existing inventory items in exchange for a partial or full credit. You won't need it and they can probably sell it to someone else. Better to pay a smaller restocking fee than to eat the entire purchase amount.

8. Talk to your customers to see if any of your products, services, and/or employees would be of interest to them. Your customers might get a great deal on something that they can use, and your employees might end up with an excellent job working for an appreciative employer. Once again, a win-win.

Hot Tip

Once you have determined the "fire-sale" value of your company, you might try talking to the previously interested buyers. For what may well be a substantially reduced price, one of these buyers might just take the whole company off your hands in a single purchase. This is faster for you, better for them, and it provides continuing employment for your employees.

9. Expect that this process will take months, and even years, depending on the level of business complexity. This is never a quick fix, but if you decide it is right for you, so be it.

It is a strange feeling to walk out the door of your business for the last time, knowing that tomorrow you will not need to come in to answer the phones, talk to customers, or deal with vendors. It is also a freeing experience in that you can now move on to doing something different or even take some well-deserved time off. Every time that I have sold or closed my past companies, I was sad for a while, but also relieved. I was sure that it was the right time, and never regretted making the decision to move on. The preparatory personal evaluation work I had already done made moving on an easier process.

The Tax Implications of Liquidating

Liquidating assets has tax implications for the company and ultimately for you, depending on the specific company structure.

Hot Tip

Remember that you can move you business's legal address to the basement of your house and still keep a legal registration with the state. Liquidate the old business, keep the cash in the company, and let it sit (invested, naturally) for a while. You might need it as funding for your next venture.

➤ Assets sold by the company will have either a short-term or a long-term gain associated with them. And the gain will be based on the depreciated value of the asset, not its sale price, so careful record keeping will help in this area.

➤ Once completely liquidated, the remaining liquid assets will then be distributed to the shareholders, who will recognize either a gain or a loss depending on the basis of their shares.

➤ Filings must be made with the state and the IRS to let them know that the company is no longer in business. It makes no sense to keep the company open, if not operational, because the longer it is a legal entity the longer it is exposed to the potential of litigation. Why take that risk, even if it is a highly remote possibility.

➤ If there is any possibility of going back into business, you might benefit from keeping the legal structure in place. Credit will be easier to obtain since the company has an established track record and the same EIN. Name recognition is on your side, even if associated with another business activity.

Different rules apply to sole proprietors, partnerships, S corporations, and C corporations. It is always best to check with your tax and legal professionals before making these final decisions. These are the general guidelines.

The Least You Need to Know

➤ Closing up is hard to do.

➤ Fire sales never make you much money.

➤ If you do not sell, expect to work extra hard at first convincing people that you are back in business to stay.

➤ Liquidating has tax implications that should be evaluated before hanging out the "For Sale" sign.

➤ ESOPs are a great way to create a winning situation for both you and your employees.

Part 7
After You Say "I Do"

Up to the closing, you have been working to get the most value for your particular company, whether you are the buyer or seller. Now it is time to work together to make the acquisition profitable for all the parties, and the employees, involved. If you have gotten this far, don't stop at this page. Finish Part Seven and learn how to make the acquisition pieces fit.

Chapter 24

Making Two Pieces Fit as One, or Maybe Two, or Even Three

In This Chapter

➤ When to merge operationally and when to keep separate

➤ Optimizing around customer sales and marketing

➤ Technology areas of importance

➤ Respecting and managing corporate cultures

➤ Maximizing brand equity after the acquisition

"I know that we are planning to merge our stock as part of the acquisition," said Jennie to Julie, her CFO. "What I want to know is your opinion about merging operations. There isn't any real reason why we HAVE to merge operations, is there? Can't we merge the stock and still keep operations separate?"

"Yes, you can," responded Julie with relief. She thought this was the right way to go about it. "Our operations and accounting systems are really incompatible, and it will require some work to get to the point where we can automatically create something as simple as a set of financial statements. Making them completely integrated would be disruptive to them and to us, and it would provide little benefit."

Jennie nodded her head in agreement. "We had looked at consolidating our sales forces, until we realized that they deal with the same companies but with completely different divisions and buyers. We plan to do some cross training over the next few years in the hopes of some day consolidating the sales and marketing departments, letting attrition take care of the headcount cuts. For now, we just want to maintain a status-quo."

"Then let's plan some simpler tasks for the near term, such as consolidating our Web sites and adding our name to their letterhead. Eventually our customers will realize that we are the same company and that things are working out fine. At that time, we will both be more ready for major changes."

Jennie and Jill smiled at each other. This was the right decision to make, and it was a lot simpler than complete integration. Simpler really was better.

You might be coming down the home stretch of your acquisition process. You know the company, its customers, employees, and overall management philosophy. You now have to consider one additional, yet critically important matter: How do you plan to integrate the newly acquired company into your parent company? If it is an asset-only purchase, the process is simple. Even if there is a stock purchase or merger as part of the negotiation, you still don't have to merge the two companies into a single operational entity. You might choose to merge the two into a single operational organization, leave them as separate operating organizations, or even subdivide the two organizations in such as way that a third is created.

Any of these options, as well as others, might be right for your situation and for any number of reasons, some of which are presented in this chapter.

You definitely want to create a transition committee and a plan that will be used as a roadmap toward the post-purchase integration process. Creating this plan before finalizing purchase negotiations allows you to build the post-purchase cost increases or reductions into your financial model. Waiting until the purchase is finalized is a little like jumping off a bridge and into a river without first checking the water depth, never a good idea.

Merging or Not Merging Cultures

Companies are comprised of people. Financial people might think of a company as assets, liabilities, goodwill, account receivable, and financial statements, but ultimately, it is the people who make a company run.

With people come cultures. With cultures come customs, norms, and expectations that may, and usually do, differ from one culture to the next.

You would think that two American companies would have similar cultures. After all, we share the same language, currency, and government. But it is just not so. Look at a Silicon Valley startup firm as compared to a well-established firm like IBM. Each brings its own attributes to the table that might be a strength for one firm but a liability for the other.

A smaller company is usually less restrictive in what it can create, produce, and offer since a smaller number of

Hot Tip

A culture consists of more than simply the dress code policy. It is the unwritten way in which a company thinks and reacts. Don't expect to understand it from a policy manual, although this can be an excellent starting point.

people can be reoriented in a shorter period of time than a company with a larger number of employees. What a smaller company lacks in administrative strengths, it makes up for in sheer creativity and energy.

Should IBM decide to purchase the smaller company, it might decide to impress its culture on the smaller company. Whether this is a good or bad action is dependent on the companies involved, but of one thing you can be sure: If IBM purchases the smaller company for its nimble creativity and then places its large company restrictions on the company, they are probably making the wrong move. Why? They are asking the company to live with both a large and a small company culture at the same time. People at the acquired company will be unhappy, will most likely cut back on the very things that made the company attractive in the first place, and may even leave the company for a more entrepreneurial environment.

Straight Talk

It is amazing how the little things can make big differences to employees. A Silicon Valley firm, where I worked in the early 1980s, had a beer bust every Friday afternoon starting at around 4:30. We had it outside, weather permitting, and frequently had visitors from other companies that stopped by to partake in the festivities. We often hired people who attended the parties because they figured that making money while working at a place that had beer busts was a solid combination. When the beer busts were cancelled, for legal reasons, every Friday afternoon had a little bit of a wake feeling about it. It is hard to put into a spreadsheet, but it is real none the less.

If, on the other hand, the smaller company has a product that can be easily sold through the IBM distribution network and the company was specifically purchased for that particular product, then assimilation might be the right thing. After all, the product already exists, and it should be easily transitioned into the IBM way of doing things. If the creativity of the people is still desired, it is feasible to set them up as a separate, rogue unit with the specific purpose of being creative. Few restrictions and open options are generally the most productive creative environments. In this way, IBM and the acquired company both win.

Sensitivity to the cultural issues cannot be overemphasized. I have seen a number of financially attractive acquisitions turn sour simply due to two dissimilar cultures trying to deny their natures with one being dominated by the other. Diversity makes us all stronger if appropriately respected and applied. The same applies to company cultures.

Determining Corporate Personnel Policies

There is no magic wand that, when waved, will provide the right corporate policy mix for two combined companies. Simply look at the two cultures, their personnel, and their benefits packages. In general, you want to keep the best of what works and to replace what is counterproductive. You might also find that purchasing economies make themselves available when you combine headcount, making it possible to provide better insurance and other benefits for a lower cost.

Straight Talk

One major car rental company recently asked some of its employees to move to another related company. The rental company provided cars to its employees as a standard part of its compensation package. Those who went to the other company, where the car benefit was not provided, received an automatic $8,000 annual salary increase to compensate them for the car benefit loss.

Any change that reduces employee benefits will cost the buyer something, or hard feeling will arise. Cutting back on benefits to increase profits while decreasing morale, or even losing key personnel since the good ones are always the first to be hired away, is a short sighted approach.

Assessing the Marketing and Sales Processes

Without sales, we can all go home because the business would disappear. I professionally cut my teeth selling advanced technology equipment, so I made my living in sales and marketing for a long time.

I contend that the sales and marketing people, and processes, must be closely examined before the acquisition is completed. If you don't have a clear picture of what will happen, with respect to customer interactions, when you announce the arrangement, you are simply asking for a lot of uneasy customers, vendors, sales, and support people. These people make hundreds of little decisions every day, and these all add up to a total sales success or failure. These people must understand and clearly project what they can and cannot expect from the combination of the two companies.

If current customers, of both companies, are expected to react favorably to a combined sales/marketing effort, which should create increased sales, then combine away. Customers might perceive that the two sales functions require completely different skill sets, like the difference between selling commercial jet aircraft and selling small, private, single engine planes. If a company tries to combine these two sales functions, it will probably wind up with a drop in the customer-perceived credibility level. This could cost you sales or, even worse, customers, and it is just not worth the risk. Have a well-defined transition strategy.

Leaving things as they were before is safe, but might sacrifice complimentary selling opportunities and add redundant costs. Combining, when the customer base will not support the combination, is like trying to put a square peg into a round hole. Determine the best way to sell to your customers and then structure the sales/marketing/ support functions so that those optimal methods are implemented.

Hot Tip

A great place to start evaluating post-purchase business combination options is with the sales/marketing functions. The underlying company structure must be set up to support the customer sales function in an optimal way, or the business cart will be placed before the customer sales horse.

Merging Customer Databases

A determination about whether or not to combine customer database information is really predicated in large part on your decisions from the preceding section. You might find that the cost of overcoming the technology hurdles associated with combining databases is greater than the expected benefits. You might also find that combining databases allows your salespeople to share leads, although selling different products to the same customers.

Once again, there is no right or wrong answer. Only the answers that best optimize your ability to use your sales force and your customer information to their optimal benefit.

Creating a New Management Team

This is often a touchy subject. The decision to create a new management structure is often made by the very people who will be part of that structure. Creating one that calls for the elimination of management positions means that a manager may have to vote to eliminate his or her own job. That is asking a lot from any person, and it often cannot be done without hard feelings.

On the other hand, adding talents could very well make the management team stronger than it was. Again, there are no hard and fast rules on the right way to do this. In an ideal world, everyone would pull together for the common good of the post-purchase organization, but idealism usually gives way to the practical realities of employment and income.

Talking about the post-purchase management structure before the purchase is finalized is the best way to ensure that all parties receive just compensation for their post-purchase role, or elimination, whichever the case may be.

Creating a New, Combined Business Face

In the case of a merger, one of the companies simply disappears to be replaced by the new, merged entity. Special attention must be paid to ensuring that credibility, goodwill, and other brand loyalties transfer to the new entity. If, on the other hand, the acquired company would be better served by leaving its old reputation behind, transferring the positives while eliminating the negatives might be the right approach. As with the other topics, there is no right answer that fits every situation. Your overall goal is to maximize shareholder wealth while taking best care of your customers and employees. Making all of these pieces fit properly is an art with few firm guidelines.

Brand Equity Retention or Sacrifice

Remember a few years ago when several people who died after taking a major drug manufacturer's over-the-counter pain reliever? We will call this company XYZ Corporation for purposes of this discussion. If XYZ had not done an effective job of defusing the negative public perception that accompanied the event, all of their other products would have been tainted, whether deserved or not. (By the way, the actual XYZ is considered to have done an excellent job of handling the problem.)

Hot Tip

Always remember that the intent is to minimize the impact of your recent acquisition on both sets of customers. It takes a lot of work to make something look easy, and that work pays off in the form of retained customers, more satisfied employees, and improved shareholder value.

If you purchased that company, you might want to adopt their safe products but attach your name instead of XYZ's. Why? Because your brand does not have a negative buyer connotation, and XYZ's might. The products work and are more saleable with your brand name instead of XYZ's. By the way, if you were XYZ, you might be tempted to purchase another company simply to use their well-respected brand on your existing, safe products. In this case, a rose by another name might look like a rose, but really isn't. How is that for a little spin doctoring?

The Department of Redundancy Department ...

It is almost guaranteed that some aspects of the two companies will overlap. Making snap decisions on what is duplicate and what is unique simply based on an organizational chart or a title is fraught with the potential for mistakes. This is particularly true if one of the companies was previously a privately owned small business that operated under its own sets of rules.

If both of the companies are in the same geographic location, or they will be moved into one after the sale, redundancy can probably be eliminated in certain operational areas. If, on the other hand, the companies will be located geographically far from each other, you might find that separate support staffs are required to make daily operations function on a smooth basis.

No matter what, you should have a careful plan outlined before the sale is finalized. Otherwise, you might find yourself struggling with the prior owners, employees, and others about future plans, which will likely drive up the estimated cost associated with the purchase.

Evaluating Location Overlaps

When competitors combine, there are almost always location issues, particularly for retail outlets. Two highly competitive retail stores might very well have locations in the same high-visibility retail locations. If the two stores merge into a single entity, the second store location is probably unnecessary since it will now sell the same products, at the same price, along with the same services as the first. One of them has to go. Which? Once again, it is a matter of individual assessment, and I suggest that you capitalize on the better location with the better sales. Regardless of which the store has the old name or the merged name, I suggest that you close the less productive store and make the more productive store the outlet location of choice.

Know and understand that you will need to train your customers, with clear maps charting the way, to understand that the old store that they frequented has not "gone away" but simply changed its name and location. I suggest that you plan this strategy over a period of several months, at a minimum, or your customers may become confused and lost in the process.

Hot Tip

The balancing act when combining companies is to optimize without sacrificing the core, mission critical aspects of the company. Stated another way, you want to trim the fat but leave the meat. If reductions have to be done, do it. But make sure drastic trimming is required before you start cutting, because once done, it is almost impossible to get those employees, customers, and/or vendors back.

Assume that you just purchased a manufacturing company, which has the same capability as your company. Now assume that its primary production plant is in another part of the country from yours and that your plant has enough surplus production capacity to manufacture the purchased company's products. It wouldn't make sense, on the surface, to keep the purchased company's production facility since it is completely surplus and redundant, not to mention a plane ride away from the new corporate headquarters.

Selling the purchased production plant allows you to recoup some of the purchase cost while also making sure that the employees stay employed after the purchase. If they remained with your company, financial pressures would probably force you to either sell or close the acquired plant, which is bad news for everyone.

This entire question should also be thought out before the purchase is finalized.

Technology Issues

In today's world, you have to evaluate technology synergies or you could be in store for some unwelcome, expensive, and disruptive surprises. Almost every aspect of a corporation is in some way dependent on technology, with the success of some companies predicated on the effective use of technology.

There is no way around it. Modern corporations must use technology or they are on their way to obsolescence. Considering the impact of technology before the purchase minimizes the likelihood of later technological surprises.

Assessing the Operations Technologies

What aspects of your operations and the purchased company's operations are dependent on technology, and is it standard or proprietary technology? This question must be answered in such a way that allows you to assess whether the two organizational technologies can be merged.

Modern manufacturing requires integrated production tracking, inspection, shipping, purchasing, and accounting capabilities. Effectively using automation is what allows these companies to compete and stay ahead of their competition. If your internal systems cannot merge with those of the acquired company, then you will likely have to purchase a new or updated version that allows for the required level of integration. To not merge the systems might substantially diminish the benefits expected by purchasing the company, which diminishes your expected return on investment and time.

Hot Tip

Don't ignore technology differences and assume that "they will just work themselves out" later after the purchase. Lack of technical compatibility could make the integration of operations difficult, prohibitively expensive, and will certainly diminish the return you expect from the purchase.

Straight Talk

Changing technologies is never easy or cheap and is always disruptive. And technology changes at an amazingly fast rate making its maintenance an integral part of corporation operation.

Operations might also include special software applications that optimize telemarketing, product development, shipping, or other business features. If the software is proprietary, you will need to determine the cost to upgrade so that integration is possible, or investigate purchasing a completely new system. The simple fact is that automation might be the very competitive advantage you just purchased. It sure would be disheartening to learn that the automation could not be integrated with your own systems, that the production processes were dependent on that automation, and that replacing it is cost prohibitive.

Assessing Communications Technologies

The ability to make a telephone call is so integral to American life that I know people who act as though they have been put into solitary confinement when their phone is out of order. For a business, critical aspects might be heavily dependent on the telephone, cellular telephone service, the Internet, or other communications-related technology.

E-mail, Web sites, 800 numbers, and notebook computers are a part of business. Period. This might not have been as true five to seven years ago, but it certainly is true today.

Assume that the both companies involved in the purchase use 800 numbers for providing service or taking orders. What happens to these 800 numbers themselves along with the people and systems who answer them? How are customers trained to dial one or the other? If you plan to have them both answered by the same people, how will these people know which company's 800 number they are answering? This is a small item, but it can turn into a large item if there is no way for employees to answer the phone with the correct name of the particular company called. And it is the small things that all come together to create large impressions.

Straight Talk

It is amazing to me the impact that simply changing your business telephone number has, as any of you in major metropolitan areas that have undergone area code changes can verify. Letterhead stationary must be changed. Web site information must be updated. Product literature, brochures, advertising, fax cover sheets, business cards, and numerous other daily necessities need updating when you change contact information. This is an expensive process, but it is necessary when changing a company's identity or method of contact. Don't forget to include it in your transition plan.

And you must consider the impact of your purchase on Internet-related activities, such as Web sites and e-mail. You really have to start thinking about Internet locations as being similar to street addresses, in that people know to "stop by" that location when they look for information.

If you plan to consolidate Web sites, how do you handle referring people from the former sites to the new one? Do you want them automatically referred, or do you want to train them to go to the new site? When they enter the new site, do they automatically come in at the parent company's home page, or do they go to the sub page that deals specifically with the former company's products or services? All of these questions must be answered to ensure a smooth and painless transition for your electronic customers.

Accounting Systems and You

We all know that the bean counters will not be happy until all of the beans are properly tracked in an accurate way. Setting up the financial systems of the two companies is a lot like setting up the operational systems. Tracking information must be based on the business model chosen as part of the purchase process.

If the two companies are to be treated as separate entities, accounting can remain relatively distinct with minimal loss. After all, there is minimal financial information interaction between the acquired company and its buyer if the operationally oriented financial data is not integrated. The only interaction might involve data required for the preparation of consolidated financial reports. Spending a lot of time and money to automate minimal data entry seems like a discretionary, not mandatory, task to me.

However, once you have merged the two companies, you must account for the assets, liabilities, income, and expenses of the two organizations, which are now sharing the same name. This consolidation process is probably worth planning and doing, or a lot of manual work will have to go into providing management with the financial reports needed to run the company on a daily basis.

The details of this process are beyond the scope of this chapter and truly require the services of a trained accountant.

Again, don't assume that this problem will just solve itself. It will have to be dealt with at some point, even if that means simply "keeping it as it is since we are remaining a separate entity."

Here are a few areas of particular note that you should consider before signing the final agreements:

> ➤ Invoicing and accounts receivable must be integrated if you plan to consolidate sales and

Hot Tip

No amount of effort will make up for under funding the consolidation effort when structuring the purchase arrangements. There is only so much a person can do to cover for an inadequate automation system. "Two hands and 40 hours," as an old boss used to say.

marketing force efforts. Keeping separate customer information databases is a guaranteed eventual trouble spot.

➤ Vendor relations and information should also be consolidated if you plan to consolidate operations. Once again, keeping separate ordering, payment, and receipt databases is a sure way to have future problems with that vendor.

➤ At some point your employee records will have to be consolidated in a merged environment, so you might as well plan this process from the beginning.

There is no easy way to determine whether your recent purchase is performing up to expectation if you do not have valid accounting and financial information. Making sure that these systems provide the information needed, in a credible and consistent manner, is an excellent strategy for spotting acquisition integration problems earlier in the process, instead of later.

The Least You Need to Know

➤ Acquired assets need only be added to the acquiring company's asset tracking and accounting system.

➤ Acquired companies that will remain stand-alone operations/profit-loss centers should require minimal system integration effort.

➤ Merging the two companies into a single operational entity means that technology systems may also require merging. This might not be a trivial task, although it is critically important to managing the transition.

➤ The decision to merge or keep separate is based on a unique combination of considerations, such as geographic locations, corporate cultures, and the optimal customer interaction model.

➤ Make sure to address all customer, vendor, and investor communication channels including phone numbers, fax numbers, e-mail accounts, and Internet Web sites.

Is It Working?

This was unbelievable. Francine, the president of the buying company, looked at yet another complaint letter about her recent approval of an employee's termination. "How could the laying off of one person create such an uproar?" she asked herself.

Greg, the terminated employee, had worked in the marketing department of the acquired company as an advertising copywriter. Francine's company already had someone in that position with more years of seniority than Greg, so she had agreed to let Greg go. It was nothing personal against Greg. In fact, she had never even met him.

What had she missed with Greg? And what could she do to correct the situation? Her staff told her that the other company's employees brought up Greg's termination in all the staff meetings. And it was quickly becoming a rallying point for discontent.

Her computer beeped indicating that she had e-mail, and sure enough, there was the letter from the acquired company's former president. And along with the letter, was her answer.

"We talked about this in our negotiations, but it probably didn't sink in at the time. Greg's family had provided the initial funding for the company over 15 years ago. We bought them

out within three years of that initial loan, but we always kept a plaque to his parents in the conference room. We gave Greg a job around five years ago, and he has easily pulled his weight. Good luck."

"Just great," sighed Francine! Now what?

The honeymoon is over. Daily life with your new acquisition, or owner, is becoming routine, for better or worse. You are now getting a realistic view of how the two companies are working with each other. It is now time to determine how well things are really going.

This chapter presents some high level ways of determining the effectiveness of the purchase and how well the relationship is performing compared to established expectations.

Did Customers Stick Around?

You can tell how good the cooking is at a local restaurant by counting the number of local license plates in the parking lot. You can also determine the success of your recent business integration by counting the number of customers who stuck with the acquired company through the acquisition and beyond.

An excellent place to start an assessment of your recent acquisition is to perform a quick overview of the existing customer base.

➤ How does it compare to the customer base the acquired company had before the acquisition?

➤ How are their purchase volumes compared to those seen before the acquisition?

➤ Have you received complaint messages or meeting requests from any of your major customers?

➤ Are your company's (the buying company) customers complaining about lack of attention? (Don't focus so much attention on keeping the acquired customers that you forget about your own prior customers.)

➤ Has the mix of products purchased by the overall customer base changed since the acquisition?

➤ Have you seen substantial turnover in the sales and marketing department since the acquisition?

These are just a few of the quantifiable ways that you can use to determine how things are going on the sales and marketing front of your acquisition.

Comparing the customer list from before and after the acquisition tells you something about the customer turnover. It is possible that the turnover is a result of something other than the acquisition, but the coincidence is too strong to completely ignore. Take into account the orders actually placed by customers since the acquisition, not those you hear about that might close.

To get these numbers, you must wait at least one complete sale *reorder cycle*, which could be several weeks to several months. Compare the frequency of purchases before the acquisition to the current frequency of purchase. If is has dropped any appreciable amount, you might have grounds for concern. If they are about the same, it is good news. If they have grown, this is great news, and it verifies your intuition that this acquisition would be a good move on both the financial and strategic fronts.

If sales have grown, take a look at the sales by product comparison. You might be really happy to find that some of the buying company's products are being sold to the acquired company's prior customers. This type of cross marketing/selling effort is the golden nugget of any company merger or acquisition. Your sales people are making calls on the same customers and they are selling more products. Now, that is great!

Terms of Acquisition

Reorder cycle   The amount of time that it takes for a customer to go from the close date of the prior purchase to the close of the next purchase opportunity. A repeat customer with a two-month reorder cycle will order from you approximately six times per year.

Sale gestation period   The time that it takes to close a sale from the point of initial customer contact to the time the deal actually closes.

If you are receiving complaints from customers or seeing a large turnover of the department's personnel, you probably have some serious personnel issues that are best addressed earlier instead of later.

Salespeople can be a fickle, temperamental lot who are often very turf protective. There are a number of things that you and other management personnel can do to get, and keep, the sales force on your side.

Getting Sales on Your Side

The simple fact is that your sales force is representing your company to your customers. If that representation is done in a positive way, great. If that representation is one of dissatisfaction with the new arrangements, disappointment with the new management or products, or dissatisfaction with other transition-related issues, this can cost you in both the short and long term.

Therefore, it is important that someone with a sales/marketing background make some sales calls with your top salespeople. This accomplishes a several things at the same time:

➤ It gives you feedback about the quality of the salespeople.

➤ It gets you face-to-face with your customers, which is always a good thing.

➤ You get to see, firsthand, how your new company and products are being presented. Sometimes the most important stuff cannot be printed, e-mailed, or faxed. You have to see it yourself.

➤ If the sales people see you or your staff taking the time to go on calls, it will mean a lot to them. It doesn't take long for these actions to filter through the sales force.

Straight Talk

I once had a founder of a startup company accompany me on a number of sales calls to my customers. I kept complaining about product deficiencies, to which he always contended the customers and I were "simply whining." So I challenged him to come out and "show me how it should be done." After a few customer calls, John told me that his attitude toward a lot of these problems had changed. In his words, "There is a big difference between reading about an accident and being the one who picks up the bodies." First hand experience cannot be replaced, and making sales calls is really the only way to get a reliable picture of what is really happening from a sales perspective.

I contend that, once the acquisition is finished, getting the sales and marketing force on your side is of critical importance if preserving the acquired customer base is important to retaining the acquired company value. Uncertainty can be dismissed quickly using face-to-face contact with the new management. This is particularly important for the key salespeople and the key customers, many of whom you might already have met as part of the due diligence process.

Keeping Customers Out of Squabbles

Again, salespeople are highly territorial. After all, most compensation programs are defined by territory, quota, and product incentives. Integrating two companies will almost always require the shifting of customers between salespeople.

It is important that the customer be kept out of any internal territorial fighting. This is not their job; it is yours. The following list outlines a few suggestions that may help make the transition a little smoother. By the way, you probably want to have these meetings before the acquisition is finalized. This way you will know what you will face afterward and be able to avoid any customer damage.

➤ Have a meeting with the sales managers of both the acquired and acquiring companies regarding territories, salespeople, and major customers.

➤ Break down revenues by customers, products, and territories.

➤ Look for areas of overlap between each company's salespeople on a customer, segment, or geographic basis.

➤ Can the account be reasonably divided between the multiple salespeople, or can one person be the lead representative with others "reporting" to him or her?

➤ Which salesperson has the best relationship and highest sales with that customer? If it comes down to a choice between the two, you might as well select the one generating the most revenue.

➤ Can the other territories be divided in such a way that nobody is let go, but simply shifted to another region, segment, or product area.

Present Your Combined, Stronger Company Face

If the intention of the acquisition is to merge the two companies into a single entity, a marketing strategy relating the two must be created. Brochures should be printed spelling out the customer benefits of the new relationship. Business cards and letterhead must be changed to reflect the new entity as the primary with some type of reference to the prior company included. For example, "XYZ Corporation, formerly ABC Company" tells customers that the two are related in a simple, yet effective way.

You are trying to tell customers, vendors, and employees that you are going to be true to your stated pre-acquisition intentions. This requires time and strategic insight on your part.

Know that there are people within the organization who have earned the respect of your target audience. There might be a special person in purchasing, who has worked with vendors over the years, whose word of endorsement is worth more than any number of mailers, flyers, and meetings. There might be a special salesperson that everyone listens to, or a key employee that can act as a barometer of acceptance. And, by the way, these people may not be, and often are not, the managers of their departments. (See Chapters 9, "Top Level View of the Proposed Acquisition," and 11, "What Do They REALLY Have Of Value?" for more information about finding these influential people who do not show up on organization charts.)

Hot Tip

Know that if you are not proactive about resolving customer/salesperson conflicts, the conflict might spill over into the customer's relationship with your company, which is almost never good news. You will get to talk to the customer, but not in the way you would prefer.

Taking these people with you when meeting with employees, customers, or vendors will help your credibility. It also shows that you understand the organization enough to know the right people to ask for information and guidance.

The flip side of this argument is also true. Firing or shuffling these people into non-critical positions can do harm in ways you may not even understand at the time. If someone is well respected by other employees but then, for no apparent reason, is treated poorly by the new management, it might engender ill will on the part of the other employees. Be careful about cutting or reorganizing staff based on an organization chart without first taking the time to assess the people involved. Involving someone from Human Resources is an almost mandatory requirement. Involving other longer-term employees in this process is often a good idea.

Firing established and respected employees may hurt not only employee morale, but also it may also create a division within the company. Not only can the single operational entity desired be compromised, but ill-advised terminations can also widen a division that might otherwise have remained nominal.

Tracking Reality to Your Projections

The pro-forma business objectives used as part of the acquisition process are the ultimate objective criteria against which to verify performance. After all, this is what everyone thought could be done, and the acquisition was valued based on these projections. If the post-acquisition performance is above that planned, the purchase price was a bargain. If the performance is under that planned, it is costing more than initially planned. This always gets people's attention, and usually not in a good way.

Before you start jumping on people to work harder, take a close look to see if they can be working smarter. After a few months working as an integrated unit, you will have a better insight into the workings of the acquired company. It might be helpful to review the assumptions associated with the original acquisition plan to see where reality varies from the projected assumptions. Not even a crystal ball gets everything right all the time. The same is true for any financial analysis.

Hot Tip

Don't treat the acquisition plan as a document that is fixed in stone. Instead treat is as a working document. One that clearly defines goals and the assumptions associated with those goals. Only the past is predictable. The future is always changing.

By seeing where reality varies from projection, you can assess whether the initial projections were unrealistic or whether changes in the current operation can create the desired level of performance. There might even be opportunities that you did not know about during the purchase stages that you now understand.

More than one businessperson has lost the financial battle by chasing good money after bad, resulting from an earlier inaccurate projection or assumption. Initially you need to keep the faith and track the performance. After a while, if you are still not hitting the projected numbers, you need to put your ego on the shelf and see if you missed something. This is a tough process, but if you don't do it, your stockholders will do it for you.

Is Everyone Making Enough Money?

Many of the items discussed in this chapter are of an intangible nature. On the other hand, money is an area that is usually well defined. Is everyone making the money agreed to when the purchase was finalized? Here are some items that you probably want to review within six months to a year of the purchase:

➤ First on the money list are the prior owners. Are the payments to them being made as agreed? Has there been any trouble with issuing the stock certificates as agreed?

➤ How did the acquired company's former employees and/or owners, who stayed on as employees of the new company, fare with respect to contingency-based payments?

➤ How has the buying company's stock performed on the public markets, and have the sellers lost or made money on the stock portion of the purchase financing?

➤ If employee stock option plans did not transfer to the acquiring company and if the acquiring company promised to establish an employee option plan during the purchasing process, has it been done?

➤ Are the acquired employees better off or worse off from a benefits perspective because of the purchase?

➤ Has there been substantial employee turnover since the acquisition? Was it planned or unexpected?

➤ Has the acquiring company received its desired level of investment return as a result of the purchase?

➤ Has the asset-secured financing (commercial bank loans) been repaid? If not, why not? It was intended as short-term financing not as a long-term line of credit.

➤ What have been the financial surprises in both positive and negative ways? Have better than expected economies of scale happened? Have certain customers cut back on purchases while others increased? Have vendors negotiated more attractive pricing for you due to your now higher purchase volumes? All of these are worth something.

➤ Compare the actual financial performance with the pro-forma predicted performance. How do they compare?

If any of the purchase agreement conditions have not been fulfilled that should already have been fulfilled, these should be resolved right away. Little things that sometimes drop through a crack during the integration process are a breeding ground for discontent and eventually for litigation. In addition, anyway, they were agreed to, and they need to be done.

Finally, how have your owners/shareholders reacted to the purchase? Are they pleased with the purchase, or are they squawking about it? After all, we all eventually work for our shareholders, and it will be easier to get the next purchase approved if this one performed as expected, keeping shareholders happy.

The Least You Need to Know

➤ Expect sales territory disputes to occur.

➤ Keep customers out of any sales disputes.

➤ Don't decrease headcount simply based on the organization chart or salaries.

➤ Pro-forma statements are a baseline for performance, not a guarantee. Use them as working documents, not as strict guidelines.

➤ Check with the major players within six months of the acquisition to ensure that everyone gets paid as expected.

➤ Present the most positive face possible to your shareholders. They directly, or indirectly, approve your next acquisition.

Gearing Up for the Next One

"OK, folks. We have had few a months working with ABC Company at this point, and I thought it time to determine how we did with that acquisition," said Ginny to her staff. They had spent almost three months working together on the ABC due diligence, financing, and negotiations. She was proud of them, but she also knew that there was always room for improvement.

Jack raised his hand while starting to speak at the same time. "I think we did better than expected, and let me tell you why. That motherboard manufacturing technology that ABC has in its Atlanta plant is actually a lot more advanced than we expected. In fact, it allows for much higher levels of performance than we have in any of our other manufacturing locations. This alone might turn out to be worth the entire cost of the company."

Ginny took a sip of her coffee and waited. Brian, from engineering, then spoke up.

"It hurts my ego a little to admit this, but their engineering staff is way underrated. They are better than us in a lot of ways, and we have been using them to teach our engineers some of their secret design techniques. These techniques really didn't come out in due diligence. Since they have always done it that way, nobody thought twice about it. They're really on to *something here. I agree with Jack. This capability should not be ignored, and might even be useful with our next acquisition choice."*

Now, this is going to be a great meeting, thought Ginny.

This chapter is really oriented more toward the buyers in the group. You sellers will typically only be able to market your companies every few years, or so, but you buyers can, and should, purchase companies just as quickly as it makes sense and your team and parent company can handle it.

It is common to think in terms of the process ending after the contracts are signed and all the lawyers have finished their paper shuffling. However, the process of integration continues long after that point, which was the subject of Chapter 25, "Is It Working?" This chapter takes a brief look at the acquisition process itself, as the purchasing company handled it. If you plan to perform this procedure on a regular basis, then reviewing the overall process will only help to make the next acquisition more efficient and reliable than the preceding ones.

Did Your M&A Process Work?

How did the last acquisition process work out? I don't simply mean the due diligence, negotiations, and closing stages. I mean the whole process from beginning to end. See Chapter 2, "Start at the Very Beginning …," for stage details, but for this analysis, let me simply divide the process into three basis stages:

1. The pre-acquisition planning stage
2. The acquisition stage
3. The post-acquisition stage

Stage 1: The Pre-Acquisition Stage

Stage One deals with the development of the initial need for an acquisition in the first place. Why should the company acquire another company? When should it happen? How much can the company afford to pay for the acquired company? What are the most important strategic and financial aspects of the acquisition?

This stage happens early in the process, and it really has nothing to do with a specific buyer (although it might recommend a specific target company). This stage lays the framework within which the other stages occur.

How did the assumptions made during this first stage work out? Did they come true or were they off by a long shot? Did the industry change in predicted ways, or were the future expectations off the mark, leading the acquisition team into unnecessary activities? Even worse, did the team start down one path only to terminate the process while deep into Stage Two?

I am not suggesting finger pointing or looking for a responsible party. I am simply suggesting that you perform an evaluation of the initial strategic decisions so that flawed assumptions don't get carried into the next acquisition.

Stage 2: The Acquisition Stage

This is the stage where you discovered the acquisition target company, made the initial introductions, performed the due diligence, came up with a price, negotiated the purchase terms, and finally closed the deal. A lot happens in this stage, and much of it is based on the work of professionals, such as your attorneys and accountants.

Did you use in-house counsel, or did you go outside for assistance? Was that a mistake, or did it work out OK? How did they do? Did you ever wish that you had their attorney instead of yours? This tells you something right there about your attorney. How did the terms and conditions of the final agreement work out when compared to those you would have ideally wanted? Overall, was it a pretty fair agreement with both parties giving up something and feeling a little bit cheated, or did one side prevail substantially over the other? Have you had to deal with pending legal issues that you feel should have been negotiated, and settled, during the negotiations?

Hot Tip

When you are in Stages Two and Three, it is easy to forget what prompted you to get there in the first place. Almost always, decisions made in Stage One moved the company to proceed into Stages Two and Three, but we often forget to return to the original assumptions that started us in a given direction in the first place.

What about your accountant? Did you use in-house financial people, or did you go outside for assistance? Did their financial analysis stand up to the scrutiny of the seller's accountant review? Did they find legitimate holes in the seller's financial arguments that were exploited to win you either a reduced sale price or more favorable terms?

How much did it cost you to perform the valuation analysis? Did you perform the valuation yourselves, or did you contract to an independent appraiser? How much did the appraiser cost? Did he or she perform as expected, or did the cost of the appraiser's services go up in small increments? Do you feel that you got an accurate, and defensible, valuation for your money? Would you use them again or refer them to someone else who is looking to have a business appraised? Did you set them up to fail based on your initial contacts so that they really couldn't succeed no matter what they did?

What if you used a business broker? Did this broker work out to your satisfaction? If so, that is great news. The broker component makes the next acquisition that much easier, since you can now set him or her out looking for the next acquisition target. If not, what would you have changed to make sure that the next broker is more to your liking? Is it possible that you don't need a broker for the next one? Do you now have the experience under your collective belts to manage the process on your own? How much would that save you, and is it worth the personnel time and money investment not to use a broker?

Hot Tip

You might think, today, that you will never forget the lessons learned from this acquisition. But you will forget most of them, along with many of the details. Think about a circumstance that was very important to you, but 10 years in the past. Now, think about the first and last names of the parties involved, where it happened, what room, time, and so on. We forget a lot over time, even if we think it is important. Write it down to be sure. Even if it is in narrative form, write it down.

Have you created a terms and conditions checklist that outlines the major points that must absolutely be in your next acquisition contract? If not, you should do that within 90 days of closing the prior acquisition. Contracts get complicated and detail oriented. You always want to make sure that your "must have" terms are included or consciously renegotiated for something more valuable. Are there terms that you did not know about that you wish had been included in this contract? Don't expect to remember them the next time around. Add them to the checklist so that you at least think about them next time.

Stage 3: The Post-Acquisition Stage

This stage is absolutely critical to a successful acquisition, and one that is often overlooked. Spend your time evaluating how well you all handled the post close activities, whether it was an asset transfer, an outright purchase, or a stock merger. Every major business change has fallout, and this acquisition is no different.

Should you have retained some members of the acquisition team as part of the transition team? Should you have left them off the transition team since they carried some bad sentiment toward the prior owners, as a result of the negotiations, that was improperly passed down to the employees? Should a transition counselor have been brought in to assist with the transition or did your people handle the situation properly?

Was it a good idea keeping the prior owners on board, or could you have done just as well, and with less hassle, if they had left with the purchase? (Watch your ego with this one, since they might have been a pain to work with but really did add a lot to the transition's success.)

Did you fail to create clearly defined success criteria for this acquisition, making it difficult to later determine if things were working as desired? In retrospect, what should that criteria have been? Write it on your checklist so that you don't forget it next time.

Did you wait too long to change things inside of the acquired company? Should you have waited a longer time? How would you determine the right time next time? Should you have promoted an acquired company employee to executive management, or was placing your own person in charge accepted by the employees and staff?

Are there people from the acquired company who would make excellent additions to your acquisition team? After all, they have also been through it from the seller's side, which provides them with a valuable perspective. And you have already worked with them and know if it worked out all right. Don't forget to use these people as a resource for your next acquisition.

What Strategically Is Needed to Improve the Company?

Life is full of surprises. Some good. Some not so good. Making the most out of the situations presented by the surprises is what differentiates the winners from the also-rans.

Your acquisition came with surprises. Hopefully more of them were wanted than unwanted. They might have come in the form of personnel with unexpected talents. Or they might have showed up as technology or expertise that was known, but unappreciated, during the acquisition process. Once you started to learn the acquisition's total implications, did you discover that the new company fit strategically well with another part of your business in a previously unexpected way?

Terms of Acquisition

Transition Counselor   A person who is trained to deal with the various personnel reactions to major change. Some counselors specialize in helping personnel deal with the changes associated with the transition of company ownership. They also guide the buying company's management toward optimal ways of dealing with the situation to minimize negative reactions.

Straight Talk

Strategic objectives are more than just a set of static line items on a piece of paper. They are dynamic destinations that change with the introduction of new technologies, legislation, and business partners. Every acquisition adds to your strategic mix, or you wouldn't have purchased the company in the first place. There are always bonuses obtained with an acquisition that you might not have expected, but they are of value if simply noticed by the buyers.

Or you might find out that an area of anticipated strategic synergy did not work out as planned. If you still need that capability, you are back to the acquisition drawing table.

It is now time to go back to your original acquisition objectives, as outlined in Stage One, and compare them against your current status after the completion of Stage Two. Which of these acquisition objectives have been achieved? Which are still lacking? Which are the most important to achieve and should be the emphasis of your next acquisition?

Is there something about the current acquisition's capabilities that, when added to what you already had in place, opens a new world of opportunities that shift your acquisition priorities?

I am not suggesting that you forget your prior objectives; simply reevaluate them in light of your newly acquired capabilities. It is likely that your strengths might have shifted in a positive way and that your future activities can enhance those strengths even further.

Some companies pursue an acquisition strategy to increase their sales and net worth to such a level that they attract the interest of a larger buyer. Many investors won't even consider an acquisition or financing venture for companies with annual sales of less than $5 million or $10 million dollars. Acquisition is a fast, proven way to increase sales to that point that the company can be sold or taken public.

How Long to Wait?

Waiting a specified period of time before proceeding with the next acquisition is probably determined more by the financial resources of the buyer than by the emotional/energy resources of the acquisition team.

Buying a company can be an intense, exhilarating, and draining experience. In addition, if your acquisition team members participate with the post-acquisition activities, their time commitment might be even longer than those who leave after closing.

There is a case to be made for waiting a while after your last acquisition, simply to make sure that you know what you bought. (See the prior section for comments in this regard.) But if you and your team are confident with the last acquisition and have particular reasons for proceeding quickly with the next, then proceed.

After all, if your strategic acquisition goal is to grow as quickly as possible, then acquiring as quickly as possible is an important part of that goal. If speedy acquisition is important, evaluating the personnel and methods involved with your acquisition process is also critical. Efficiency makes for more reliable, quicker, and less expensive acquisitions.

Just beware that you don't grow so quickly that you forget that your company must operate profitably to remain a financially healthy investment. Yours wouldn't be the first company to grow so quickly that it ran out of money and was forced to divest itself of the very companies it acquired, simply to maintain a financially solid base.

The Least You Need to Know

➤ A post acquisition review and/or report is good business.

➤ A thorough review of the acquisition team members, both employees and professional contractors, is a good idea.

➤ If you found yourself wishing that you had their attorney, you should hire that attorney for your next acquisition team.

➤ Reviewing strategic goals after the acquisition is finished is sound business. Goals might shift with the addition of the acquired company's personnel and/or capabilities.

➤ There is really no "right length of time" to wait before proceeding with the next acquisition.

Glossary of Terms

accounting profit   A profit that appears on the financial statements that is the result of an administrative or accounting procedure or change, as opposed to resulting from an actual change in operation.

acid test   An accounting ratio for measuring the amount of liquid assets a company has on hand for paying its short-term bills.

acquisition target   A company that you decide to investigate in earnest for potential purchase.

active customer   A customer who has purchased within a timeframe defined by two or three purchase phases.

advertising   Mass market exposure for your company, usually in newspapers or magazines, on TV or radio, or in the yellow pages.

assets   Items owned by a company that have some value, such as cash, account receivable, inventory, buildings, equipment, goodwill, and other tangible or intangible items.

bad debt ratio   The ratio of the un-collectable funds divided by total sales, expressed as a percent.

bailing   The act of removing water from a sinking boat and of extracting yourself from a sinking business.

bean counter   An accountant who, with the sharp analytical eye of someone paid to avoid risk, ruthlessly proves that your idea is far too risky.

brand equity   The asset value associated with a particular trademarked name, such as Ford, Coca-Cola, Kleenex, or Yahoo!. Increasing the perceived market value of products bearing the brand name increases its equity.

breakeven   This is the point at which you are making just enough money to cover your expenses. You are just living at a subsistence level, paying the rent, and putting food on the table with no extra money for movies and popcorn.

brutal honesty   The process of saying all of those things to yourself that you would hate someone else for saying to you. You can thank yourself for the candor.

business inertia   Resistance to change even though the business needs it.

Business Judgement Rule   A legal foundation that assumes management and board members operate from a "good faith" basis in making decisions that they feel are best for the company and its shareholders. A conflict of interest situation puts this protection in jeopardy.

calendar fiscal year   When the company's financial reporting period is the same as the calendar year, extending from January 1 to December 31.

close   A request by the salesperson for a specific action on the part of the customer. Asking for the order is the ultimate close, but smaller closes occur at each stage of the selling process.

comparative budget analysis   Defined budget that is compared to the current period.

context   The interrelated conditions in which something exists or occurs.

contingency plan   A plan of attack that kicks in if the initial plan does not work out as expected. If we cannot get airline tickets, we can drive, but we will have to leave earlier than expected. Driving is the contingency plan for this particular situation, and it has its own set of requirements.

contract   A legal agreement between the buyer and the person providing a product or service.

corporation   A separate legal business entity with a board of directors and shareholders.

cost plus pricing   When the offering price is calculated using the offering cost plus whatever profit margin is desired. So a widget that costs $1 to produce added to a desired 50 percent profit margin would sell for $2 ($1/.5 = $2).

current assets   Assets that can be converted into cash within a 12-month period.

current assets and liabilities   Current assets are easily used to pay off debts. Current liabilities have duration of 12 months or less.

current liabilities   Debts that must be paid off within a 12-month period.

cyberspace   A generic term used to describe the new computer networking technology.

debt financing   Occurs when a company takes out a loan to pay for things, such as special research projects, expansion, or the company purchase.

depreciation   The percentage of the initial purchase price of an asset that it is assumed to devalue in a given year of operation. For example, a piece of equipment might cost $25,000 and might have an assumed depreciable accounting life of five years. This means that the equipment devalues, or depreciates, by $5,000 ($25,000/5 years) per year.

direct mail   A piece of marketing literature that is mailed to a specific group of people to get a specific response.

disclosure document   A required filing with the Federal Trade Commission and many state regulatory agencies.

discount   The decrease in price from the list price for a product or service.

discount factor   The amount used to decrease the current effect of a future financial event. The larger the discount the less the current effect.

discount rate   The percentage amount that a financial company takes for providing you with cash for your account receivables. This is also called *factoring*.

diversification procedure   The business practice of spreading important business purchases or sales activities over multiple companies. In this way, should one company have trouble, the others can be relied on until an alternative new source is found. Without diversification, a single company on which you are heavily dependent could go under, taking your company with it.

double taxation   When the business pays taxes on its annual profits and then passes the income to you who again gets taxed at the personal level. The same dollar has been taxed twice.

due diligence   The evaluation process performed by the buyer to verify the underlying, often hidden, aspects of a seller's company. This phase of the acquisition process requires in-depth exposure to typically proprietary company operations and confidential information.

Employer Identification Number (EIN)   A number given to any company that has employees other than its owner. All corporations must have an EIN, since all personnel are officially employees. Call the IRS to get your EIN and Federal Tax Deposit Coupon book (IRS Form 8109).

equity stake   The transfer of a percentage of company ownership, usually in the form of a stock transfer, in exchange for the financial investment.

expenses   The amount of money that you spend to operate your business for fiscal period.

factoring   The percentage amount that a financial company takes for providing you with cash for your account receivables. This is also called *discounting*.

finished goods   Items that are ready for sale to a customer. Notice that raw inventory combined with some type of process creates finished goods.

295

fiscal period   The period of time over which the finances of a company are monitored. It can be for any period, but generally, it is assumed to be a month, a quarter (three months), or a year.

fiscal quarter   A three-month period that existed during a given company's fiscal year, which includes 12 months, or four quarters.

fiscal year   The 12-month period over which a company tracks its financial performance. Most companies use a fiscal year that matches the calendar year, but it is not an absolute requirement. For example, the Federal Government has a fiscal year that starts on October 1 and ends on September 30.

fixed costs   Costs that remain constant and that are independent of the sales level. Typical fixed costs include mortgage payments, utilities, executive salaries, and state licensing fees. This may be expressed either as a dollar figure or as a percentage of sales.

fixed expense   An expense that occurs whether you sell something or not.

float   The timeframe over which you are paying bills out of your own funds that should have been paid by client funds if received on time. Float, generically, refers to the timing between financial transactions.

franchisee   The person or company that purchases the proprietary business model.

franchiser   A company that offers to replicate its proprietary business model for others in exchange for an initial fee and a recurring franchise royalty (fee).

good faith   That intangible quality that is difficult to describe and yet very real. Without it, distrust shows up, and most negotiations will be seriously disrupted or simply fail. With it, many obstacles can be overcome, but it usually requires flexibility on the part of both parties in the negotiations.

goodwill   The value attached to the good name of a company. Just having the company name associated with an organization is worth something, and that value is tracked as goodwill.

gross margin   Subtract the cost of producing the product or service from the amount of money someone paid you to provide the offering.

growing market   A market with total revenues that increase from one year to the next, preferably over a five-year period or so.

guesstimate   Your best guess (estimate) about the specifics of a future event.

highly leveraged   When a company has committed so much of its value (and cash flow) to loan agreements, that it has little left over to pay for anything else.

holding company   A company that owns enough shares of stock in a particular company that it has effective control over its disposition. A firm can be a holding company for several companies at once.

horizontal acquisition   Where one competitor acquires another within the same industry.

income   This is the amount of money that you actually take home after everyone is paid. This should be calculated both before and after taxes are taken out.

input   Refers to the various items and/or skills required to make a process work properly.

intellectual property (capital)   Asset items owned by a company that are not tangible in nature, but that have commercial value. Typically, these assets involve legal protections, such as patents, trademarks, and copyrights.

inventories   Items used in the generation of income, which could be either finished products that are ready for sale or the components that are involved in the manufacture of finished goods.

job description   A detailed listing of the duties to be performed by the person filling the job in question, and a listing of the required skills, education and certification levels, and other criteria directly related to the job in question.

liabilities   Money owed by the company to some other company or person. These may include loans for the purchase of equipment or a building, a credit card debt, a bank line-of-credit, or unpaid payroll taxes. If it is owed to someone, it is a liability.

linear regression   Assumes that past and future values will fall along a straight line. Works well for numbers that change at a fixed rate.

loan to value ratio   The total percentage of an asset's value against which a loan will be provided. For example, an asset worth $1,000 against which the bank will loan up to a 60 percent loan to value ratio, means that you can borrow up to $600 using this asset as collateral.

Local Area Network   Technology used for connecting several computers together. A LAN allows the sharing of data and printers.

M & A   Merger and Acquisition.

mail order   Where your customers order from a catalog or other mailed information piece. Person to person selling is not involved.

majority shareholder   The person or company that owns most of the outstanding shares in a corporation.

manipulation   To control or change, especially by artful or unfair means, so that you achieve a desired end.

market driven pricing   Pricing a product or service at a level comparable to the competitive market as opposed to pricing that is based on product cost.

market niche   A segment of the market that has an existing need for a product or service that nobody is currently offering.

market positioning   Creating a beneficial perception in the minds of potential and existing customers. When they think about your company and/or its offerings, they immediately correlate it with a simply understood message that conveys an associated benefit to them.

market segmentation   Dividing the total available market (everyone who might ever buy) into smaller groups, or segments, by specific attributes, such as age, sex, location, industry, or other pertinent criteria.

market share   The percentage of total market segment revenues attributed to the target company's sales activities.

marketing   The background work that makes selling easier. Marketing includes research, pricing decisions, product or service design, and literature preparation.

materiality   1) An accounting term that designates a number or accounting assumption as having a substantial impact on the final results. The larger the impact the more "material" it is assumed to the analysis. 2) When including or deleting a number from financial statements will make a substantial difference to the resulting statements.

merchant number   A number given to your company that is used for all credit card related transactions. This number is given to you by the transaction service provider and used by the credit card companies, such as American Express.

need to know   Refers to when a person reveals information only to those people who absolutely must know that particular piece of information.

non-linear regression   Assumes that past and future values fall along a curve instead of a straight line. This method is used for predicting values if using rapidly changing values, as are often seen with new, emerging technology companies.

on-line services   Services that are accessed by computer and companies that provide services, such as electronic mail and information retrieval.

opportunity cost   The profit that would have been gained by pursuing another investment instead of the one currently in process. For example, if you go out on a date with one person, you lose the potentially good time you could have had with someone else. Sound familiar? That is opportunity cost.

output   The final result of the process.

paper profit   A profit that appears on the financial statements which are the result of an administrative or accounting procedure or change, as opposed to resulting from an actual change in operation.

parent company   A company that owns the majority, or all, of the stock in another company. For example, a company that purchases all of the stock in another company would become the purchased company's parent company.

partnership   A legal form of business in which two or more people share the business's legal obligations.

perceived value   The overall value that the customer places on the offering. This includes much more than price, and it considers other features, such as delivery lead-time, quality of salesmanship, service, style, and other items less tangible than the price. Customers rarely buy on price alone, except in purely commodity markets where all products and companies are perceived as identical.

personal computer   A term applied to computers that an individual uses for word processing and other applications.

policies   The internal "laws" around which employees operate. These typically include guidelines for vacation, sick leave, and other rules.

prepaid expenses   Expense items paid in advance of when they are actually due, such as taxes or credit balances with vendors.

price-earnings ratio   Compares the price of a stock to its last 12 month's earnings.

procedures   Deal with operational topics, such as the creation of a final report, performing an audit, or testing a particular product. They often include detailed, step-by-step instructions for performing specific tasks.

pro-forma financial statements   Statements that predict the future based on a combination of historical performance and projected (guesstimated) future performance. Used to project a company's financial statements as they might appear months, or years into the future. These are often not used when selling a company for liability reasons since they might possibly be construed as a commitment of future performance instead of somebody's best guess.

prospectus   A document that outlines the opportunity presented by a specific investment. Fundamentally, it is a sales document, aimed at potential investors.

public relations   Work done on your part to secure media coverage—including newspaper, radio, television, and magazine—of you, your company, and/or its offerings. Any form of media applies.

purchase phase   The length of time between purchases. For large capital equipment, this might be a very long time, whereas commodity products, such as sugar, might have a short purchase phase.

quick ratio   An accounting ratio for measuring the amount of liquid assets a company has on hand for paying its short-term bills.

ratio analysis   Comparing one set of financial numbers to another to determine a ratio. This ratio is then compared against past performance or industry standard ratios to determine a business's financial health.

raw inventory   Asset items that were purchased so that they can be combined to create a finished product. These include items like screws, nuts, paper, ink, wire, and other basic materials.

recasting   The process of removing unnecessary expenses from historical financial statements so that they more accurately reflect a realistic financial assessment of performance. Often done by small companies to remove "special" expenses incurred to decrease net income and taxes.

regression analysis   The process of mathematically determining a future value based on existing data. The procedure, usually performed on a computer, determines an equation that matches the existing data. It then inserts future values into the equation to mathematically estimate future values.

reorder cycle   The amount of time that it takes a customer to go from the close date of the prior purchase to the close of the next purchase opportunity. A repeat customer with a two-month reorder cycle will order from you approximately six times per year.

revenue   The total sales for the company expressed for a fiscal period, such as a quarter or a total year.

revenue matching   The accounting procedure that ensures that sales revenues and associated expenses for a given time period are tracked and recorded so that they appear on financial statements for the same fiscal period.

risk   1) The possibility that things will not turn out as you expect and that it could cost you a portion or all of your investment. 2) The uncertainty associated with an action or investment. The higher the risk the more reward the investor expects.

routine tasks   Things that you do that are much the same as the last time you did them, except for minor variations. The level of personal or business risk associated with the task is small, and the outcome of the task is definite.

sale gestation period   The time that it takes to close a sale from the point of initial customer contact to the time the deal actually closes.

sales   The activities directly associated with getting the customer to pay cash for your product or service.

SCORE   A part of the Small Business Administration (SBA) that provides experienced, often retired, executives who will consult with small business owners on a wide variety of business matters. Contact the SBA for a local SCORE office.

service mark   Similar to a trademark except related to a service procedure instead or a particular product. These are commonly used by service organizations, such as consulting, accounting, and training companies.

shareholder wealth   The underlying value of a share of stock as determined by its assessed market value. Actions that increase market value increase shareholder wealth.

sniff test   An unwritten, non-numeric, yet very real test that we all undergo and perform when negotiating something important. If the other person or the situation just doesn't "feel" right, it failed the test. This is never a good sign for future relations.

sole proprietorship   The simplest form of business to establish where the owner is responsible for all legal liabilities.

specifically vague   Providing information that is general in nature, but specific enough to answer the other party's initial questions. Stating the general facts without much detail attached.

Standard Industrial Code (SIC)   A numbering system used to categorize companies by their primary business activities. It is helpful in comparing companies from the same industry since they can be grouped by SIC.

stock   1) The legal device used to determine ownership of a corporation. People or companies that own stock are called shareholders. 2) The portion of a corporation that is sold to a shareholder.

stock dilution   Offering more company stock for sale when the net income of the company does not increase. The extra shares have the effect of dividing the same net income by more shares. This, in turn, decreases the earnings per share. This decrease will typically decrease the stock price via the price-earnings ratio.

strategic plan   A business plan that sets the overall direction of a company over a future three- to five-year period.

strategy   A careful plan or method; devising or employing plans toward a goal.

subordinate lender   A lender who is paid only after some other lender is paid in full.

sunk cost   An expense already incurred based on past events that cannot be easily recovered. Often used in conjunction with events that, negatively, turned out differently than initially expected.

system   A process of turning daily routines that you or your employees "Just know" how to do into specific procedures that someone else can learn and follow.

tactical   Of or relating to the small actions that relate to a larger overall purpose or goal.

target marketing   A marketing approach that defines a special group of potential buyers. All marketing and sales efforts are based on convincing this group to purchase your company's offerings.

telemarketing   A marketing approach using the telephone for quick access to sales prospects or existing customers with the intent of closing more business.

tire kickers   People who appear interested in buying a car (or your business), who ask a lot of questions (kick the tires), and who take up lot of your time only to ultimately find out for themselves that they really aren't interested.

transition counselor   A person who is trained to deal with the various personnel reactions to major change. Some counselors specialize in helping personnel deal with the changes associated with the transition of company ownership. They also guide the buying company's management regarding optimal ways of dealing with the situation to minimize negative reactions.

triangular merger   A merger involving the target company and a subsidiary corporation of the buyer's corporation.

Uniform Franchise Offering Circular (UFOC)   A detailed set of franchise information disclosure guidelines adopted by many states.

up economy   A period of positive overall economic growth.

variable cost   A cost of doing business that varies directly with the sales level, such as paper and ink costs for a newspaper business. This may be expressed as a dollar figure or as a percentage of sales, depending on the analysis being performed.

variable expense   An expense that varies with the amount of product or service sold.

vertical acquisition   Where one company acquires either a supplier or a customer creating a strategically unfair alliance that precludes competition.

wealth   Defined as the money obtained divided by the money needed. If wealth ratio is greater than 1 then you are wealthy. If wealth ratio is less than 1 then you are courting financial disaster.

work in progress   Designates asset items that are in the process of being converted from raw materials into finished goods that can then be resold. This is sometimes called WIP by manufacturing folks.

Reference Materials

General Business

Paulson, Ed, and Marcia Layton. *The Complete Idiot's Guide to Starting Your Own Business*. 2nd ed. New York: Alpha Books, 1998.

Strategic Planning

Hickman, Craig R. *The Strategy Game*. New York: McGraw-Hill, Inc., 1993.

Porter, Michael E. *Competitive Strategy*. New York: The Free Press, 1998.

Porter, Michael E. *Competitive Advantage*. New York: The Free Press, 1998.

Steiner, George A. *Strategic Planning*. New York: The Free Press, 1979.

Buying and Selling

Buono, Anthony F. and Bowditch, James L.. *The Human Side of Mergers and Acquisitions*. San Francisco, CA: Jossey-Bass, Inc., 1989.

Leimberg, Rosenbloom, and Yohlin. The Corporate Buy-Sell Handbook. Chicago, IL: Dearborn Financial Publishing, Inc., 1992.

Lipman, Frederick D. *How Much Is Your Business Worth?* Rocklin, CA: PRIMA Publishing, 1996.

Sherman, Andrew J. *Mergers and Acquisitions From A to Z*. New York: AMACOM, 1998.

Snowden, Richard W. *The Complete Guide to Buying a Business*. New York: AMACOM, 1994.

Sperry, Paul S. and Mitchell, Beatrice H. *The Complete Guide to Selling Your Business.* Dover, NH: Upstart Publishing Company, Inc., 1992

Wasserstein, Bruce. *Big Deal: The Battle for Control of America's Leading Corporations.* New York: Warner Books, Inc., 1998.

Valuing The Business

Copeland, Tom and Koller, Tim and Murrin, Jack. *Valuation.* New York: John Wiley & Sons, 1991.

Horn, Thomas. *Business Valuation Manual.* Lancaster, PA: Charter Oak Press, 1990.

Nunes, Morris A. *The Right Price for Your Business.* New York: John Wiley & Sons, 1988.

Financial Basics

Bernstein, Peter L., ed. *The Portable MBA in Investment.* New York: John Wiley & Sons, 1995.

Blechman, Bruce and Levinson, Jay Conrad, *Guerrilla Financing.* Boston, MA: Houghton Mifflin Company, 1991.

Field, Drew. *Take Your Company Public.* New York: New York Institute of Finance, 1991.

Gates, Sheldon. *101 Business Ratios.* Scottsdale, AZ: McLane Publications, 1993.

Livingstone, John Leslie, ed. *The Portable MBA in Finance and Accounting.* 2nd ed. New York: John Wiley & Sons, 1997.

Nickerson, Clarence B. *Accounting Handbook for Non-Accountants.* 2nd ed. Boston, MA: CBI Publishing Company, Inc.,1979.

Rachlin, Robert and Sweeny, Allen. *Accounting and Financial Fundamentals for NonFinancial Executives.* 2nd Ed. New York: AMACOM, 1996.

Rao, Ramesh K.S. *Financial Management.* New York: Macmillan Publishing Company, 1987.

Seglin, Jeffrey L. *Financing Your Small Business.* New York: McGraw-Hill, Inc., 1990.

Simini, Joseph Peter. *Balance Sheet Basics for Nonfinancial Managers.* New York: John Wiley & Sons, 1990.

Welsch and Short. *Fundamentals of Financial Accounting.* Homewood, IL: Irwin, 1987.

Van Horne, James C. *Financial Management and Policy*, 8th Edition. Englewood Cliffs, NJ: Prentice-Hall, Inc., 1989.

ESOPs

Blasi, Joseph R. *Employee Ownership.* Cambridge, MA: Ballinger Publishing Company, 1988.

Sample Financial Statements

ABC Corporation
Income Statement
For Years Ended December 31, 1999 and 2000

	2000	1999
Operating Income and Expenses		
Sales	$ 2,209,731,000	$ 1,937,556,000
Cost of goods sold	$ 883,892,400	$ 794,397,960
Operating Income (gross margin)	**$ 1,325,838,600**	**$ 1,143,158,040**
Fixed Expenses		
Selling expenses	$ 441,946,200	$ 387,511,200
Salaries	$ 530,335,440	$ 465,013,440
Interest expense	$ 16,990,000	$ 14,897,323
Depreciation	$ 12,134,000	$ 10,639,442
Utilities	$ 98,760,000	$ 86,595,622
Total Fixed Expenses	$ 1,100,165,640	$ 964,657,027
Net Income Before Income Tax	$ 225,672,960	$ 178,501,013
less income taxes paid	$ 112,836,480	$ 89,250,507
Net Income	**$ 112,836,480**	**$ 89,250,507**
Dividends paid	**$ 18,575,480**	**$ 2,060,487**
Retained earnings	**$ 94,261,000**	**$ 87,190,020**
Earnings per share	**$ 17.46**	**$ 16.15**

(Based on 5,400,000 outstanding shares.)

ABC Corporation
Balance Sheet
December 31, 1999 and 2000

Assets	2000	1999
Current Assets:		
Cash	$ 44,668,000	$ 42,256,000
Marketable securities, at cost which approximates market value	$ 242,300,000	$ 190,382,000
Receivables	$ 252,445,000	$ 211,124,000
Inventories	$ 161,167,000	$ 144,274,000
Prepaid Expenses	$ 6,006,000	$ 6,414,000
Total Current Assets	**$ 706,586,000**	**$ 594,450,000**
Property and Equipment, at cost:		
Land	$ 16,950,000	$ 16,808,000
Buildings	$ 113,120,000	$ 109,409,000
Equipment and improvements	$ 401,434,000	$ 378,937,000
	$ 531,504,000	$ 505,154,000
Less accumulated depreciation and amortization	$ 287,861,000	$ 270,910,000
Total Property and Equipment	**$ 243,643,000**	**$ 234,244,000**
Other Assets	$ 37,772,000	$ 44,330,000
Total Assets	**$ 988,001,000**	**$ 873,024,000**
Current Liabilities:		
Accounts payable	$ 96,733,000	$ 95,889,000
Accrued liabilities	$ 147,702,000	$ 132,253,000
Accrued income taxes	$ 105,900,000	$ 88,100,000
Current portion of long-term debt	$ 5,192,000	$ 4,709,000
Total current liabilities	**$ 355,527,000**	**$ 320,951,000**
Long-term debt	$ 313,350,000	$ 315,457,000
Deferred income taxes	$ 58,000,000	$ 65,800,000
Other long-term liabilities	$ 10,066,000	$ 9,863,000

Assets	2000	1999
Shareholder's Equity:		
Preferred stock	$ 516,000	$ 516,000
Common stock	$ 32,340,000	$ 32,340,000
Additional paid-in capital	$ 445,885,000	$ 432,360,000
Retained earnings	$ 601,262,000	$ 507,001,000
	$1,080,003,000	**$ 972,217,000**
Less treasury stock at cost	$ 457,595,000	$ 466,007,000
Total shareholders' equity	**$ 622,408,000**	**$ 506,210,000**
Total Liabilities and Shareholder's Equity	**$ 988,001,000**	**$ 837,024,000**

Index